A NEW GLOBAL DEAL

The **Foundation for European Progressive Studies (FEPS)** is the think tank of the progressive political family at EU level. Our mission is to develop innovative research, policy advice, training and debates to inspire and inform progressive politics and policies across Europe. We operate as hub for thinking to facilitate the emergence of progressive answers to the challenges that Europe faces today.

FEPS works in close partnership with its members and partners, forging connections and boosting coherence among stakeholders from the world of politics, academia and civil society at local, regional, national, European and global levels.

Today FEPS benefits from a solid network of 68 member organisations. Among these, 43 are full members, 20 have observer status and 5 are ex-officio members. In addition to this network of organisations that are active in the promotion of progressive values, FEPS also has an extensive network of partners, including renowned universities, scholars, policymakers and activists.

Our ambition is to undertake intellectual reflection for the benefit of the progressive movement, and to promote the founding principles of the EU – freedom, equality, solidarity, democracy, respect of human rights, fundamental freedoms and human dignity, and respect of the rule of law.

This book has been published in cooperation with:

 **Earth4All**   C/o The Club of Rome, Lagerhausstrasse 9, 8400 Winterthur, Switzerland (www.earth4all.life)

 Fondation Jean-Jaurès   12 Cité Malesherbes, 75009 Paris, France (www.jean-jaures.org)

 **Fundación Pablo Iglesias**   Calle de Quintana 1–2° A, 28008 Madrid, Spain (www.fpabloiglesias.es)

 Friedrich-Ebert-Stiftung – New York   747 Third Ave., Suite 34D, New York, NY 10017, USA (https://ny.fes.de)

 **Karl-Renner-Institut**   Karl-Popper-Straße 8, A-1100 Vienna, Austria (www.renner-institut.at)

 **Olof Palme International Center**   Sveavägen 68, 111 34 Stockholm, Sweden (www.palmecenter.se)

 **TASC – Think-tank for Action on Social Change**
28 Merrion Square N., Dublin 2, Ireland (www.tasc.ie)

A NEW GLOBAL DEAL

REFORMING WORLD GOVERNANCE

Edited by Maria João Rodrigues

Book published in May 2024 by the Foundation for European Progressive Studies in association with London Publishing Partnership

FOUNDATION FOR EUROPEAN PROGRESSIVE STUDIES (FEPS)

Avenue des Arts 46 – 1000 Brussels, Belgium
www.feps-europe.eu
@FEPS_Europe

Supervision: Maria João Rodrigues and Christian Salm
Project coordination: Christian Salm, David Rinaldi, Thainá Leite and Andriy Korniychuk
Layout and editing: T&T Productions Ltd, London

GOBIERNO DE ESPAÑA

MINISTERIO DE ASUNTOS EXTERIORES, UNIÓN EUROPEA Y COOPERACIÓN

Cooperación Española

Actividad organizada por la Fundación Pablo Iglesias con financiación del Ministerio de Asuntos Exteriores, Unión Europea y Cooperación en el marco de una convocatoria de subvenciones abierta a todas las fundaciones dependientes de partidos políticos.

This book was published with the financial support of the European Parliament and the Spanish Foreign Ministry. It does not represent the view of the European Parliament or the Spanish Foreign Ministry.

A catalogue record for this book is available from the British Library
978-1-916749-15-3 (paperback)
978-1-916749-16-0 (iPDF)
978-1-916749-17-7 (ePUB)

Table of contents

Preface

This book was prepared by a group of European policymakers and experts with a long and diverse body of experience and in dialogue with their counterparts across the world. They felt they should speak out at this historical juncture of European and world history marked by the UN Summit of the Future. But this is just an initial contribution to a much-needed global debate. They want to go on listening to others and engaging with them in a long-term undertaking: reinventing global governance for the 21st century. The book is part of the FEPS "UNited for" flagship project in the thematic area of Europe and the world and devoted to a New Global Deal in 2023 and 2024.

Maria João Rodrigues

Introduction

The current global order is undergoing a large-scale transformation: emerging existential challenges for all humankind, increasing inequalities within and between countries and generations, competing global strategies between great powers, fragilities of the multilateral system and major military conflicts.

There is a clear gap between the global challenges in front of us and the current global governance system. A Summit of the Future to reform global governance and adopt a Pact for the Future with commitments to policy goals and the solutions to deliver them was convened by the United Nations secretary-general to take place in September 2024. It was preceded by a summit on the Sustainable Development Goals (SDGs) in 2023 and to be followed by a World Social Summit in 2025. This unique political sequence provides a once-in-a-generation opportunity and should be used to its full potential by all actors who want to change the global order for a better future.

Triggered by the report Our Common Agenda, presented by the UN secretary-general for his second mandate, the preparatory process for the Summit of the Future started with a High-Level Advisory Board on Effective Multilateralism, composed of personalities from all continents, and went on, with a plethora of contributions expected from UN member states and regional organisations such as the European Union, as well as civil society stakeholders, NGOs, businesses, trade unions, think tanks and academia.[1]

The purpose of this book is to present an organised contribution to this global debate from renowned European progressive experts and policymakers, with the aim of inspiring the EU's official positions and further dialogue with other countries across the world. This book is focused, from a progressive perspective, on the possible content of the Pact for the Future, which should include a New Global Deal between countries and between generations.

---

1   See www.un.org/en/common-agenda and https://highleveladvisoryboard.org.

The Foundation for European Progressive Studies – as a European political foundation financed by the EU budget, and as the central hub for European progressive thinking, which also holds UN ECOSOC (Economic and Social Council) status – is an active member of these different networks. With this book, we want to discuss the kind of New Global Deal that will be necessary to enable many more countries to implement the SDGs, and to enable all generations to improve their life chances. Let us underline that over the last four years there have been a general backsliding and increasing inequalities in the implementation of the SDGs.

To start with, some key questions can already be identified. A New Global Deal should truly be a deal, with give and take from all parties involved, with trade-offs and synergies, and with a general win-win outcome. Below are some of the important questions to be addressed.

- How can foresight on long-term trends and possible scenarios help to identify possible choices? (See chapter 1.)

- How should this New Global Deal be translated in key policy fields, notably climate, digital, access to knowledge, education and social welfare? (See chapters 2–7.)

- How can this New Global Deal be translated into trade agreements and new financial and tax arrangements? (See chapters 8–10.)

- What are the main changes to be introduced in the global governance system in order to deliver on this New Global Deal? (See the chapter 11.)

- In what general terms can this New Global Deal emerge as a key ingredient of a Pact for the Future? (See the conclusion.)

Let us set the scene for this discussion by addressing some background issues.

Multilateralism for the 21st century: why we need to reinvent it

Throughout the last few decades, new challenges and aspirations have emerged and forced the multilateral system to develop new ramifications to cope with them, thus creating a complex architecture that now has several significant inconsistencies and flaws.

Furthermore, the range and dynamics of the relevant global actors are now very different, because these actors include many new countries that joined the UN system after decolonisation, as well as new great powers, regional organisations, multinational corporations, civil society organisations and global citizenry.

These new challenges and new actors have generated a large set of global initiatives that create a very complex landscape of global governance: plurilateral platforms (such as the G20), comprehensive bilateral agreements (notably in trade), regional political organisations (such as the EU and the African Union) and multiactor coalitions focusing on particular issues (such as the environment).

Competition between the great powers is also evolving. After the long US–USSR bipolar period, and the US unipolar phase after the fall of the Berlin Wall, American hegemony now seems to have been weakened by the emergence of new great powers, notably China. More recently, this multipolar world and this new great-power game seem to be reaching the level of systemic competition between different potential global orders.

Nevertheless, human history is now entering a new phase. Humankind is not only united by common aspirations – peace, development, democracy, human rights, and access to culture, knowledge and new technologies. It is also confronted with new common global challenges that are perceived as vital – human health, living conditions, general security and survival on this planet. Global governance needs to be reinvented to cope with this new situation.

Which are the main scenarios for the global order?

The first scenario would be a kind of Western revival, particularly due to the replacement of President Trump by President Biden in the United States. Biden's presidency might not have significantly changed the American attitude to trade, but it has brought a new American attitude to climate change and human rights standards, as well as an American reengagement with the UN system. Russia's invasion of Ukraine may spur on this scenario.

The second scenario would involve a recognition that we now have a new world and would likely see the ongoing fragmentation of the current global order and the emergence of a polycentric structure with zones of influence, including the new zone of influence connected with China. These different poles and zones of influence may also tend to become more inward-looking and to use a weakened multilateral system for their particular needs.

Since the invasion of Ukraine by Putin's Russia, a third scenario should be considered, particularly if China becomes more aligned with Russia: a new Cold War and a major internal fracture in the existing multilateral system.

Therefore, a fourth scenario is needed: renewed international cooperation with an updated multilateral system for the 21st century should be the way to go. The chances for such a scenario depend on building a large coalition of forces involving willing states, regional organisations, civil society entities of different kinds, and also willing citizens wherever they are in the world, even under authoritarian and antimultilateral political regimes. This would be a global coalition of progressive forces, which could count on a core of strongly committed forces as well as on a variable geometry of partners, according to the different objectives.

Hence, the Alliance for Multilateralism proposed by progressive actors remains a good starting point to prevent the risk of a major division of global governance between the competing leaderships of the US and China. The EU should remain a central force in this alliance.

How far are UN and EU agendas aligned on renewing the multilateral system?

The EU and UN need one another if they are to fulfil their own promises now more than ever. They have been confronted with a sequence of shock waves: first of all the global financial crisis; then peace and development tensions triggering larger migration flows; increasing manifestations of climate change; recently, an unprecedented pandemic bringing a new economic recession; and, today, explosive military conflicts involving risks of escalation.

A new Common Agenda was presented by the UN Secretary-General António Guterres after his reelection for a second mandate at the helm of the United Nations. At the same time, the EU started developing stronger instruments of European sovereignty in the budgetary, economic, social and environmental fields, but also started asserting itself as a political entity with a vital interest in defending and updating a multilateral system at the global level, and in building up a global coalition of allies.

Let us start by identifying and assessing the bridges between the UN's Common Agenda and the European agenda, both in their design and in their ongoing relevance.

Health

First of all, the international fight against Covid-19 has strengthened the One Health approach, showing the interdependence between the health of humankind and that of the rest of the planet.

Access to updated vaccination was perceived as a new public good, but there is still a lot to do to ensure global access so as to control future pandemics. The EU improved its capacity for internal coordination and external cooperation but has been hesitating on the way towards supporting capacity building and access to intellectual property rights in developing countries. The EU might be confronted again with this kind of dilemma around global solidarity.

The environment

The same dilemma for the EU is visible in the case of climate change. At the last few sessions of the Conference of the Parties it was possible to approve the rulebook for implementing the Paris Agreement and a new loss-and-damage instrument, but it was not possible to sufficiently strengthen the Global Green Fund to support adaptation and mitigation in developing countries. The EU is now committed to stepping up its decarbonisation, but success will depend on its capacity to support the same efforts in developing countries. Ultimately, this will be a condition for the success of the European Green Deal and the new EU package Fit for 55.

Sustainable development

And the same dilemma is taking place in the implementation of the SDGs and the UN's 2030 Agenda. In the EU the so-called European Semester process to coordinate member states' national policies is moving from austerity towards recovery, resilience and stronger alignment with the SDGs. The national recovery plans are being supported by a stronger European budgetary capacity relying on the common issuance of debt backed by new resources of taxation. Nevertheless, a qualitative leap is still missing when it comes to supporting developing countries with substantial means to invest towards the SDGs. The most obvious example is the current partnership between the EU and Africa. Furthermore, EU trade agreements should be more active in promoting the SDGs.

Digital issues

The digital transformation is another policy field where the bridge between the UN and the EU can become very fruitful. The UN is promoting a Global Digital Compact to make the best of digital solutions in order to implement the SDGs.

On its side, the EU is striving to define its own way for digitalisation – one different from those of America and China – and it has recently adopted an important set of legislative instruments (such as the General Data Protection Regulation, Driver Monitoring Systems, the Digital Markets Act, the Artificial Intelligence Act and the Platform Work Directive). The differences can be very relevant, first of all because the European way should be particularly focused on providing better products and services to meet people's needs, and on ensuring universal access to public services. This requires that their reorganisation be supported by reskilling providers and users and by developing artificial intelligence algorithms in line with European values.

Another striking difference concerns the protection of privacy, which, in line with the European tradition of regulated capitalism, should be translated into a change in business models, particularly for the big digital platforms. The same applies to the working conditions that are being regulated to ensure fundamental workers' rights, including access to social protection. Finally, another big difference concerns taxation, since the EU is debating the terms of a coordinated digital tax, beyond the minimum corporate tax that was recently agreed on at the international level.

A New Social Contract

The UN's Common Agenda proposes two key concepts to improve global governance: a New Social Contract and a New Global Deal. A New Social Contract should involve labour market regulations as well as social protection to ensure internal cohesion at the national level. When it comes to the EU, relevant developments are taking place to implement the recently proclaimed European Pillar of Social Rights. This is paving the way for a phase of social Europe that is based not only on policies for economic, social and regional cohesion, but also on building up the foundations of European citizenship in terms of some fundamental rights: a minimum wage, a minimum income, access to lifelong learning, employment protection in case of crisis, the Child Guarantee, the Youth Guarantee and a work–life balance.

A New Global Deal

The UN's concept of a New Global Deal aims to translate this social contract to the global level in order to reduce the gap between developing and developed countries. One lesson might be learned from the European experience: the reduction of social inequalities depends first of all on the efforts deployed by each country, with good governance, a fight against mismanagement and corruption, and internal wealth redistribution. But better opportunities should also be given to developing countries with better framework conditions, notably by promoting fair trade, fair global taxation, debt relief and global financing, particularly when these countries make a real effort to implement the SDGs.

*

Hence, in spite of several shortcomings, it is possible to identify several important bridges and synergies between the UN's agenda and the EU's.

Furthermore, the EU should organise itself as a global political actor that is able to influence the international game, pushing for rules-based global governance and safeguarding multilateral institutions. In the current situation, it is vital to isolate Putin's Russia, build up a large coalition of forces and neutralise other ambiguous ones such as China. An approach of the "West against the rest" would be the wrong one. We are in a new world, and if we want the multilateral system to have a future, we need to build up a much larger coalition of forces, eventually with variable geometries. The compelling common challenges facing humankind as a whole can only be addressed by inclusive global governance.

In order to preserve the multilateral system and regain the conditions for implementing Our Common Agenda, including the outcomes of the Summit on the Future of Global Governance, the EU should actively promote global public goods and work for a New Global Deal, while redoubling efforts to bring back peace to the European continent.

The Summit of the Future: a window of opportunity for a New Global Deal

Ahead of the 75th anniversary of the UN, Secretary-General Guterres launched a Global Conversation, which spurred more than 3,000 civil society dialogues worldwide and surveys involving some 1.5 million people in 195 countries. The UN75 Office reported that the Global Conversation showed "overwhelming public support for international cooperation" and for a more people-centered multilateralism.

These civil-society-led consultations fed into and shaped intergovernmental negotiations on the UN75 Declaration, adopted during High-Level Week at the start of the General Assembly's 75th session, in September 2020. With the UN75 Declaration, governments renewed their commitment to tackling global challenges such as climate change, the Covid-19 pandemic, extreme poverty, armed conflict, disarmament and disruptive technologies. At the same time, the declaration directed the secretary-general "to report back" within a year "with recommendations to advance our common agenda and to respond to current and future challenges".

Figure 0.1. Our Common Agenda.
Source: United Nations (2021) "Our Common Agenda".

In September 2021, the Our Common Agenda report was released. Emphasising ways to accelerate the SDGs and implementation of the Paris Climate Agreement, and benefiting from four tracks of consultations (which sought input from youth, thought leaders, civil society and governments), the report outlined some 90 distinct recommendations across four pillars: a renewed social contract, a focus on the future, protecting the global commons and delivering global public goods, and an upgraded UN. Recommended ideas for advancing this agenda included three global summits, seven high-level tracks and the High-Level Advisory Board on Effective Multilateralism.

The SDG Summit as a starting point

The SDGs are a common reference for all UN member states and for humankind, but they are not on track for their time horizon of 2030.

The sequence of summits on SDGs (2023), on the future of global governance (2024), on social development and on finance (2025) offers a unique opportunity to put them on track. Nevertheless, the risk of failure would remain high as long as different frameworks were proposed to organise their preparation, such as the Our Common Agenda tracks, the UN secretary-general's policy briefings, the report of the High-level Board on Effective Multilateralism and the Global Sustainable Development Report, just to name the most relevant ones. To overcome this, on 30 August 2023, the scope of the Summit of the Future was defined in UN Resolution A/77/L.109 (see Appendix A).

Moreover, the report of the secretary-general on "Progress towards the Sustainable Development Goals" from May 2023 presented the clearest proposal yet of a common framework for these UN summits. Letters sent by the deputy secretary-general to all member states were also instrumental in proposing a clearer common framework and paving the way, in spite of difficult negotiations until the last few days, for the final approval of a declaration on the SDG Summit in September 2023 (see Appendix B).

*

A foresight exercise will be presented in Chapter 1 of this book to highlight strong arguments showing why we need to move to a new development model everywhere. There are two main reasons: the current model is no longer sustainable, taking into account the planet's boundaries and population trends; and the current model is unfair, widening social inequalities within countries, between countries and between generations.

SDG implementation is at a crossroads. We are in a Too Little Too Late scenario, but we have a choice: to move to a Giant Leap scenario. Nevertheless, this is only possible with stronger efforts from all member states, but also with much higher international cooperation – a New Global Deal for a new development model.

We need this New Global Deal for three main reasons.

- To organise the joint and coordinated action needed to provide public goods that can only be provided at the global level: countering climate change, pandemics, large natural and human disasters, global economic recessions, and nuclear and digital threats.

- To include the future generations' concerns – and the survival of humankind – in all public and private governance systems at all levels, on the basis of foresight and public debate about possible choices.

- To deepen cooperation between developed and developing countries according to a win-win approach. If developing countries act to move to a new development model, they should be supported by developed countries. If developed countries agree to support developing countries, they should benefit from new economic opportunities, and also from the improvement of the global context, with more sustainability and fairness.

But what should the more precise terms be for this New Global Deal in different policy fields, if we keep in mind the global negotiations already taking place in all of them and creating interactions between them?

The purpose of the following chapters of this book is precisely to identify proposals for a New Global Deal, going through various policy fields and their interactions. These proposals will cover new approaches, strategic priorities and concrete measures, but also the means to deliver them and the necessary reforms in the multilateral system.

Johannah Bernstein, David Collste,
Sandrine Dixson-Declève and Nathalie Spittler

1 | SDGs for all: strategic scenarios
Earth4All system dynamics modelling of SDG progress

This chapter was written by Earth4All, a vibrant collective of leading economic thinkers, scientists and changemakers convened by the Club of Rome, BI Norwegian Business School, the Potsdam Institute for Climate Impact Research and the Stockholm Resilience Centre. The information presented here equips policymakers with solutions designed to accelerate implementation of the Sustainable Development Goals (SDGs) and to respond to the planetary emergency.

This report is not only a direct response to the call from United Nations Secretary-General António Guterres for more rigorous strategic analysis and foresight to support policymaking. It also responds to the secretary-general's call for climate action as the 21st century's greatest opportunity to drive forward all the SDGs.[1] Taken together, the Earth4All modelling outputs and deep insights combined with our policy proposals provide the basis for structured emergency plans that enable and even strengthen SDG implementation. At the same time, they ensure a just response to today's triple planetary crisis: climate disruption, nature and biodiversity loss, and pollution and waste.[2]

In this chapter we take the Earth4All model developed for *Earth for All: A Survival Guide for Humanity* and reapply it to examine SDG progress in the light of Earth4All's five "extraordinary turnarounds" – poverty,

---

1   "Harnessing climate and SDGs synergies". United Nations Department of Economic and Social Affairs website (https://sdgs.un.org/climate-sdgs-synergies).

2   United Nations (2022) "Ambitious action key to resolving triple planetary crisis of climate disruption, nature loss, pollution, Secretary-General says in message for International Mother Earth Day". Press release, 21 April (https://press.un.org/en/2022/sgsm21243.doc.htm).

inequality, empowerment, food and energy – and against the backdrop of the two scenarios that lie at the core of the model.[3]

Too Little Too Late: a scenario exploring the path of economic development and unsustainable consumption if societies continue on the same course as the last 40 years.

Giant Leap: a scenario exploring a path that sees societies make extraordinary decisions and investments today through five extraordinary turnarounds that enhance social cohesion, build trust and establish a New Social Contract between people and the state.

We also consider SDG progress when each extraordinary turnaround is undertaken alone, as opposed to simultaneously in the Giant Leap.

The urgency of the Earth4All turnarounds

Achieving the five Earth4All extraordinary turnarounds will require governments to take unprecedented measures to transform economies in order to enable widespread increases in human welfare within earth's natural boundaries.[4] It will also require a massive acceleration in the scale and speed of transformative change if we are to rise to the challenge of the growing existential threats to humanity and the planet posed by predicted future shocks and stresses.

Evidence of these threats has never been more terrifying. In the summer of 2023, climate emergencies were declared in more than 2,300 jurisdictions and local government areas in 40 countries, impacting more than 1 billion citizens.[5] Now more than ever, the words of Pope Francis from 2015 ring particularly true: in its handling of climate change, the world

---

3 Dixson-Declève, S., O. Gaffney, J. Ghosh, J. Randers, Rockstrom and P. E. Stoknes (2022) *Earth for All: A Survival Guide for Humanity* (Gabriola, Canada: New Society Publishers).

4 Ghosh, J. (2022) "Achieving earth for all". *Project Syndicate*, 12 July (www.project-syndicate.org/commentary/club-of-rome-report-sustainable-wellbeing-five-shifts-by-jayati-ghosh-2022-07).

5 "Climate emergency declarations in 2,355 jurisdictions and local governments cover 1 billion citizens". Climate Emergency Declaration website, 22 February 2024 (http://climateemergencydeclaration.org/climate-emergency-declarations-cover-15-million-citizens/).

is on a path to suicide.[6] More recently, UN Secretary-General Guterres called upon all countries to declare a state of climate emergency until the world has reached net-zero CO_2 emissions.[7]

Our proximity to so many tipping points is undeniable. If we do not take action, we face an unthinkable default option of "environmental devastation, extreme economic disparities and fragilities, and potentially unbearable social and political tensions".[8] In this chapter we identify the myriad of solutions under the Giant Leap scenario. It provides us with a pathway forward – a pathway of hope – but it also reinforces that time is of the essence.

About the Earth4All system dynamics model

This chapter uses the unique Earth4All system dynamics model, future scenarios and recommended pathways for change that were developed for the 2022 book *Earth for All*. The book and programme of work were launched as a 50-year follow-up to *The Limits to Growth* (1972).

In *The Limits to Growth* the authors argued that earth's finite natural resources could not support ever-increasing consumption, and they warned of likely ecological overshoot and societal collapse if the world did not recognise the environmental costs of unlimited exponential growth in resource use and waste on a finite planet. Today, scientists have concluded that, as a result of this growth, we are exceeding six of the nine planetary boundaries. Climate tipping points, once considered a distant risk, may be crossed within a few decades. We cannot rule out the possibility that some climate tipping points may have already been crossed.

It is against that backdrop that we ran an extensive system dynamics modelling exercise and then ensured proper stress testing by the Earth4All Transformational Economics Commission (consisting of economic thinkers and scientists from across the globe). This three-year

6   Chokshi, N. (2015) "Pope Francis: the world is near 'suicide' on climate change; 'it's now or never'". *Washington Post*, 30 November (www.washingtonpost.com/news/worldviews/wp/2015/11/30/pope-francis-the-world-is-near-suicide-on-climate-change-its-now-or-never/).

7   Harvey, F. (2020) "UN secretary general urges all countries to declare climate emergencies". *The Guardian*, 12 December (www.theguardian.com/environment/2020/dec/12/un-secretary-general-all-countries-declare-climate-emergencies-antonio-guterres-climate-ambition-summit).

8   Ghosh, J. (2022) "Achieving earth for all".

process, combined with deep thinking by the Earth4All partners around a well-grounded yet hopeful narrative, resulted in *Earth for All*. The central conclusion, which is extremely pertinent for the SDGs, is that wellbeing for all can be achieved while respecting planetary boundaries, but only if five extraordinary turnarounds are implemented simultaneously for poverty, inequality, empowerment, food and energy. We also considered SDG progress when each extraordinary turnaround is undertaken alone, as opposed to simultaneously in the Giant Leap.

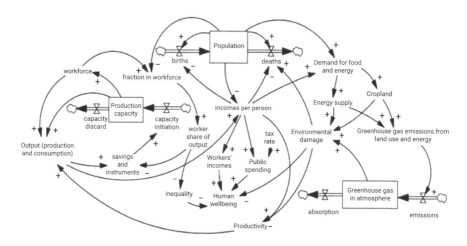

Figure 1.1. The Earth4All system dynamics model.

A note on this chapter's methodology

In this chapter we have clustered the 17 SDGs under the five extraordinary turnarounds. The inequality and empowerment turnarounds are considered jointly because of their particular synergies. The choice of which SDGs to include in separate clusters was based on the combinations of SDGs that are particularly synergistic and that closely relate to particular turnarounds. By clustering the SDGs in this way, we can also explore dependencies and potential trade-offs between these goals.

About our choice of indicators

Another important methodological point to highlight is that we mostly examined SDG progress using indicators that could easily be derived from variables that were already included in the Earth4All model or that could easily be added. For reasons related to the architecture of the model, and because of the limited availability of modellable indicators, we used only one indicator per SDG. Each of the 17 SDGs encompasses several targets and indicators, but not all of these indicators were available, or relevant for the global level of modelling that was originally carried out. Additionally, it should be emphasised that we scoped and designed the Earth4All model to answer the fundamental research question of how we can maximise human wellbeing within planetary boundaries up to 2100. Therefore, indicators were originally selected with this objective in mind.

The Earth4All model was not designed with the objective of assessing SDG progress; nevertheless, we have decided to use it to understand SDG progress up to 2050. No new variables or structures were added to the model indicators, which were not changed for the purposes of this chapter. However, we have taken great care to select suitable indicators given the 2030 Agenda scope and structure of the model. We have chosen indicators to reflect the dynamics of each individual SDG and the synergies between them. Together, they are designed to reflect the overarching challenge of the 2030 Agenda.

In each of the graphs throughout this chapter, the y-axis always reflects the indicator. For example, in our graph on poverty levels (Figure 1.2), where we use the fraction of the population living below $6.85 per day as the indicator, the numbers on the y-axis reflect population percentages. The lines labelled "Green threshold" in the graphs represent the highest level of attainment in relation to the actual goal, while those labelled "Red threshold" represent only partial attainment of the goal.

In the next phase of our work we will be retrofitting the Earth4All model to enable greater granularity in the indicators in order to assess macro regions. In parallel, we are cooperating with the Millennium Institute to assess the Too Little Too Late and Giant Leap scenarios at the national level.

The detailed results of the modelling are presented in the section on "Policy interventions". We provide a snapshot below.[9]

---

9   A more technical documentation of the model, data sources and indicators can be found in Collste, D., N. Spittler and F. Barbour (2023) "Policy coherence beyond the 2030 Agenda: Global Trajectories towards 2050". OSF preprint. DOI: 10.31219/OSF.IO/SB2NA

Key findings

Finding 1: the Giant Leap delivers concrete wins for many of the SDGs

Because of the architecture of the Earth4All model, we have modelled single indicators for a relevant cluster of SDGs. Greater granularity and additional indicators will be applied in the next phase of this project, when macro regions and nation states will be analysed under the Too Little Too Late and Giant Leap scenarios. Nevertheless, the present work has already generated important insights, which reinforce how much further the Giant Leap gets us by 2050 compared with the Too Little Too Late scenario.

We turn poverty around

Using the fraction of the population living below $6.85 per day as the indicator for poverty, we see massive differences between the Too Little Too Late and Giant Leap scenarios.[10] In the Too Little Too Late scenario, close to 20% of the global population will continue to live in poverty by 2050. In the Giant Leap, this figure drops steeply to 6.7%. This translates to 1 billion fewer people in poverty by 2050.

Wellbeing for all is achieved

We measure wellbeing with Earth4All's Average Wellbeing Index, which is based on dignity, natural health, the strength of institutions, fairness and equality, and citizen participation. Under Too Little Too Late, wellbeing drops far below its 2015 level, when the SDGs were adopted. By 2050 it could plummet to historically low levels because of increased poverty, inequality, social tensions and worsened climate change. The good news is that under the Giant Leap wellbeing soars to historic highs by 2050, far exceeding the highest levels reached in recent history, prior to the financial crash in 2008.

---

10   For the poverty threshold, we have used the $6.85 threshold instead of $1.90 because it better represents the new international consensus on what it actually takes to escape poverty, as noted by Fanning, A. L., D. W. O'Neill, J. Hickel and N. Roux (2021) "The social shortfall and ecological overshoot of nations". *Nature Sustainability*, 5: 26–36 (www.nature.com/articles/s41893-021-00799-z).

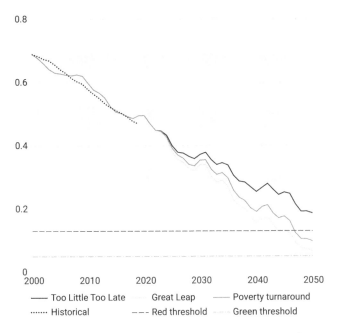

Figure 1.2. Fraction of the population living below $6.85 per day.

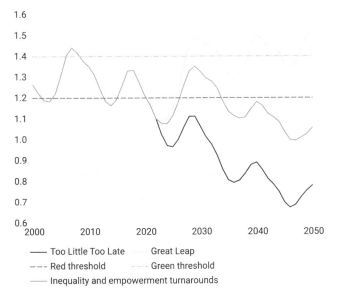

Figure 1.3. Average Wellbeing Index.

Income inequality is massively reduced

Our chosen indicator of income inequality – the ratio of owner incomes to worker incomes – is particularly relevant because, for the first time this century, global real wage growth has become negative, meaning that it is not keeping up with inflation. In 2022 we saw "the largest gap recorded since 1999 between real labour productivity growth and real wage growth in high-income countries"; this covers a period that includes the most significant economic crises of the 21st century so far.[11]

Measuring the ratio of owner incomes to worker incomes is also relevant given the deeply concerning North American trends whereby CEO salaries have skyrocketed 1,460% since 1978.[12] In 2021, CEOs were paid 399 times as much as a typical worker. In our Too Little Too Late scenario, income inequality increases, with owners accounting for 75% of incomes and workers for only 25% by 2050. Under the Giant Leap scenario we reach parity, with owners and workers each accounting for 50% of incomes by 2050. This has a massive impact for improved standards of living, access to basic human needs, social justice and cohesion.

CO_2 intensity is lowered to negative levels

The Giant Leap scenario demonstrates a greater improvement in CO_2 intensity than Too Little Too Late, with the CO_2 intensity of the economy declining rapidly by the 2040s. This indicator highlights the importance of upgrading infrastructure and retrofitting industries to make them more resource-efficient.

Emissions per person also decline rapidly in the Giant Leap scenario

By 2050 the Giant Leap enables an annual per capita drawdown of 0.58 tonnes of carbon, or a total of 5 billion tonnes of carbon globally.

---

11 International Labour Office (2022) "Global Wage Report 2022–23: the impact of inflation and Covid-19 on wages and purchasing power" (www.ilo.org/wcmsp5/groups/public/---ed_protect/---protrav/---travail/documents/publication/wcms_862569.pdf).

12 Gelles, D. (2021) "CEO pay remains stratospheric, even at companies battered by pandemic". *New York Times*, 24 April (www.nytimes.com/2021/04/24/business/ceos-pandemic-compensation.html).

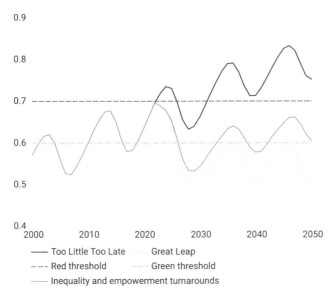

Figure 1.4. Ratio of owner incomes to worker incomes.

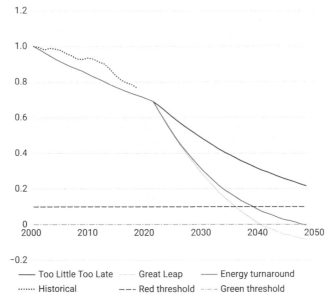

Figure 1.5. CO$_2$ intensity (indexed to 2000).

This is in stark contrast to the Too Little Too Late scenario, which results in 16.7 billion tonnes of carbon emitted globally in 2050.

The steady increase in fertiliser use is reversed

The global production and use of nitrogen fertiliser for food production accounts for approximately 5% of greenhouse gas emissions. This is why the dramatic decrease in fertiliser use in the Giant Leap is so important for the climate change battle. Reduction in fertiliser use is also key for the transition to more sustainable and responsible food production systems and for restoring the nitrogen cycle. Considered an important planetary boundary, the nitrogen cycle has been dramatically altered by the overloading of ecosystems with nitrogen through the burning of fossil fuels and an increase in nitrogen-producing industrial and agricultural activities. Under the Giant Leap, the global decline in fertiliser use continues its rapid downward trend towards 2050. It lands at 25 million tonnes per year, representing one quarter of the volume of fertiliser use in the Too Little Too Late scenario, which hovers at 100 million tonnes per year by 2050.

Public spending per person increases dramatically

Government investment in public infrastructure, health, education, electricity and other basic services is directly relevant to the aim of promoting peaceful, fair and inclusive societies. In the Giant Leap scenario, public service spending has a significantly upward trend. Compared with 2019 levels of $2,700 per person, by 2050 public spending will increase to $6,000 per person per year. This represents an additional $8.8 trillion spent globally on public services per year, an amount equivalent to twice the GDP of Germany. The Giant Leap is in stark contrast to the Too Little Too Late scenario, in which public service spending per person per year increases to only $4,800 by 2050. By way of comparison, India currently spends almost $1,800 per capita, a stark contrast to Norway, which spends over $30,000 per capita.[13]

---

13   Ortiz-Ospina, E., and M. Roser (2016) "Government spending: what do governments spend their financial resources on?" *Our World in Data*, 18 October (https://ourworldindata.org/government-spending).

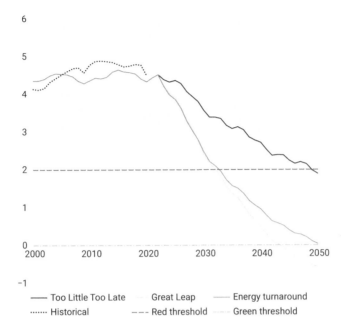

Figure 1.6. Emissions per person (in tonnes of CO_2 per year).

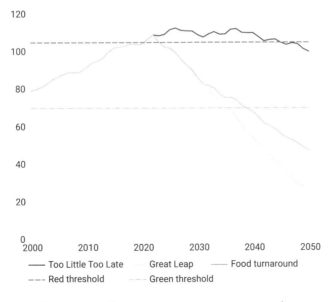

Figure 1.7. Fertiliser use (in megatonnes per year).

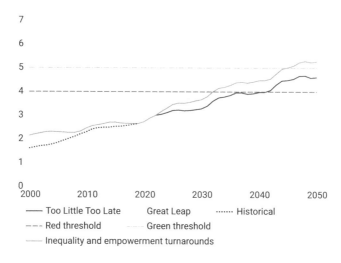

Figure 1.8. Total public services per person (in thousands of dollars per year).

Finding 2: the Giant Leap can only be achieved with simultaneous policy turnarounds

We explored SDG progress on the basis of implementing one extraordinary turnaround at a time and found that, when undertaken individually, the turnarounds do not get us anywhere near the Giant Leap trajectory of wellbeing for all within planetary boundaries.

This reinforces the critical point that the Giant Leap for the SDGs can only be attained if we act simultaneously on all five extraordinary turnarounds and operationalise all of the policy interventions that we identify later in this chapter.

The Giant Leap scenario is the only way out of the current planetary emergency and the only pathway for attaining most of the SDGs by 2050. If we are to support humanity with a fighting chance to cope with likely future shocks and stresses and to reduce the risk of crossing tipping points, we need to urgently embark on a radical transformation. This entails a shift away from today's extractive economy dominated by GDP growth and towards wellbeing economies that place value on people, the planet and prosperity. This means pivoting away from growth at all costs to a new growth paradigm, which embraces economic development fostering prosperity for the many – not just the few – within planetary boundaries.

Finding 3: despite the Giant Leap's hopeful pathways, there are two very important red alerts that emerge from our modelling

Red Alert 1: the gender gap is 230 years behind schedule

The dire situation of gender inequality in both scenarios is greatly concerning. Current numbers show that the share of female pretax labour income increases from 35% to 40% by 2050 under the Too Little Too Late scenario before levelling off and showing no signs of improvement. Under the Giant Leap scenario, there is only a marginal improvement to 42% by 2050, and only a further 4% increase by 2100.

At current rates, it would take approximately 257 years to reduce the overall gender gap, meaning that we are 230 years behind schedule. These numbers need to be a wake-up call for governments to start delivering on the promise of gender equality and ensuring the delivery of the Giant Leap, since gender equality is a key turnaround for creating more resilient and prosperous wellbeing economies.

Red Alert 2: climate goals will not be reached under either scenario

The reality of overshooting climate goals in both the Too Little Too Late scenario and the Giant Leap scenario gives serious cause for concern and calls into question the lack of emergency planning to address climate change, including growing shocks and stresses. Even with massive emissions reductions, global warming is on track to reach 1.5 °C in the early 2030s.[14] It is time to heed the call from UN Secretary-General Guterres for all countries to declare a state of climate emergency until the world has reached net-zero CO_2 emissions.[15]

Equally important is the need for governments to step up their levels of ambition at the 29th session of the Conference of the Parties (COP29) and agree to fast-track our global transition to clean energy and decarbonisation by

---

14   Garthwaite, J. (2023) "Earth likely to cross critical climate thresholds even if emissions decline, Stanford study finds". *Stanford News,* 30 January (https://news.stanford.edu/2023/01/30/ai-predicts-global-warming-will-exceed-1-5-degrees-2030s/).

15   Harvey, F. (2020) "UN secretary general urges all countries to declare climate emergencies".

- accelerating fossil energy phase-out and fossil energy subsidy repurposing,
- supporting vulnerable communities in adapting to the transition,
- transforming climate finance to support the rebuilding of vulnerable communities.

Finding 4: the Earth4All turnarounds and their related policy interventions are key to wellbeing for all

The synergistic effects of the policy interventions that underpin the Giant Leap's five extraordinary turnarounds are crucial for success in accelerating the SDGs and responding to the global planetary emergency.

Below, we identify the most important policy interventions, which are further elaborated in the final section of this chapter.

- Significant new investments are essential and must be accompanied by massive increases in public spending, along with higher taxation of extremely wealthy individuals and private corporations.

- We need a fundamental reform of the IMF's process for allocating special drawing rights (SDRs) to ensure they reach the countries that need them most. Creating global liquidity with new issuances of SDRs is not enough. Dealing with the sovereign debt overhang is also essential to give low-income countries more fiscal space. Until recently, not a single debt-burdened country had been given any form of relief.

- Governments must also quickly reverse the steady erosion of workers' rights and implement new safety nets such as a universal basic dividend.[16] Governments must massively scale up investment in women and girls to reverse the huge declines in income, safety, education and health, all of which have been exacerbated by cascading global crises. The world is at a tipping point for women's rights and gender equality.

---

16   A universal basic dividend is a regular payment given to all in society, usually without means testing, distributed as a dividend of common natural resources from companies who exploit those resources, such as companies in the oil or gas industries.

- Global food systems must be radically transformed, starting with the repurposing of agricultural subsidies towards supporting low-carbon and regenerative agricultural practices in order to improve the efficiency and sustainability of food production. Food supply chains must shift towards localised food production, and farmworkers' rights must be prioritised and protected.

- Global energy systems must shift from inefficient fossil energy systems to a clean and optimised energy system that reduces consumption in high-income countries and enhances efficiency across the global energy system. This will entail global acceleration in the phase-out of fossil energy and the repurposing of fossil energy subsidies in order to guarantee a just transition. All efforts must continue to scale up towards a 50% cut in greenhouse gas emissions, net-zero biodiversity loss by 2030 and net-zero carbon by 2050, thereby ensuring sustainable and affordable energy for all.

Table 1.1 presents a summary of the five extraordinary turnarounds under the Giant Leap scenario, along with the clusters of indicators that we have modelled under each turnaround. We have also identified the policy interventions that are essential for the turnarounds and, throughout this chapter, we have further adapted the original policy interventions from our 2022 book to address the results of our SDG modelling. The results of the modelled indicators for the inequality and empowerment turnarounds have been addressed together because of the important synergies between the policy interventions related to these two turnarounds.

Policy interventions needed for the five turnarounds

The poverty turnaround

In this subsection we highlight the specific policy interventions that are necessary to achieve the three SDGs that we cluster under the poverty turnaround. As with all the other turnarounds, these policy interventions are deeply interconnected and must be implemented together in order to optimise their inherent synergies.

The three most urgent interventions for turning poverty around are listed below.

Table 1.1. The five turnarounds, their SDG clusters and related policy interventions.

	Poverty	Inequality*	Empowerment*	Food	Energy
SDGs considered under the turnaround	SDG 1: poverty SDG 2: zero hunger SDG 6: clean water and sanitation	SDG 3: good health and wellbeing SDG 4: quality education SDG 5: gender equality SDG 8: decent work and economic growth SDG 10: reduced inequalities SDG 16: peace, justice and strong institutions SDG 17: partnership for the goals		SDG 12: sustainable consumption and production SDG 14: life below water SDG 15: life on land	SDG 7: clean energy SDG 9: industry, innovation and infrastructure SDG 11: sustainable cities and communities SDG 13: climate action
Indicators modelled under the turnaround	• Fraction of population living below $6.85 per day • Prevalence of under-nourishment • Safe water access • Safe sanitation access	• Average Wellbeing Index • School life expectancy • Female pretax labour income share • Worker disposable income • Ratio of owner incomes to worker incomes • Total public services per person (in thousands of dollars per year) • Social tension		• Fertiliser use (in mega-tonnes per year) • pH of ocean surface • Expansion of cropland (in millions of hectares)	• Electricity access • CO_2 intensity • Emissions per person • Observed warming (°C)
Overall aim of the turnaround	A GDP growth rate of at least 5% for lower-income countries until GDP per person is greater than $15,000 per year.	By 2030, the wealthiest 10% take less than 40% of national income.	Full gender equity in terms of agency, rights, resources and power in both law and employment.	A regenerative, sustainable food system that works for all within planetary boundaries.	Improved energy access for citizens of lower-income countries. Zero emissions by 2040 through low-carbon energy sources and efficiencies.

*The inequality and empowerment turnarounds are modelled together, so the same SDGs and indicators are examined for each.

	Poverty	Inequality	Empowerment	Food	Energy
Call to action of the turn-around	Reform of the international financial system and trade regulations to support lower-income countries – reducing multidimensional poverty and enabling sustainable economic progress for all.	Governments should increase taxes (income and wealth) on the wealthiest 10% in societies until they take less than 40% of national incomes.	Empower women and others disadvantaged in current systems to have equal access to education, economic and social rights, power and assets by 2030 – stabilising the world's population immediately and unleashing the potential of all.	Shift the food system towards regenerative and sustainable agriculture. Enhance locally grown and healthy diets without destroying the planet – halting biodiversity loss and protecting the global commons to ensure food for all.	Transform our inefficient fossil energy system into a clean and optimised energy-efficient system, reaching a 50% cut in greenhouse gas emissions by 2030 and net-zero fossil carbon and biodiversity loss by 2050 – thereby ensuring access to sustainable energy for all.
Policy interventions needed to activate the turnaround	• Expand the fiscal space of lower-income countries • Transform the current global financial architecture to expedite debt relief and improve allocation of special drawing rights • Transform global trade dependencies to reduce trade deficits in low-income countries • Improve access to knowledge, technology and leapfrogging • Develop new economic indicators	• Strengthen progressive taxation of both income and wealth for individuals and corporations • Strengthen labour rights and trade unions' negotiating power • Establish safety nets and innovation nets to share prosperity and provide security, such as the universal basic dividend	• Recognise that gender equality is a fundamental right and an essential precondition for economic prosperity and social cohesion • Massively scale up investment to meet 2030 education targets and guarantee the right to education for women and girls • Ensure gender equality in leadership positions in public and private bodies • Guarantee universal social protection and adequate universal pension systems	• Remove perverse agricultural subsidies • Shift food production from industrial to sustainable and regenerative agricultural practices • Prioritise and protect localised consumption, food sovereignty, and farmworkers' rights • Improve efficiency across the supply chain	• Triple investment in renewables and efficiency • Provide climate financing as concessional grants and not as loans • Make renewable energy affordable by redirecting fossil fuel subsidies • Support a global price on carbon and guarantee access to clean, safe and affordable energy for all

- Governments must definitively bridge the financing divide. Overseas development assistance (ODA) must be massively scaled up so that it actually matches the real need on the ground.

- The IMF must reform the process for issuance and allocation of SDRs, especially because of their potential to free up much-needed fiscal space for low-income countries to finance the SDGs.

- The international community must urgently scale up debt relief efforts. Debt relief is absolutely critical and urgent because of the record number of indebted countries that are either in or near debt default, and equally because they are paying exorbitant debt service payments that are crushing their ability to provide basic human needs to their populations.

Governments must definitively bridge the financing divide

The solution for unlocking finance and bridging the ever-growing financing divide for the poverty turnaround is actually very simple. Governments have to honour the financing commitments that were made over 40 years ago but continue to be unmet. In 2022, high-income countries mobilised only $204 billion in ODA, which represented a mere 5% of the annual needs of low-income countries. If governments can match their firepower in mobilising the trillions that they were able to find to address Covid-19, the war in Ukraine and recent banking failures, we can potentially bridge the financing divide. However, this will require not just efforts by the public sector but also a massive increase in private investment going to the right sectors and the areas of the world that need investment most urgently. For example, when it comes to ensuring universal access to water, overall investments must be quadrupled.[17]

At the same time, it is critical that private investment in the improvement of water infrastructure be massively scaled up, especially in those

---

17   World Health Organization (2022) "Universal access to safe drinking water requires increased investment backed by strong government institutions – WHO, UNICEF, World Bank". News article, 24 October (www.who.int/news/item/24-10-2022-universal-access-to-safe-drinking-water-requires-increased-investment-backed-by-strong-government-institutions--who--unicef--world-bank).

countries that are fraught with droughts and floods.[18] Moreover, even though access to education is addressed in the empowerment turn-around, it is worth noting here that, alongside broken ODA promises, a lack of funding for education is actually part of a larger systemic economic challenge. For example, due to decades of World Bank austerity measures, indebted countries have been required to divert domestic resources away from education and other basic human needs in order to service loan payments. This continues to be the case today, with the debt service payments of the world's poorest countries representing 10.3% of their export of goods and services and 1.8% of their gross national product.[19]

The process for issuance and allocation of SDRs must be transformed

Governed by the IMF quota system, SDRs are not fairly allocated and have not yet reached the countries most in need. While we recognise that the 2021 SDR issuance of $650 billion was the largest in the IMF's history, approximately two thirds of the SDRs went to high-income countries because SDR allocation is undertaken on the basis of the IMF quota system as opposed to actual need. There has been no reform of the governance of the IMF since the institution was established in 1945. Its decision-making processes must be radically overhauled if resources are to flow equitably to those countries that need them most.

Another complicating factor related to SDRs that must be urgently addressed is the slow and cumbersome process of the two IMF trust funds – the Poverty Reduction and Growth Trust and the Resilience and Sustainability Trust – through which recycled SDRs are meant to be channelled. It is important to recall that, in 2021, high-income countries agreed to reallocate 30% of their SDRs to low- and middle-income countries (totalling $100 billion). However, not only has it taken over two years for high-income countries to actually honour their SDR-recycling commitments, but the reality on the ground is that neither of these two trust funds has disbursed any recycled SDRs. This situation must be reversed urgently, especially since the whole premise of SDRs is to provide urgent

---

18   Mao, B. (2022) "Low-income communities lack access to clean water. It's time for change". World Economic Forum, 2 August (www.weforum.org/agenda/2022/08/access-clean-water-inequality-financing/).

19   World Bank (2022) "Debt-service payments put biggest squeeze on poor countries since 2000". Press release, 6 December (www.worldbank.org/en/news/press-release/2022/12/06/debt-service-payments-put-biggest-squeeze-on-poor-countries-since-2000).

liquidity to low-income countries. If it takes this long to increase the fiscal space of low-income countries, they will be driven deeper and deeper into debt, from which they might never be able to escape.

The international community must urgently scale up debt relief efforts

To avoid another lost decade of development, the international community must, as a critical step, urgently reform the Debt Service Suspension Initiative and the Common Framework for Debt Treatment to ensure that countries' requests for treatment are met and that debt treatment is equally available to highly indebted middle-income countries. In 2021, 26 low-income nations individually paid more to service debts than they actually received in climate finance. Instead of agreeing to cancel partial debt, many big banks and hedge funds continue to insist on receiving payments in full, including high-interest payments. This is driving an unprecedented number of indebted countries into a downward poverty spiral, which will take decades to emerge from.

The June 2023 Paris Summit on the Global Financing Pact highlighted just how low the appetite is among high-income countries and private sector creditors to reform the debt architecture, which until only recently had not granted any requests for debt treatment. This has to change urgently, and the forthcoming annual meetings of the World Bank and the IMF must take bold steps to reform the inequitable and inefficient international debt architecture, not to mention the larger systemic inequalities in the global financial system that continue to be inadequately addressed – not only by the World Bank and the IMF, but also by the recent G7 meeting in Hiroshima and the Paris Summit. They have all failed to embrace a reform path to ensure that the unaccountable, undemocratic international financial system is retrofitted for a world that is very different from the one in which it was first created. Reform of the international financial architecture is highly relevant for the poverty turnaround because today's flawed architecture is blocking resources from going to the low-income and vulnerable countries that need them most.

The inequality turnaround

Here, we highlight the specific policy interventions that are necessary to achieve the inequality turnaround. The policy interventions for the closely related empowerment turnaround are presented in the next subsection.

The Earth4All inequality turnaround recognises that countries in which citizens are economically more equal function better. They have greater social cohesion and perform better in all areas of human wellbeing and achievement than countries with divisive levels of income inequality. More equal countries (especially the Nordic countries) tend to have better outcomes for trust, education, social mobility, longevity, health, obesity, child mortality and mental health, among other areas.

The most urgent interventions for turning around inequality are listed below.

- Governments must tax the rich, with more progressive taxation of both income and wealth of individuals and corporations.
- Governments must urgently reverse the steady erosion of workers' rights, through the strengthening of labour rights and trade unions' negotiating power.
- Governments must implement new safety nets and innovative approaches for sharing prosperity, such as the universal basic dividend.

Governments must tax the rich

Earth4All asserts that taxing the super-rich is not just essential for reducing inequality, ensuring democracy and guaranteeing political and economic stability but also plays a vital role in the climate crisis (see the energy turnaround). Climate change and its effects are disproportionately driven by the investments and emissions of the wealthiest people. The richest 1% – over 80 million people – are the fastest-growing source of emissions by far: on average their investments result in a million times more emissions than one average person. Despite the continued resistance by the international community to wealth taxation, we believe that its potential for redressing wealth inequality is greater than ever. In addition to the growing evidence on the increase and impact of wealth inequality, there is, on the part of the general public, a growing awareness of and diminished tolerance for tax avoidance and evasion by wealthy individuals and multinational companies at a time when the cost of living has increased for so many due to the polycrisis of interrelated challenges that the world faces today. With 2024 as a critical election year in many countries, including the United States and countries within the EU, we believe that the increase in perceived inequality will translate into stronger demands for redistributive tax policies. There is a risk that a lack of effort by governments to redistribute wealth and ensure a just transition will create greater instability and exacerbate the backslide away from democracy.

Governments must urgently reverse the steady erosion of workers' rights

The importance of rigorous laws to strengthen workers' rights and trade unionisation are critical because, in a time of profound transformation, workers need economic protection and new opportunities for skill development. This is essential for renewing equality within societies – especially between workers and employers, since rising CEO pay is a major contributor to rising inequality. This widening pay gap is fuelling the growth of the top 1% and top 0.1% of incomes, "leaving fewer gains of economic growth for ordinary workers and widening the gap between very high earners and the bottom 90%".[20] Reversing the erosion of workers' rights will require efforts by governments to strengthen labour rights and the negotiating power of workers in order to increase the worker share of national income. Governments must also renew collective bargaining rights after decades of erosion of union and worker power. Finally, governments must empower more workers with co-ownership and seats in the boardroom to influence decisions and to give them a stake in companies' futures.

Governments must implement a universal basic dividend

The universal basic dividend (UBD) is an underexplored policy lever that can help to fundamentally redress inequality within societies. It entails investing a portion of the profits made by large corporations through publicly subsidised innovations into a public fund disseminated using a basic dividend, similar to what stock traders might receive.[21] The UBD is premised on the assertion that resources in the global commons cannot be legitimately owned by private individuals or enterprises. This means that any financial benefit derived from the exploitation of these resources must be shared with the general public.[22] The UBD is also grounded in the

---

20   Bivens, J., and J. Kandra (2022) "CEO pay has skyrocketed 1,460% since 1978". *Economic Policy Institute*, 4 October (www.epi.org/publication/ceo-pay-in-2021/).

21   Project ALTER (2019) "Universal basic dividend vs income: the policy that could forge a path beyond money". *Data Series*, 31 July, Medium (https://medium.com/dataseries/universal-basic-dividend-vs-income-19f04f7136ac).

22   UCL Institute for Innovation and Public Purpose (2023) "Universal basic dividend as a form of welfare". *UCL IIPP Blog*, 12 July, Medium (https://medium.com/iipp-blog/universal-basic-dividend-as-a-form-of-welfare-e11ed4349b07).

belief that, in most cases, wealth is produced collectively and privatised by those with the power to do so, notably the corporate elite. This under-pins the general public's right to a share of the capital stock and associ-ated dividends, reflecting society's investment in corporations' capital.[23]

The UBD proposal is based on proven, effective ways to transfer a por-tion of the wealth extracted from common resources such as fossil fuels, land, real estate or social data. In addition to redistributing wealth more fairly, this will provide essential individual economic security during the transformation of societies, and it is likely to spur creativity, innovation and entrepreneurship.

The empowerment turnaround

In this subsection we highlight the specific policy interventions that are necessary to achieve the empowerment of women and other disadvan-taged groups. This turnaround is about enabling women, girls and other disadvantaged groups to access

- education, health services and lifelong learning;
- financial independence and leadership positions;
- economic security through universal social protection.

Empirical data shows that economies that support greater equality score highest in global rankings of wellbeing and human development. Gender equality is about removing discrimination in order to achieve greater inclusiveness and equity in society. These are fundamentally the conditions that build social cohesion and embed fairness and justice more deeply in society. In turn, societies become more resilient to shocks such as financial crises, pandemics and food price volatility.

Shockingly, gender equality (SDG 5) – which we explore through income disparity (the percentage of pretax labour income held by women) as our indicator – will not be achieved in the next two centuries. Indeed, the UN estimates that, at the current rate of "progress", it will take

- 286 years to close gaps in legal protection and remove discrimina-tory laws,
- 140 years for women to be represented equally in positions of power and leadership in the workplace and
- 40 years to achieve equal representation in national parliaments.

---

23   Ibid.

Against this backdrop, the most urgent policy interventions for the empowerment turnaround are as follows.

- Governments must reverse the lack of progress on gender equality.
- Donor governments must massively scale up investment to meet 2030 education targets.
- Governments must guarantee the right to education for women and girls.

Governments must reverse the lack of progress on gender equality

The world is at a tipping point for women's rights and gender equality. Governments must massively scale up investment in women and girls to reverse the regressions in their lives in terms of income, safety, education and health, all of which have been exacerbated by cascading global crises. Gender equality is at the heart of all SDGs, and governments must now rally to significantly increase investment and rigorously implement legal systems that ban violence against women, protect women's rights in marriage and the family, guarantee equal pay and benefits at work, and guarantee their equal rights to own and control land. The reality is that the longer governments take to carry out these urgent actions, the more it will cost and the more difficult it will be to change course in order to achieve full gender equality and a more thriving economic system that delivers prosperity for all before the next millennium.

Donor governments must massively scale up investment to meet 2030 education targets

Even before the Covid-19 pandemic, the world was already way off track in achieving its education targets under SDG 4. Currently, only one in six countries will meet SDG 4 and achieve universal access to quality education by 2030.[24] A total of 57 million primary-aged children remain out of school, with "more than half of them in sub-Saharan Africa".[25]

We know that scaling up investment will be critical for getting SDG 4 back on track by 2030. Earth4All supports the UN in its call for an infusion

---

24   "Goal 4". United Nations Department of Economic and Social Affairs website (https://sdgs.un.org/goals/goal4).

25   "Goal 4: quality education". United Nations Development Programme website (www.undp.org/sustainable-development-goals/quality-education).

of $148 billion in annual financing to bridge the financing gap if low- and lower-middle-income countries are to meet SDG 4 by 2030. As UNESCO asserts: "Additional costs due to Covid-19 related school closures risk increasing this current financing gap by up to one-third." Investment now could reduce this additional cost by up to 75%.[26]

In addition to the much-needed immediate mobilisation of resources, we must also address the reality that education is a systemic economic challenge. The early years of austerity-imposed lending by the IMF and the World Bank meant that many low- and middle-income countries were required to introduce user fees, with many poor populations having to spend over 10% of their yearly income just to send two children to school. This reality underscores the importance of Earth4All's call for debt relief under the poverty turnaround in order to free up fiscal space for low-income countries to fund the necessary social and educational programmes for the next generation of children to thrive, not just survive.

Governments must guarantee the right to education for women and girls

Although we analyse SDG 4 in terms of school life expectancy as the indicator, we must highlight the importance of gender parity in primary, secondary and tertiary education. Gender parity in education is an important policy lever in the empowerment turnaround. However, despite the fact that all member states have made commitments to realise the right to education for all, the reality is that "fewer than half of the world's countries" have achieved gender parity in primary education.[27]

Moreover, as recently as January 2023 the UN confirmed that 130 million girls around the world continue to be denied the human right to education. This is unconscionable and must be rectified by government action to operationalise the right to education for women and girls by repealing laws that block girls from accessing quality education; regularly reviewing and evaluating constitutional guarantees and legislative and policy frameworks to counter discrimination; ensuring gender-sensitive

---

26   Global Education Monitoring Report Team (2020) "Act now: reduce the impact of Covid-19 on the cost of achieving SDG 4". Policy Paper 42, September, UNESCO Global Education Monitoring Report (https://unesdoc.unesco.org/ark:/48223/pf0000374163/).

27   Office of the High Commissioner for Human Rights (2023) "The world is failing 130 million girls denied education: UN experts". Press release, 23 January, United Nations (www.ohchr.org/en/press-releases/2023/01/world-failing-130-million-girls-denied-education-un-experts).

budgeting for girls' education; and, importantly, ensuring that the right to education is justiciable, and that girls are aware of their rights and have access to sensitive and safe judicial and nonjudicial remedies.

The food turnaround

In this subsection we highlight the specific policy interventions that are necessary to achieve the food turnaround. These are as follows.

- Governments must repurpose perverse agricultural subsidies.
- Food production must shift from industrial to sustainable and regenerative agricultural practices.
- Localised consumption, food sovereignty and farmworkers' rights must be prioritised and protected.
- Improvements to efficiency must be made across the supply chain, including waste reduction.

As with all the turnarounds, these interventions have been adapted to the results of our indicator modelling.

Governments must repurpose perverse agricultural subsidies

Direct agricultural subsidies are estimated at over $635 billion a year and are driving the excessive use of environmentally harmful subsidies. More than 90% of these subsidies damage human health, fuel the climate crisis, destroy nature and drive inequality by excluding smallholder farmers, many of whom are women. Without reform, agricultural subsidies could rise to over $1 trillion per year by 2030.[28] A recent World Bank report estimates that subsidies for soya beans, palm oil and beef are responsible for 14% of forest loss every year.[29] Beef and milk receive

---

28   Carrington, D. (2021) "Nearly all global farm subsidies harm people and planet – UN". *The Guardian*, 14 September (www.theguardian.com/environment/2021/sep/14/global-farm-subsidies-damage-people-planet-un-climate-crisis-nature-inequality).

29   World Bank (2023) "Trillions wasted on subsidies could help address climate change", press release, 15 June (www.worldbank.org/en/news/press-release/2023/06/15/trillions-wasted-on-subsidies-could-help-address-climate-change). Damania, R., E. Balseca, C. de Fontaubert et al. (2023) *Detox Development: Repurposing Environmentally Harmful Subsidies* (Washington, DC: World Bank) (www.worldbank.org/en/topic/climatechange/publication/detox-development).

the biggest subsidies, which is not surprising given that their production represents the biggest sources of greenhouse gas emissions in the agricultural sector.

There are ample models of best practice for subsidy reform and repurposing perverse subsidies, not just in agriculture but also in energy and other extractive sectors. Regarding agricultural subsidies, we emphasise that these should be repurposed towards low-carbon and regenerative agricultural techniques and towards empowering smallholder farmers to ensure rural prosperity within planetary boundaries.[30] At the same time, the shift away from chemical agriculture must be carried out through a carefully planned transition, especially for smaller farmers, by providing them with special subsidies for agro-ecological practices.[31]

Circling back to our modelling of fertiliser use, we highlight that profits of chemical fertiliser companies grew exponentially from $14 billion before the Covid-19 pandemic to $28 billion in 2021, and further increased to $49 billion in 2022. These unconscionable levels of profit underpin the strong case for a windfall profit tax (as called for in the subsection on the inequality turnaround), which should be sufficiently high as to discourage further attempts by multinational companies to yet again raise prices.[32]

Food production must shift from industrial to sustainable and regenerative agricultural practices

As we highlight above, governments must repurpose perverse subsidies that promote dependence on chemical inputs. But we also need a massive transformation of the global food system, which is currently dominated largely by multinational corporations and trade as opposed to providing guaranteed access to food as a universal human right. The whole system is predicated on high-carbon, unsustainable and unhealthy production and consumption patterns, with enormous waste across all stages of production and distribution.

---

30   Ding, H., A. Markandya, R. Feltran-Barbieri et al. (2021) "Repurposing agricultural subsidies to restore degraded farmland and grow rural prosperity". World Resources Institute (www.wri.org/research/farm-restoration-subsidies).

31   Ghosh, J., and L. Fries (2023) "Subsidizing chemical fertilizers is counterproductive". Institute for New Economic Thinking, 13 July (www.ineteconomics.org/perspectives/blog/subsidizing-chemical-fertilizers-is-counterproductive).

32   Ibid.

As Earth4All Transformational Economics Commission member Jayati Ghosh asserts:

> The global food system also produces massive greenhouse gas emissions, thereby inflicting substantial ecological damage, and deprives small-scale farmers in many countries of secure and viable livelihoods. Perhaps worst of all, food access remains profoundly unequal, causing extreme hunger to increase rather than decline.[33]

The transition to sustainable and regenerative agricultural practices will take time, and it will in some cases be more expensive, which is why perverse subsidies must be redirected to free up investment in healthier, sustainable and – most importantly – regenerative practices. The production of food using cleaner and more sustainable technologies and practices will also drastically reduce the need for chemical fertilisers,[34] which are the main factors in the transgression of planetary boundaries in relation to the nitrogen and phosphorus cycles.[35]

Localised consumption, food sovereignty and farmworkers' rights must be prioritised and protected

Localised food production not only supports planetary health but also encourages greater community cohesion, resilience and connection. This is directly related to the call for food sovereignty as "the right of each nation to maintain and develop its own capacity to produce its basic foods respecting cultural and productive diversity".[36]

Additionally, the Food and Agriculture Organization emphasises that fair and equitable working conditions for those who grow, sell and process food are essential to achieving true food security: "Challenges are particularly aggravated for migrant, undocumented and seasonal workers, who may lack access to legal protection and face further discrimination due to language and cultural differences or their inability

---

33   Ibid.

34   This is shown by the decrease in chemical fertiliser use – the indicator used for the modelling of SDG 12 – under the Giant Leap.

35   "Planetary boundaries". Stockholm Resilience Centre website (https://bit.ly/49wEmu6).

36   "The 1996 Rome Food Sovereignty Declaration in postcards". La Via Campesina website, 22 November 2021 (https://bit.ly/4cJlafv).

to seek justice."[37] Gender considerations are hugely important as well; while women make up 43% of agricultural workers, they represent only 15% of landowners, despite an estimate that giving women equal access to food-related support and resources could provide sufficient nourishment for 100–150 million people.[38] Justice and human rights considerations must therefore be central to policy decisions around food system reform.

As a bare minimum, governments have a responsibility to regulate companies and ensure the implementation of workers' rights across the supply chain,[39] and mechanisms of accountability and improvement must be conceived and implemented that place the voices and wellbeing of workers at their core. The Coalition of Immokalee Workers, for example, has created the Fair Food Program,[40] a partnership between farmworkers, growers and buyers that the UN stated "must be considered as an international benchmark"[41] for action against agricultural exploitation in order to ensure worker dignity and create an ethical supply chain.[42] The encouragement and protection of such partnerships are essential to the realisation of food sovereignty and sustainability supportive of health and dignity for all.

Improvements to efficiency must be made across the supply chain, including waste reduction

Approximately one third of crops produced globally is wasted. This means that close to 2 billion tonnes of food never makes it to consumers. In 2017

---

37   High Level Panel of Experts on Food Security and Nutrition (2022) "Critical, emerging and enduring issues for food security and nutrition". Committee on World Food Security, July (www.fao.org/3/cc1867en/cc1867en.pdf).

38   See "These numbers prove that rural women are crucial for a better future. But they're not getting what they need to succeed", International Fund for Agricultural Development website, 7 March 2022 (www.ifad.org/en/web/latest/-/these-numbers-prove-that-rural-women-are-crucial-for-a-better-future). This is also related to SDG 8 (decent work and economic growth).

39   As noted in the *Earth for All* chapter on the food turnaround, "regulations should at least require implementation of the OECD/ILO Human Rights Due Diligence (HRDD) process".

40   See https://fairfoodprogram.org.

41   Coalition of Immokalee Workers (2017) "UN expert: FFP 'must be considered an international benchmark' in fight against modern-day slavery!" Blog post, 3 January (https://ciw-online.org/blog/2017/01/un-expert-ffp/).

42   This is also related to SDG 8 (decent work and economic growth).

food-waste emissions measured 9.2 billion tonnes of CO_2-equivalent, approximately as much as the total emissions that year of the United States and United Kingdom combined,[43] and many fisheries throw away more fish than they keep.[44]

Interventions to reduce and prevent food waste are thus crucial for reducing waste and emissions and increasing the food available for a growing world population. Improving storage and cooling facilities among small-scale farmers and reducing intermediaries in the supply chain, particularly in low- and middle-income countries, will decrease one of the root causes of food waste[45] and also provide more income to farmers directly, thus strengthening rural livelihoods and small-scale farming operations. Behavioural interventions focused on consumers could be one way to address household-level food waste, particularly when they target attitudes and social norms.[46] A study by the European Commission found that up to 10% of annual food waste (8.8 million tonnes) was related to food "use by" dates,[47] supporting the idea of policy interventions that revise or clarify this label on packaging.[48]

The energy turnaround

The energy turnaround must address the specific challenges faced by low-income and middle-income countries when transitioning to clean energy, because these countries often pay more for electricity, "cannot

43   Dwyer, O. (2023) "Food waste makes up 'half' of global food system emissions". *Carbon Brief*, 13 March (www.carbonbrief.org/food-waste-makes-up-half-of-global-food-system-emissions/).

44   "Sustainable seafood". World Wildlife Fund website (www.worldwildlife.org/industries/sustainable-seafood).

45   Balaji, M., and K. Arshinder (2016) "Modeling the causes of food wastage in Indian perishable food supply chain". *Resources, Conservation and Recycling*, 114: 153–167 (www.sciencedirect.com/science/article/abs/pii/S0921344916301902).

46   Stancu, V., P. Haugaard and L. Lähteenmäki (2016) "Determinants of consumer food waste behaviour: two routes to food waste". *Appetite*, 96: 7–17 (https://pubmed.ncbi.nlm.nih.gov/26299713/).

47   Directorate-General for Health and Food Safety (2018) "Market study on date marking and other information provided on food labels and food waste prevention". European Commission (https://op.europa.eu/en/publication-detail/-/publication/e7be006f-0d55-11e8-966a-01aa75ed71a1/language-en).

48   Shen, G., Z. Li, T. Hong et al. (2023) "The status of the global food waste mitigation policies: experience and inspiration for China". *Environment, Development and Sustainability* (https://link.springer.com/article/10.1007/s10668-023-03132-0).

access clean energy projects, and are locked into fossil fuel dependency".[49] This is exacerbated by the fact that the "top 10% of the richest in the world account for more than half of all emissions". In addition, "within-country inequality in carbon emissions is now greater than between-country inequality".[50]

At the outset it is extremely important to spotlight the continued resistance of the international community to addressing these systemic challenges and to truly shifting away from burning fossil energy, the number one cause of human-made climate change. The lack of willingness among governments to address the need for an immediate transition to clean energy was brought into sharp relief at the recent gathering of the G20 in Goa. Since the G20 countries collectively account for more than three quarters of global emissions and GDP, their cumulative effort to decarbonise is crucial for the climate battle. However, they could not reach agreement on the urgency of reducing the use of fossil fuels, instead preferring to focus on carbon-capture technology. Just as worryingly, governments could not agree on the tripling of renewable energy capacity by 2030. In fact, Saudi Arabia, Russia, China, South Africa and Indonesia specifically opposed this goal.

Below, we highlight the policy interventions that are necessary to ensure the energy turnaround.

- Triple investment in renewables to at least $4 trillion per year and ensure comparable investment in energy efficiency.
- Commit to increasing concessional climate finance.
- Make renewable energy affordable by redirecting fossil fuel subsidies, which currently amount to $0.5 trillion per year.
- Support a global price on carbon by establishing an internationally agreed price floor to significantly accelerate the world's transition to renewable energy sources and ensure equitable access to energy for all.

---

49   World Bank (2023) "Breaking down barriers to clean energy transition". News article, 16 May (www.worldbank.org/en/news/feature/2023/05/16/breaking-down-barriers-to-clean-energy-transition).

50   Ghosh, J. (2023) "It's not just analysis, it's a call for action". Interview by Sorcha Brennan, *Frontiers*, April 24 (https://blog.frontiersin.org/2023/04/24/jayati-ghosh-its-not-just-analysis-its-a-call-for-action/).

Investment in renewables must be tripled and energy efficiency must be intensified

A report prepared for India's G20 presidency estimated the cost of the energy transition at $4 trillion per year globally and stressed the need for increased climate finance for low- and middle-income countries.[51] Official World Bank figures indicate that in 2020 renewable energy did in fact dominate climate finance. The share of climate finance going to renewable energy over the past decade is even higher, at 70%. While a good start, this is nowhere near enough. We support the UN secretary-general in his call for a tripling of public and private investments in renewable energy to at least $4 trillion per year.[52] We also highlight that according to UNCTAD's World Investment Report 2023, low-income countries receive far less foreign direct investment in sustainable energy than high-income countries.[53] Low-income countries need annual renewable energy investments of about $1.7 trillion, but in 2022 they received only $544 billion. We also emphasise that climate investment does not always flow towards climate mitigation or adaptation, and in particular not to renewables or energy efficiency projects. A recent Reuters special report found that large sums of reported climate finance were going to projects that had absolutely nothing to do with climate (e.g. chocolate stores in Italy, hotel expansion in Haiti, film projects in Belgium and, most worryingly, Japanese financing of coal plants in Bangladesh and airport expansion in Egypt).[54] The underlying problem is that the original climate pledges made in 2009 are not governed by official guidelines as to which activities count as climate finance.

Tripling investment in renewables must also be accompanied by increased global progress on energy efficiency. The latter is essential if

51 Mooney, A. (2023) "G20 deal on fossil fuels blocked after Saudi opposition". *Financial Times*, 22 July (www.ft.com/content/fd30b0d2-2990-4531-9ed3-e91db0f4e47e).

52 Li., B. (2023) "Scaling up climate finance for emerging markets and developing economies". Speech at EIB Group Forum 2023, International Monetary Fund (www.imf.org/en/News/Articles/2023/02/28/sp022823-scaling-up-climate-finance-for-emerging-markets-and-developing-economies).

53 United Nations Conference on Trade and Development (2023) "UNCTAD calls for urgent support to developing countries to attract massive investment in clean energy". News article, 5 July (https://unctad.org/news/unctad-calls-urgent-support-developing-countries-attract-massive-investment-clean-energy).

54 Rumney, E., I. Casado Sánchez, J. Dowdell et al. (2023) "Rich nations say they're spending billions to fight climate change. Some money is going to strange places". *Reuters*, 1 June (www.reuters.com/investigates/special-report/climate-change-finance/).

we are to double the rate of improvement in energy efficiency globally by 2030, as called for by SDG 7.3. Currently the world is not on track, with the rate of energy intensity improvement having dropped to 0.6% in 2020, in large part due to Covid-19.[55] While this figure is expected to increase, the annual improvements in energy intensity must average 3.4% if we are to make up for lost time and meet SDG 7.3 by 2030.[56]

Governments must commit to increasing concessional climate finance

The Intergovernmental Panel on Climate Change estimates that the current level of climate finance spending is about $630 billion. This is just a fraction of what is really needed – and very little goes to low- and middle-income countries.[57] In addition to broken climate finance promises, donor governments have actually overestimated their spending, claiming to have mobilised $83.3 billion in 2020 when the actual value was at most $24.5 billion.[58] On top of this, donor countries are repurposing up to one third of official aid contributions as climate finance, rather than putting forward new and additional money.[59]

Besides overestimating their spending, donor governments are supplying the bulk of their climate finance commitments in the form of loans rather than grants. More than half of all climate finance going to the world's poorest countries is provided as loans, adding to the debt burdens of already heavily indebted countries. The reality is that not only is the flow of private investment inadequate (approximately $14 billion

55   ETEnergyWorld (2023) "World not on track to achieve Sustainable Development Goal for energy by 2030: report". *Economic Times*, 6 June (https://energy.economictimes.indiatimes.com/news/renewable/world-not-on-track-to-achieve-sustainable-development-goal-for-energy-by-2030-report/100795564).

56   United Nations Economic and Social Council (2023) "Sustainable renewable energy key to unlocking developing countries' potential, achieving global goals, speakers tell High-Level Political Forum". Meetings coverage, 12 July (https://press.un.org/en/2023/ecosoc7136.doc.htm).

57   Georgieva, K., and T. Adrian (2022) "Public sector must play major role in catalyzing private climate finance". *IMF Blog*, 18 August (www.imf.org/en/Blogs/Articles/2022/08/18/public-sector-must-play-major-role-in-catalyzing-private-climate-finance).

58   Oxfam International (2023) "Rich countries' continued failure to honor their $100 billion climate finance promise threatens negotiations and undermines climate action". Press release, 5 June (www.oxfam.org/en/press-releases/rich-countries-continued-failure-honor-their-100-billon-climate-finance-promise).

59   Ibid.

annually goes to climate mitigation efforts), but the actual distribution of climate finance is skewed, with investment directed primarily to Asian and middle-income countries as opposed to the lowest-income countries in sub-Saharan Africa, despite their significantly greater vulnerability to climate change.[60]

And there is of course the continued investment in fossil fuels by the World Bank. The World Bank and all of the multilateral development banks (except the European Investment Bank) have a poor record in leveraging private investment for climate and development infrastructure and services. The World Bank, for example, has continued to invest over $16 billion of project finance in fossil fuels since the 2015 Paris Agreement. Reliance on private investment to fight climate change is deeply problematic when the fossil fuel industry has not only contributed most to the climate crisis but also profiteered in the worst possible way and now all but abandoned its net-zero commitments.

Renewable energy must be made affordable by redirecting fossil fuel subsidies

Government subsidies for fossil fuels are one of the biggest obstacles to the energy turnaround. Each year, governments around the world invest $0.5 trillion into artificially lowering the price of fossil fuels. The IMF has found that prices for fossil fuels were "at least 50% below their true costs for 99% of coal, 52% of diesel and 47% of natural gas in 2020". It further concluded that the "fossil fuel industry benefits from subsidies of $11m every minute", with five countries responsible for two thirds of the subsidies: China, the United States, Russia, India and Japan.[61] Currently, governments spend three times more on fossil fuel subsidies than they invest in renewables. This highlights the extent to which government intervention is skewing prices – and therefore market incentives – in favour of fossil fuels, rather than against them.[62]

---

60   Belianska, A., P. Mitra, S. Jain et al. (2023) "Closing the gap: concessional climate finance and sub-Saharan Africa". Analytical note, April, International Monetary Fund (www.imf.org/-/media/Files/Publications/REO/AFR/2023/April/English/ ClimateNote.ashx).

61   Carrington, D. (2021) "Fossil fuel industry gets subsidies of $11m a minute, IMF finds". *The Guardian*, 6 October (www.theguardian.com/environment/2021/oct/06/fossil-fuel-industry-subsidies-of-11m-dollars-a-minute-imf-finds).

62   Ghosh, J., S. Chakraborty and D. Das (2022) "Climate imperialism in the twenty-first century". *Monthly Review*, 1 July (https://monthlyreview.org/2022/07/01/climate-imperialism-in-the-twenty-first-century/).

The inequity is that while billions of people are suffering from high energy prices, the oil and gas industry is actually making billions in windfall profits from a distorted market, which the UN secretary-general refers to as scandalous.[63] These profits are also being made on the back of growing energy poverty, thus creating greater inequalities across our societies and a risk of destabilising democracies. Without action, subsidies will rise to $6.4 trillion in 2025.[64] The first step to creating viable sustainable energy and electricity markets is redirecting these subsidies and windfall profits, freeing up trillions of dollars for investment in the shift towards renewables.[65]

There is another important equity issue with regard to fossil fuel subsidies. Namely, as with agricultural subsidies, in many low-income countries most of the subsidies that lead to lower market prices for oil and gas are often intended to help the poor. These subsidies must be redirected towards renewable energy pathways that are fair and equitable.

Governments must support a global price on carbon and bridge the energy access gap

Another important barrier to the energy turnaround is the lack of agreement on a fair carbon price that takes into consideration the damage incurred due to greenhouse gas emissions. An internationally agreed price floor for carbon could significantly accelerate the world's transition to renewable energy sources. Despite the effectiveness of this tool to redirect spending towards renewables and other low-carbon practices, many countries fear a loss of international competitiveness, notably in high-emission sectors. We support an international carbon price floor with tiered price floors based on income levels.[66] Although not a panacea, carbon pricing is an essential part of mitigation efforts to unlock

---

63   United Nations Secretary-General (2022) "Secretary-General's video message on the launch of the World Meteorological Organization's State of the Global Climate 2021 Report". Speech, 18 May (www.un.org/sg/en/content/sg/statement/2022-05-18/secretary-generals-video-message-the-launch-of-the-world-meteorological-organization%E2%80%99s-state-of-the-global-climate-2021-report-scroll-down-for-languages).

64   Carrington, D. (2021) "Fossil fuel industry gets subsidies of $11m a minute".

65   Ahmed, N. (2022) "The clean energy transformation: a new paradigm for social progress within planetary boundaries". Deep Dive Paper 8, August, Earth4All (www.clubofrome.org/wp-content/uploads/2022/08/Earth4All_Deep_Dive_Ahmed.pdf).

66   Chateau, J., F. Jaumotte and G. Schwerhoff (2022) "Why countries must cooperate on carbon prices". *IMF Blog*, 19 May (www.imf.org/en/Blogs/Articles/2022/05/19/blog-why-countries-must-cooperate-on-carbon-prices).

the trillions of dollars in private capital necessary to reach emissions reduction targets.[67]

A further important priority action for governments is to urgently bridge the energy access gap. The International Energy Agency estimates that without a massive increase in investment, 1.9 billion people will be without clean cooking and 660 million people without electricity access by 2030.[68] In addition to increased foreign investment flows, debt relief must be accelerated to increase low-income countries' fiscal space to make the domestic investments necessary for a just and clean energy transition.

Conclusions

It is clear from our analysis that the Too Little Too Late scenario condemns future generations to a dangerously destabilised planet. The climate system will likely cross multiple tipping points, and social tensions are likely to increase. By contrast, the Giant Leap scenario significantly reduces this risk – but it does not eliminate it. However, social tensions are likely to fall and wellbeing is likely to improve significantly, thereby contributing to the greater resilience of societies. It must be emphasised that the Earth4All extraordinary turnarounds must be implemented simultaneously if we are to achieve the Giant Leap towards the SDGs. One of the novel features of our integrated systems modelling approach is that economic, demographic, ecological and social drivers are fundamentally interconnected and give us a vision of what is possible in the long term. When we explored SDG progress on the basis of one extraordinary turnaround at a time, we found that, undertaken individually, the turnarounds do not get us anywhere near the Giant Leap trajectory. This reinforces the critical point that the Giant Leap for the SDGs can only be attained if we act simultaneously on all five extraordinary turnarounds and operationalise all of the policy interventions that we have identified.

We recognise that many of the policy interventions for each of the five turnarounds are well known. These interventions are all elaborated in our 2022 book *Earth for All* and in previous papers and reports published by the Earth4All partners.

---

67   World Economic Forum (2023) "Carbon pricing standards needed to accelerate green energy". News article, 19 January (www.weforum.org/press/2023/01/carbon-pricing-standards-needed-to-accelerate-green-energy/).

68   ETEnergyWorld (2023) "World not on track to achieve Sustainable Development Goal for energy by 2030".

In this chapter we have adapted our policy interventions to relate specifically to the results of our SDG modelling work. Against that backdrop, the new insight that we bring to the SDG Summit is that governments must implement all of these policy interventions simultaneously, starting well before 2030 if we are to achieve the SDGs by 2050 and get close to an earth for all at a time when humanity is facing its greatest existential risk. This is an unfathomable challenge, but our analysis shows that if we are to achieve the Giant Leap by 2050, we must do things in a radically different way. Table 1.2 provides an overview of the policy interventions necessary to achieve a Giant Leap for all the SDGs – the only trajectory that enables humanity to get closer to thriving rather than just surviving.

Table 1.2. Overview of all the policy interventions necessary to achieve a Giant Leap for the SDGs.

Poverty	Inequality	Empowerment	Food	Energy
• Expand the fiscal space of lower-income countries • Transform the current global financial architecture to expedite debt relief and improve allocation of SDRs • Transform global trade dependencies to reduce trade deficits in low-income countries • Improve access to knowledge, technology and leapfrogging • Develop new economic indicators	• Strengthen progressive taxation on both income and wealth for individuals and corporations • Strengthen labour rights and trade union negotiating power • Establish safety nets and innovation nets to share prosperity and provide security, such as the universal basic dividend	• Recognise that gender equality is essential for economic prosperity and social cohesion • Massively scale up investment to meet 2030 education targets and guarantee the right to education for women and girls • Ensure gender equality in leadership positions in public and private bodies • Guarantee universal social protection and adequate universal pension systems	• Remove perverse agricultural subsidies • Shift food production from industrial to sustainable and regenerative agricultural practices • Prioritise and protect localised consumption, food sovereignty, and farmworkers' rights • Improve efficiency across the supply chain	• Triple investment in renewables and efficiency • Provide climate financing as concessional grants and not as loans • Make renewable energy affordable by redirecting fossil fuel subsidies • Support a global price on carbon and guarantee access to clean, safe and affordable energy for all

The reality of overshooting the green and red thresholds for climate action under SDG 13 in both the Too Little Too Late scenario and the Giant Leap scenario is extremely worrying in light of the lack of global and national emergency plans currently in place to address rapidly worsening climate change and predicted growing shocks and stresses. It is time to heed the calls from UN Secretary-General Guterres to put in place the policy interventions and systemic shifts necessary to address today's planetary emergency.

We recommend both declaring and then adopting clear planetary emergency plans integrating the five extraordinary turnarounds and implementing the above policy recommendations. Collectively this is the greatest insurance plan for humanity to not only survive but eventually thrive. Implementing this plan to achieve SDGs for all will ensure an earth for all.

Enrico Giovannini

2 | The New Global Deal: a key tool to achieve the Sustainable Development Goals

After being a key contributor to its preparation, the European Union has been at the forefront of implementation of the United Nations' 2030 Agenda for Sustainable Development. Especially since 2019, after the election of the European Parliament and the establishment of the new European Commission, EU institutions have adopted an impressive and unprecedented number of legal acts, strategies, recommendations and action plans to transform the European economy and European society and make them more sustainable and equitable, according to the principles embedded in Article 3 of the Treaty on the Functioning of the European Union (TFEU):

1. The Union's aim is to promote peace, its values and the well-being of its peoples.

2. The Union shall offer its citizens an area of freedom, security and justice without internal frontiers, in which the free movement of persons is ensured in conjunction with appropriate measures with respect to external border controls, asylum, immigration and the prevention and combating of crime.

3. The Union shall establish an internal market. It shall work for the sustainable development of Europe based on balanced economic growth and price stability, a highly competitive social market economy, aiming at full employment and social progress, and a high level of protection and improvement of the quality of the environment. It shall promote scientific and technological advance. It shall combat social exclusion and discrimination, and shall promote social justice and protection, equality between women and men, solidarity between generations and protection of the rights of the child. It shall promote economic, social and territorial cohesion, and solidarity among

Member States. It shall respect its rich cultural and linguistic diversity, and shall ensure that Europe's cultural heritage is safeguarded and enhanced.

4. The Union shall establish an economic and monetary union whose currency is the euro.

5. In its relations with the wider world, the Union shall uphold and promote its values and interests and contribute to the protection of its citizens. It shall contribute to peace, security, the sustainable development of the Earth, solidarity and mutual respect among peoples, free and fair trade, eradication of poverty and the protection of human rights, in particular the rights of the child, as well as to the strict observance and the development of international law, including respect for the principles of the United Nations Charter.

6. The Union shall pursue its objectives by appropriate means commensurate with the competences which are conferred upon it in the Treaties.

Under the strategic frameworks of the European Green Deal and the European Pillar of Social Rights, the European Commission led by Ursula von der Leyen put the 2030 Agenda at the core of its strategy, which has included setting up governance rules explicitly aimed at implementing the 2030 Agenda and achieving the Sustainable Development Goals (SDGs). This is why the EU experience could be used to identify practices that are useful for designing the New Global Deal and the New Social Contract proposed by the UN secretary-general.

There are four areas where the EU experience, as well as the practices implemented by its member states, could be especially useful (particularly in light of the proposals made by the UN secretary-general in preparation for the 2024 Summit of the Future):

- the adoption of sustainable development as a key principle driving public policies, business strategies and private behaviours;
- the design of a monitoring system to evaluate the progress towards the SDGs at the local, national and supranational levels, as well as evaluating the impact that public policies have on them;
- the adoption of the 2030 Agenda as *the* framework for designing and assessing the impact of both public policies and business strategies, making it the cornerstone of public and corporate governance;
- the design of public policies using strategic foresight tools and the concept of "transformative resilience" as the new compass for policies and business strategies, in order to face future shocks, reduce

risks and identify future opportunities, and to put the world onto a more sustainable pathway.

These four areas show how the transformative power of the 2030 Agenda can become effective only through a set of actions that profoundly change the way in which socioeconomic systems work and public policies are designed and carried out.

The implementation of the 2030 Agenda in the EU

The EU and the goals of the 2030 Agenda

The EU represents the most advanced geopolitical area with respect to the goals of the 2030 Agenda, and many of the best-performing countries in international rankings based on the SDGs are European. From 2010 onwards, the EU has made progress towards most of the SDGs, although this progress is insufficient to hope to fully achieve the SDGs by the end of this decade. According to the composite indicators calculated by the Italian Alliance for Sustainable Development (ASviS) using the data published by Eurostat (see Figure 2.1),[1] between 2010 and 2021 the increase for 12 of the goals was very close to 5% (the composite index was not calculated for SDG 14 – marine ecosystems – due to a lack of information), while only in one case is there a significantly higher increase (for SDG 5, gender equality). For three goals, the indicators show a decrease. Between 2015 – the year of the approval of the 2030 Agenda – and 2021, most composite indicators show slight improvements, except for SDG 5 and SDG 8 (decent work), which show improvements greater than 5%. Only SDG 15 (terrestrial ecosystems) worsens, while SDG 11 (sustainable cities) and SDG 17 (partnership) remain substantially stable.

One of the central objectives of the 2030 Agenda is the reduction of inequalities, as stated in the principle "Leave no one behind". Looking at the evolution of the national composite indicators over the period 2010–2021, a reduction in inequalities between countries is significant only for eight goals, while for three goals there is no change and five see inequalities between countries increase. Grouping the goals according to the four pillars that the 2030 Agenda itself suggests (environmental, social, economic and institutional), we can note that, among the five goals for

---

1 ASviS (2023) "L'Italia e gli Obiettivi di Sviluppo Sostenibile" (https://asvis.it/public/asvis2/files/Rapporto_ASviS/Rapporto_ASViS_2023/RapportoASViS_2023_final.pdf).

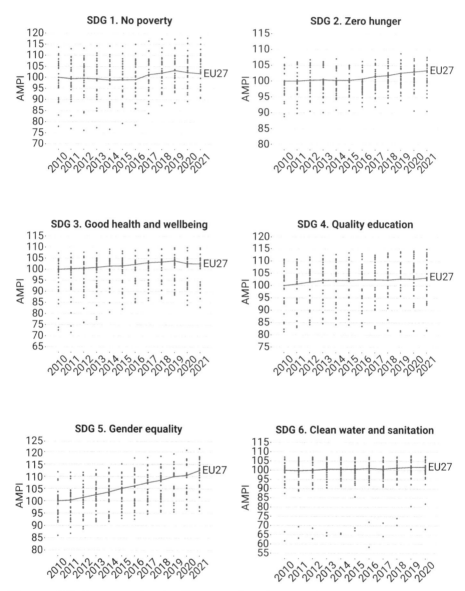

Figure 2.1. Composite indicators for the EU (2010 = 100). [1 of 3]

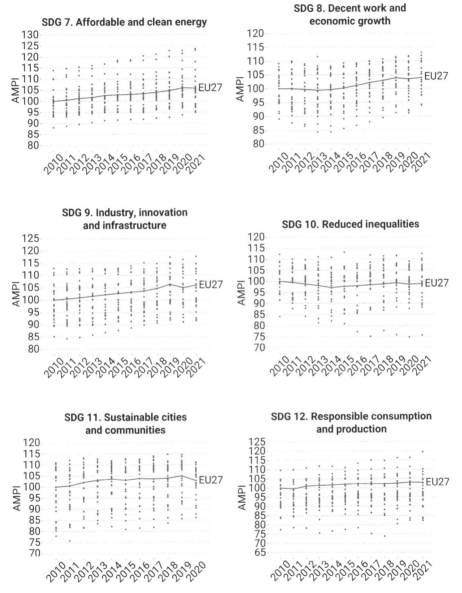

Figure 2.1. [2 of 3]

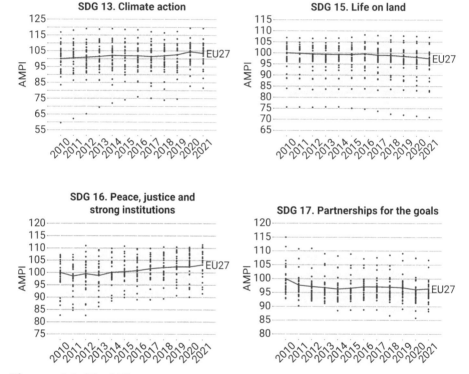

Figure 2.1. [3 of 3]

Source: ASviS (2023) "L'Italia e gli Obiettivi di Sviluppo Sostenibile". The charts show both the composite indicators – AMPI – concerning the European average (solid line) and those of the 27 member states (each point corresponds to the value of the composite index for that country). The grey area highlights the range within which member states fall. The composite index was not calculated for SDG 14 – marine ecosystems – due to a lack of information.

which differences have increased, two, SDG 5 and SDG 10 (reducing inequalities), belong to the social pillar; another two, SDG 7 (renewable energy) and SDG 15, belong to the environmental pillar; and one, SDG 12 (the circular economy), belongs to the economic pillar. Moreover, inequalities between countries increased over the last 10 years for most of the goals.

The 2030 Agenda as key driver of EU policies

In her first speech at the European Parliament, President of the European Commission Ursula von der Leyen expressed a clear commitment to the implementation of the 2030 Agenda.[2] Since then, the EU has adopted an impressive set of strategies, regulations and directives clearly related to the 17 SDGs.[3] The 2030 Agenda framework and the commitment to implementation of the Paris Climate Agreement were confirmed during the current legislature by all EU institutions, to the point that the aim of achieving the SDGs also guided the design of the measures launched in response to the Covid-19 pandemic through Next Generation EU, which financed the National Recovery and Resilience Plans, and the design of the REPowerEU programme, launched in response to the Russian invasion of Ukraine.

The commitment to achieving the SDGs was also confirmed in documents agreed in 2023, as is clear from reading the first EU Voluntary Review, published by the European Commission on 15 May and presented to the UN High-Level Political Forum on 19 July.[4] In particular, the resolution of the European Parliament of 15 June[5] and the conclusions of the

2   Von der Leyen, U. (2019) "Opening statement in the European Parliament Plenary Session by Ursula von der Leyen, candidate for President of the European Commission". Speech, 16 July, European Commission (https://ec.europa.eu/commission/presscorner/detail/en/SPEECH_19_4230).

3   ASviS (2023) "L'Italia e gli Obiettivi di Sviluppo Sostenibile".

4   European Union (2023) "EU Voluntary Review on the implementation of the 2030 Agenda for Sustainable Development" (https://commission.europa.eu/system/files/2023-06/SDG-Report-WEB.pdf).

5   European Parliament (2023) "European Parliament resolution of 15 June 2023 on the implementation and delivery of the Sustainable Development Goals" (www.europarl.europa.eu/doceo/document/TA-9-2023-0250_EN.html).

Council of the European Union of 20 July[6] expressed EU institutions' support for the acceleration of the political processes necessary to achieve the SDGs considering the setbacks that have occurred in recent years due to the pandemic and the war in Ukraine, and as a tool to respond to the growing geopolitical instability.[7]

To transform the above declarations into practice, the EU defined a set of rules to integrate the SDGs into all European policies.[8] In particular, the 2030 Agenda was used as part of the process for the coordination of macroeconomic policies (the European Semester) and in the ex ante evaluation of EU legislation (the Better Regulation initiative), by which every new proposal has to be assessed in terms of its contribution to the implementation of the 2030 Agenda. Especially important in this perspective is the verification of adherence to the "Do no significant harm" (DNSH) principle in relation to the environment, a principle that has been placed at the core of the European Green Deal, the Next Generation EU programme and the projects financed by the Cohesion Fund.[9]

All the innovations and good practices developed by the EU in this field could be shared with other countries, especially developing ones, and eventually become elements of future cooperation agreements to be signed by the EU in the context of initiatives devoted to nonmember countries.

On the other hand, the EU should pay much more attention to the negative spillover effects that its economic choices produce in other

---

6   Council of the European Union (2023) "EU priorities at the 78th UN General Assembly: Council approves conclusions". Press release, 20 July (www.consilium.europa.eu/en/press/press-releases/2023/07/20/eu-priorities-at-the-78th-un-general-assembly-council-approves-conclusions/).

7   The European Parliament remarked that "the SDGs are the only globally agreed and comprehensive set of goals on the major challenges ahead for both developed and developing countries and Agenda 2030 should therefore serve as a guiding light when navigating through the current uncertainties". Even the consultative institutions of the Union (i.e. the Economic and Social Committee and the Committee of the Regions) have contributed over the last four years, through various recommendations and opinions, to stimulating the European debate on policies aimed at the implementation of the 2030 Agenda. They have continually asked for a greater coherence of policies and a stronger commitment from colegislators, to be achieved in part through the participatory involvement of civil society organisations as well as regional and local authorities.

8   For a full review of EU policies vis-à-vis the 2030 Agenda, see ASviS (2023) "L'Italia e gli Obiettivi di Sviluppo Sostenibile", Chapter 2.

9   "2023 Flagship Technical Support Project: Technical Support Instrument". European Commission website (https://reform-support.ec.europa.eu/integration-environmental-dimensions-public-finances_en).

countries and at a global scale. Eurostat and OECD indicators on spillover effects[10] should be published with greater emphasis and be considered when the European Commission's economic forecasts are prepared,[11] in order to provide a more comprehensive assessment of the EU impact on environmental and social global trends.

Four proposals for designing the Global Green Deal and the New Social Contract

Based on the experience of the EU over the last few years, this chapter highlights four proposals aimed at reinforcing the proposals put forward by the UN secretary-general in preparation for the 2024 Summit of the Future.

1. Put sustainable development principles into national constitutions

The Brundtland Commission's definition of sustainable development underlines the right of future generations to meet their own needs.[12] Unfortunately, data and models clearly show that this right is not respected at all, due to the characteristics of the socioeconomic model established over the last century, which undermined and still undermines the key elements of economic, social and environmental sustainability. According to this model, private and public decision-making processes are aimed at achieving short-term results (GDP, profits, capital gains, elections, etc.), a historical tendency that has accelerated over the last 30 years in all parts of the world, due in part to the role of finance, which is interested in maximising profits and capital gains in the very short run, and due as well to the revolution in the communication and information world brought about by the increasing role of social media.

---

10   "Estimating spillover effects of EU consumption", Eurostat website (https://ec.europa.eu/eurostat/statistics-explained/index.php?title=Estimating_spillover_effects_of_EU_consumption); OECD (2021) *Understanding the Spillovers and Transboundary Impacts of Public Policies. Implementing the 2030 Agenda for More Resilient Societies* (Paris: OECD).

11   See, for example, Pfeiffer, P., J. Varga and J. in 't Veld (2021) "Quantifying spillovers of Next Generation EU investment". European Economy Discussion Paper 144, July, European Commission (https://economy-finance.ec.europa.eu/system/files/2021-07/dp144_en.pdf).

12   World Commission on Environment and Development (1987) *Our Common Future* (Oxford: Oxford University Press and the United Nations) (https://sustainabledevelopment.un.org/content/documents/5987our-common-future.pdf).

According to the proposal put forward by the UN Secretary-General António Guterres, the New Global Deal has to change these trends, and several proposals for doing so have been put forward for discussion at the 2024 Summit of the Future. One of them concerns the recognition of the rights of future generations through new legal and governance frameworks. Namely, in the policy brief "To think and act for future generations", Guterres recalls that:

> Commitments to future generations are integral to customs, cultures and religions around the world, including Indigenous knowledge systems. Such commitments are increasingly referenced in national constitutions, legislation and judicial decisions, especially on the environment and safeguarding cultural and biological diversity [...] By some estimates, nearly half of all written constitutions now contain references to future generations [...] Others have mechanisms to understand the future impact of all public policy decisions and to embed long-term thinking into their policymaking processes. Countries have passed legislation acknowledging the responsibility to safeguard the future and, in some cases, creating institutions with explicit mandates to represent the future or establishing ombudspersons or parliamentary committees or commissions with explicit mandates to advocate for or act on behalf of future generations.[13]

In terms of concrete actions, the UN secretary-general calls on member states to

> take meaningful steps to safeguard the interests of future generations and to preserve their ability to effectively enjoy their human rights, drawing on the models that now exist at the national level and the strong commitments already made. I invite Member States to consider two specific steps in this regard, namely: (a) to adopt a declaration making concrete the commitment to future generations; and (b) to establish a dedicated intergovernmental mechanism for debating and sharing best practices.[14]

As already mentioned, Article 3 of the TFEU, devoted to illustrating the aims of the Union, makes two references to "sustainable development". Moreover, reading the article, one can find aims corresponding to almost all the 17 SDGs. This is quite a remarkable characteristic of the text, partially explained by the fact that the TFEU was agreed in 2007 – 20 years after the publication of the Brundtland Report and a few years after the

---

13   United Nations (2023) "To think and act for future generations". Our Common Agenda Policy Brief 1, March (www.un.org/sites/un2.un.org/files/our-common-agenda-policy-brief-future-generations-en.pdf).

14   Ibid.

Millennium Declaration[15] – when the key elements of sustainable development were well established and understood at the international level.

To close the gap between the TFEU and national constitutions (often written several decades ago), several EU member states over the last few years have modified their constitutions to include, directly or indirectly, a reference to sustainable development or to the rights of future generations, following an exponential trend observed worldwide.[16] For example, in 2022, for the first time ever, Italy changed the key principles embedded in its constitution, with Article 9 changed to state:

> The Republic promotes the development of culture and scientific and technical research. It protects the landscape and the historical and artistic heritage of the nation. [It protects] *the environment, biodiversity and ecosystems, also in the interest of future generations. State law regulates the methods and forms of animal protection.*[17]

Moreover, Article 41 was changed to recognise that:

> Private economic initiative is free. It cannot take place in conflict with social utility or in such a way as to cause damage *to health, the environment*, safety, freedom or human dignity. The law determines the appropriate programs and controls so that public and private economic activity can be directed and coordinated for social *and environmental* purposes.[18]

In a few EU countries, high courts have recently been asked to condemn governments for not having done enough to protect the basic rights of both current and future generations, especially as far as environmental conditions are concerned, or for having failed to fully implement international agreements (such as the Kyoto Protocol on cutting greenhouses emissions), which is exactly what happened in Germany and the Netherlands. In these cases, the presence of a reference to sustainability or to the rights of future generations made a big difference in the way the courts made their decisions.

---

15   United Nations (2000) "United Nations Millenium Declaration". General Assembly Resolution A/RES/55/2, 18 September (www.un.org/en/development/desa/population/migration/generalassembly/docs/globalcompact/A_RES_55_2.pdf).

16   Araújo, R., and L. Koessler (2021) "The rise of the constitutional protection of future generations". LPP Working Paper 7-2021, Legal Priorities Project (www.legalpriorities.org/research/constitutional-protection-future-generations.html).

17   Addition in italics.

18   Additions in italics.

In conclusion, based on the EU experience, we believe that the proposals made by the UN secretary-general should be strengthened in order to push all UN countries to committing themselves to embedding the concept of "sustainable development" or the "protection of the interests of future generations" in their national constitutions.

2. Redesign national and international statistical systems to monitor progress towards the SDGs and go "beyond GDP"

The adoption of the 2030 Agenda placed a lot of pressure on national statistical systems to measure progress towards the SDGs. Two targets of SDG 17 in the 2030 Agenda reference statistics:

17.18. By 2020, enhance capacity-building support to developing countries, including for least developed countries and small island developing States, to significantly increase the availability of high-quality, timely and reliable data disaggregated by income, gender, age, race, ethnicity, migratory status, disability, geographic location and other characteristics relevant in national contexts.

17.19. By 2030, build on existing initiatives to develop measurements of progress on sustainable development that complement gross domestic product, and support statistical capacity-building in developing countries.

For the first target, a lot of progress has been made, as highlighted by the special edition of the UN's 2023 SDG report:

In just seven years, the global SDG database has expanded significantly [...] In 2016, a concerning 39% of the SDG indicators lacked internationally established methodology or standards. By March 2020, all indicators had a well-established and internationally agreed methodology [...] The proportion of indicators that are conceptually clear and have good country coverage has increased significantly from 36% in 2016 to 66% in 2022.[19]

However:

While these achievements are worthy of celebration, we cannot ignore the persistent gaps that still challenge our data landscape. Geographic coverage, timeliness,

---

19 United Nations (2023) "The Sustainable Development Goals report 2023: special edition" (https://unstats.un.org/sdgs/report/2023/The-Sustainable-Development-Goals-Report-2023.pdf).

and disaggregation remain areas of concern. For several crosscutting goals such as climate action (Goal 13), gender equality (Goal 5), and peace, justice, and strong institutions (Goal 16), less than half of the 193 countries or areas have internationally comparable data since 2015. This stark reality serves as a reminder that we must prioritize gathering essential information on these critical issues that profoundly impact our future and our planet. Furthermore, a significant challenge lies in the timeliness of data, with less than 30 per cent of the latest available data from 2022 and 2023, while over half of the latest data comes from 2020 and 2021. As we embark on delivering a rescue plan for people and planet at the SDG Summit, accelerated action for data is imperative.[20]

In this area too, the EU is at the forefront at the world level. Since 2017, Eurostat has published annual reports on the progress of the EU and its member states towards the SDGs, using a wide range of indicators, whose numbers have increased over the years.[21] The reports highlight the pace at which the EU has progressed towards each of the 17 SDGs, taking into account, among other things, the policy background at the global and EU levels. The detailed monitoring results are presented in 17 chapters, preceded by an analysis of how the recent crises, such as the Covid-19 pandemic and Russia's invasion of Ukraine, have influenced the EU on its way towards achieving the SDGs, followed by an analysis of spillover effects. The reports close with a "Country overview" chapter on the status of EU member states' progress towards the SDGs.

This excellent monitoring system, based on 100 indicators, is extremely important for evaluating the state of specific phenomena, but it is unable to fully acknowledge and take into account the highly interrelated nature of the different dimensions of sustainability. As recognised by the European Commission:

Avoiding the disruption of critical natural systems, such as the water cycle, respecting planetary boundaries, and halting biodiversity loss, are thus essential preconditions for resilient societies and sustainable economies. As this interdependence between the economy and the environment is becoming increasingly clear, it also becomes a matter of intergenerational fairness: adapting the economic model will be the foundation for the wellbeing and material wealth of future generations, including the way

---

20   Ibid.

21   Eurostat (2023) "Sustainable development in the European Union: monitoring report on progress towards the SDGs in an EU context" (https://ec.europa.eu/eurostat/en/web/products-flagship-publications/w/ks-04-23-184).

economic gains are distributed [...] However, the above-mentioned issues call for additional ways to capture progress and prosperity beyond Gross Domestic Product (GDP) [...] Additional work should also be pursued to improve monitoring tools by developing robust model-based indicators (for instance on planetary boundaries or the social-environment-economy nexus), and better integrated assessment models for projections and scenario analysis.[22]

This is why the EU is also seriously working to achieve SDG 17.19, benefiting from the availability of high-quality sets of national accounts, that for several member states also cover environmental phenomena. After several years of work by the OECD, Eurostat and other international organisations, in 2023 the European Commission decided to launch a project to build "Sustainable and Inclusive Wellbeing" metrics to complement GDP. As described in the Strategic Foresight Report:

> Beyond-GDP metrics should be further developed and progressively embedded into EU policymaking. This will help monitor progress towards wellbeing, facilitate the communication of political challenges, and design the strategies to address them in a people- and planet-centred manner, while ensuring that economic growth does not destroy its very foundations [...] To further inform policies, statistical standards for national accounts need to be complemented by additional indicators to better reflect the interdependence between economic activity, people's wellbeing, and the environment.[23]

One of the very first results of the project, led by the Joint Research Centre of the European Commission, was the estimation of the health-adjusted GDP (per capita) for the EU, the United States, China and India in 2000, 2020 and 2040, based on life expectancy as a proxy for the health dimension of wellbeing (Figure 2.2). Future work will develop other complementary "beyond GDP" indicators to reflect selected factors such as inequalities or environmental damages.

---

22 European Commission (2023) "Strategic Foresight Report 2023" (https://commission. europa.eu/strategy-and-policy/strategic-planning/strategic-foresight/2023-strategic-foresight-report_en).

23 Ibid.

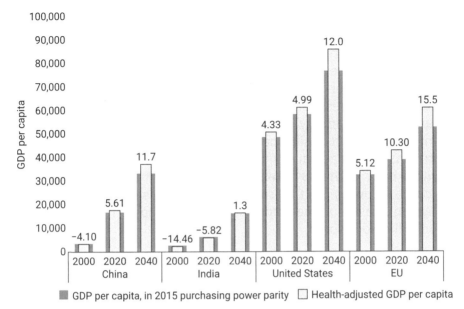

Figure 2.2. Adjusting per capita GDP for life expectancy leads to a larger upward change (in %) for the EU in comparison with the United States, China and India.

In the policy brief "Valuing what counts: framework to progress beyond gross domestic product", the UN secretary-general made three proposals to member states:

(a) A renewed political commitment to create a conceptual framework that can accurately "value what counts" for people, the planet and the future, anchored in the 2030 Agenda and the commitment set out therein to leave no one behind;

(b) The elaboration of a robust technical and scientific process, informed by sound and disaggregated data, resulting in a United Nations value dashboard of a limited number of key indicators that go beyond GDP;

(c) A major capacity-building and resourcing initiative to enable Member States to use the new framework effectively.[24]

---

24 United Nations (2023) "Valuing what counts: framework to progress beyond gross domestic product". Our Common Agenda Policy Brief 4, May (www.un.org/sites/un2.un. org/files/our-common-agenda-policy-brief-beyond-gross-domestic-product-en.pdf).

Actually, the policy brief was based on a document approved in 2022 by the Chief Executives Board (CEB) of the United Nations system, which was much more ambitious in presenting why the international community needs to go "beyond GDP".[25] Moreover, the document proposed an integrated framework aimed at evaluating three key outcomes – "wellbeing and agency", "respect for life and the planet" and "reduced inequalities and greater solidarity" – as well as three "process elements", namely, "from vulnerability to resilience", "participatory governance and stronger institutions" and "innovative and ethical economies".

On the basis of the EU experience, we believe that a more courageous approach, following the CEB recommendations, should be taken by the UN system, based on the below two steps in addition to the three proposed in the policy brief.

- By the end of 2023, a high-level commission should be established, composed of the best experts in the field, to develop in a couple of years a tentative new conceptual framework for a new system of national accounts aimed at measuring "Sustainable and Inclusive Wellbeing", focusing on the wellbeing of people and of the planet and overcoming the outdated vision of the world still embedded in the current System of National Accounts (SNA).
- On the basis of this commission's work, by 2025 (the year in which the SNA will anyway be adjusted, but without any radical change) the UN General Assembly should give a mandate to the Intersecretariat Working Group on National Accounts (composed of the "custodians of the system", i.e. the UN, the OECD, Eurostat, the World Bank and the IMF) to develop a brand new system by 2030.

3. Adopt the 2030 Agenda as *the* framework for public and private decisions

As already mentioned, sustainable development and the 2030 Agenda have been taken up as a key reference point by the European Commission and the European Parliament since the presentation of the 2019–2024

---

25   High-Level Committee on Programmes Core Group on Beyond GDP (2022) "Valuing what counts: United Nations system-wide contribution on progress beyond gross domestic product (GDP)". Report, 17 August, Chief Executives Board for Coordination, United Nations System (https://unsceb.org/sites/default/files/2023-01/Valuing%20 What%20Counts%20-%20UN%20System-wide%20Contribution%20on%20Beyond%20 GDP%20%28advance%20unedited%29.pdf).

political program "A more ambitious Union" at the plenary session of the European Parliament on 16 July 2019. The European Commission is implementing the 2030 Agenda through a "whole-of-government" approach, integrating the SDGs into all proposals, policies and strategies (see Figure 2.3). Since 2020, the Commission's annual work programmes have put the SDGs at the heart of EU policymaking. They are reflected, in particular, in flagship initiatives such as the European Green Deal and Next Generation EU. These involve large amounts of funding – for example, through the Recovery and Resilience Facility, which supports reforms and investments that concretely contribute to making progress on SDGs.

Figure 2.3. The Commission's whole-of-government approach.

The European Commission has also integrated the SDGs into the European Semester, the EU's framework for economic and fiscal policy coordination. As described in the 2023 EU Voluntary Review on the implementation of the 2030 Agenda:

> The current strategy to fully deliver on the SDGs consists in advancing the headline ambitions through concrete initiatives set out in the annual Commission work programmes. Since 2020, every Commission work programme put the SDGs at the heart of EU policymaking [...] The SDGs are thus mainstreamed into EU policies and they guide policymaking and law-making in the EU. Proposed legislation must include an assessment of how it contributes to delivering on the SDGs.[26]

---

26 European Union (2023) "EU Voluntary Review".

In particular, in addition to the European Semester cycle, the process that guides the elaboration of the Better Regulation legislative proposals has been designed to ensure that each legislative proposal contributes to the implementation of the 2030 Agenda. Extremely important in this context is the verification of adherence to the DNSH principle and of consistency between new legislative proposals and the contents of the annual Strategic Foresight Reports published by the European Commission.

Moreover:

> The EU pays particular attention to such interlinkages and integrated actions that can create mutual benefits and meet multiple objectives in a coherent way. It is actively assessing synergies and trade-offs as it progresses towards sustainable development in an integrated manner, balancing the economic, social and environmental dimensions. This is also a central requirement to fulfilling the commitment to ensure policy coherence for sustainable development.[27]

The EU is also strengthening its external role to support the implementation of the 2030 Agenda in nonmember countries. Since December 2021 the EU has been rolling out Global Gateway, its strategy for mobilising sustainable investments in infrastructure in partner countries. Global Gateway will directly contribute to progress on a range of interlinked SDGs, notably through investment in transport, energy and digital infrastructure, as well as health and education. Moreover, at least 20% of the €79.5 billion budget of the Neighbourhood Development and International Cooperation Instrument, known as Global Europe, will contribute until 2027 to human development and the principle of leaving no one behind, targeting people living in the poorest and most vulnerable situations and crisis contexts.

To identify best practices for incorporating the 2030 Agenda into public governance frameworks, the EU experience could be considered alongside the most interesting approaches followed by other UN member states and presented over the years at the High-Level Political Forum on Sustainable Development. In particular, the UN secretary-general could mandate a high-level group to identify best practices and derive possible recommendations for member states as to

- ex ante and ex post evaluation frameworks for public policies (especially those implemented through new legislation) vis-à-vis the 2030

---

27   Ibid.

Agenda – this work would be especially important for designing a post-2030 Agenda based on more effective and efficient public governance systems for sustainable development;

- frameworks put in place to ensure the policy coherence of sustainable development, as defined by the OECD guidelines;
- systems for monitoring progress towards the implementation of the 2030 Agenda and their role in the design of public policies;
- models and approaches to evaluate trade-offs between alternative policies aimed at achieving the SDGs, reducing risks and increasing the resilience of socioeconomic and environmental systems.

4. Design public policies using strategic foresight tools and the concept of "transformative resilience"

In the policy brief "Strengthening the international response to complex global shocks" the UN secretary-general put forward a series of proposals to better equip the UN system and its member states to face global shocks:

Global shocks in the twenty-first century have taken on new and worrying characteristics. They are becoming more complex, their impacts are more global, and the need for international cooperation to respond to them is therefore even more critical. Today, the complexity and acuity of the potential global shocks we face outstrip the existing capacity of the multilateral system to sufficiently manage those risks.[28]

Moreover, according to the policy brief:

We also need to better anticipate shocks. At the twenty-seventh session of the Conference of the Parties to the United Nations Framework Convention on Climate Change, I called for investments to ensure that everyone on the planet had access to early warning systems by 2027. Furthermore, in Our Common Agenda, I committed to enhancing the capability of the United Nations to better anticipate risks by improving our strategic foresight, pursuing anticipatory action, establishing a "Futures Lab" and issuing a Global Risk Report. Strengthening our response to shocks and building people's awareness, preparedness and resilience are mutually reinforcing goals.

---

28   United Nations (2023) "Strengthening the international response to complex global shocks: an emergency platform". Our Common Agenda Policy Brief 2, March (www.un.org/sites/un2.un.org/files/our-common-agenda-policy-brief-emergency-platform-en.pdf).

Several proposals described in the policy brief build on the work done over the last decade by the United Nations Development Programme, the OECD and the EU. For example, the 2014 Human Development Report highlighted the need both to promote people's freedom of choice and to protect human development achievements, underlining that "vulnerability threatens human development, and unless it is systematically addressed, by changing policies and social norms, progress will be neither equitable nor sustainable".[29]

The report also proposed a possible policy approach to enhance the resilience of socioeconomic systems to future shocks:

At its core, resilience is about ensuring that state, community and global institutions work to empower and protect people. Human development involves removing the barriers that hold people back in their freedom to act. It is about enabling the disadvantaged and excluded to realize their rights, to express their concerns openly, to be heard and to become active agents in shaping their destiny [...] This Report highlights some of the key policies, principles and measures that are needed to build resilience – to reinforce choices, expand human agency and promote social competences. It also indicates that achieving and sustaining human development progress can depend on the effectiveness of preparedness and response when shocks occur.

In 2019 the OECD Council adopted a set of recommendations on "Policy coherence for sustainable development" aimed at enhancing policy coherence

under three main pillars: a strategic vision for implementing the 2030 Agenda underpinned by a clear political commitment and leadership to enhance policy coherence for sustainable development; effective and inclusive institutional and governance mechanisms to address policy interactions across sectors and align actions between levels of government; a set of responsive and adaptive tools to anticipate, assess and address domestic, transboundary and long-term impacts of policies.[30]

The first recommendation says that, in order to define, implement and communicate a strategic long-term vision that supports policy coherence

---

29   United Nations Development Programme (2014) "Sustaining human progress: reducing vulnerabilities and building resilience". Human Development Report (https://hdr.undp.org/content/human-development-report-2014).

30   "Recommendation of the Council on policy coherence for sustainable development". OECD website (https://legalinstruments.oecd.org/en/instruments/OECD-LEGAL-0381).

and orients the government and stakeholders towards the SDGs, member countries should, among other things

> use existing tools such as strategic foresight, scenario development and systems thinking approaches in the formulation and implementation of policies, to identify, prevent and mitigate actual and potential adverse impacts on the wellbeing and sustainable development prospects of future generations.

Over the last decade the EU has undertaken important initiatives strengthening its capacity to anticipate future shocks, address vulnerability and increase its resilience. In particular, after the two events organised in October 2015 by the European Commission on the resilience of the EU in the context of the 2030 Agenda, a network of experts (led by the author at the Joint Research Centre of the European Commission) was established to study the issue, which led to the publication in 2017 of the paper "Building a Scientific Narrative towards a more resilient EU society", in which a conceptual model was proposed that could aid in redesigning public policies around the concepts of vulnerability and resilience:

> Thinking about changes brought about by the digital innovation, demographic change, climate change, globalization or migration, it would be illusionary to believe that we can eliminate crises, shocks or persistent structural changes (slow burn processes) in the future. On the contrary, the number of potential shocks could even increase. Since we will not be able to avoid them, we have to learn from distressful experiences and set up policies that prepare citizens, companies, societies and institutions to overcome them with the minimum damage possible. Therefore, the role of policy institutions, such as governments or supranational institutions, is crucial in fostering policies towards a positive socio-economic-environmental outcome of sustainability, cohesion and prosperity of the society. In the context of a stormy future becoming the "new normal", enhancing resilience might become one of the most important tasks of policy institutions.[31]

Specifically, the paper's proposals included adopting a "systems thinking" approach to public policies, based on the literature around "closed systems" such as the earth system in which we live, as well as

---

31   Manca, A. R., P. Benczur and E. Giovannini (2017) "Building a Scientific Narrative towards a more resilient EU society: part 1; a conceptual framework". EUR 28548 EN, Joint Research Centre, European Commission (https://publications.jrc.ec.europa.eu/repository/handle/JRC106265).

an innovative view of what "transformative resilience" means for socio-economic systems; designing policies with the aim of strengthening the capacity of socioeconomic systems to respond to shocks by "bouncing forward" towards a new development path (and not "bouncing back", as the classical concept of resilience implies); and replacing the classical approach to economic, social and environmental policies with a classification of interventions based on five categories: prevention, preparation, protection, promotion and transformation.

In a second paper, "Time for transformative resilience: the Covid-19 emergency",[32] the five-category policy framework was applied to the concrete case of the pandemic shock, showing how the framework could be usefully used to frame the policy responses put in place at national and EU levels. The proposed approach was adopted by the EU to design the response to the pandemic: this is why the EU instrument to finance national plans was called the Recovery and Resilience Facility and national programmes designed to respond to the crisis were called National Recovery and Resilience Plans.[33]

In 2019, when the current European Commission led by Ursula von der Leyen was established, the research work focusing on resilience and strategic foresight led the president to allocate to one of the vice-presidents the responsibility for "interinstitutional relations, better policymaking and strategic foresight". Since 2020 an annual Strategic Foresight Report has been published by the Commission. In the first report, the abovementioned approach to vulnerability and resilience was fully embraced:

> The central theme of this first report is resilience, which has become a new compass for EU policies with the COVID-19 crisis. Resilience is the ability not only to withstand and cope with challenges but also to undergo transitions in a sustainable, fair, and democratic manner. Resilience is necessary in all policy areas to undergo the green and digital transitions, while maintaining the EU's core purpose and integrity in a dynamic and at times turbulent environment. A more resilient Europe will recover faster,

---

32   Giovannini, E., P. Benczur, F. Campolongo, J. Cariboni and A. Manca (2020) "Time for transformative resilience: the COVID-19 emergency". EUR 30179 EN, Joint Research Centre, European Commission (https://publications.jrc.ec.europa.eu/repository/handle/JRC120489).

33   See "A roadmap for recovery: towards a more resilient, sustainable and fair Europe", available on website of the Council of the EU and of the European Council (www.consilium.europa.eu/media/43384/roadmap-for-recovery-final-21-04-2020.pdf).

---

emerge stronger from current and future crises, and better implement the United Nations' Sustainable Development Goals.[34]

The report also presented the first set of "prototype dashboards" on vulnerability and resilience, based on statistical indicators. For each variable, a scale of colours indicates countries' relative situation in the last year for which data is available versus the pooled values of available data since 2007. The dashboards were developed for the social and economic dimension of resilience, and then extended to other domains (such as trade and value chains, security, green issues and digitalisation)[35] and also used in the context of the European Semester, the EU tool to coordinate the economic policies of member states. Moreover, in 2030 the global resilience dashboard was published, shown here in Figures 2.4 and 2.5. In these figures, variations from the shade of grey marked "Medium capacities/vulnerabilities" indicate countries that, in the latest available year, performed at least one standard deviation worse or better than the average. Finally, to illustrate the overall performance of the countries in terms of vulnerabilities and resilience capacities in each of the four dimensions, the dashboards are complemented by synthetic resilience indexes (Figure 2.6).

In this field too, the EU experience could be used to implement, and demonstrate the feasibility of, the proposals put forward by the UN secretary-general. In particular, the European Commission should make available its models, data and researchers to ensure the establishment of the proposed UN foresight centre, providing adequate financial support not only in the start-up phase but also afterwards, in order to make the centre an example of excellence at the world level.

---

34   European Commission (2020) "2020 Strategic Foresight Report: charting the course towards a more resilient Europe" (https://commission.europa.eu/strategy-and-policy/strategic-planning/strategic-foresight/2020-strategic-foresight-report_en#documents).

35   "Resilience dashboards", European Commission website (https://commission.europa.eu/strategy-and-policy/strategic-planning/strategic-foresight/2020-strategic-foresight-report/resilience-dashboards_en); Joint Research Centre (2023) "Resilience dashboards: global comparison; update summer 2023", European Commission (https://jeodpp.jrc.ec.europa.eu/ftp/public/JRC-OpenData/RESILIENCE-DASHBOARDS/Summer2023Update/GlobalDashboard_SummerUpdate_2023.pdf).

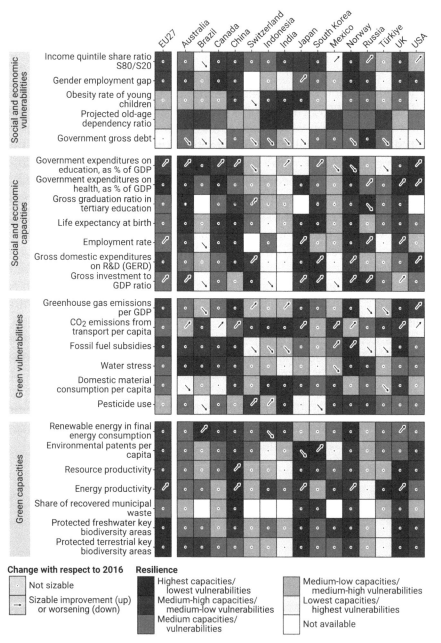

Figure 2.4. Global resilience dashboard for the social and economic dimension and the green dimension.

Source: Joint Research Centre (2023) "Resilience dashboards".

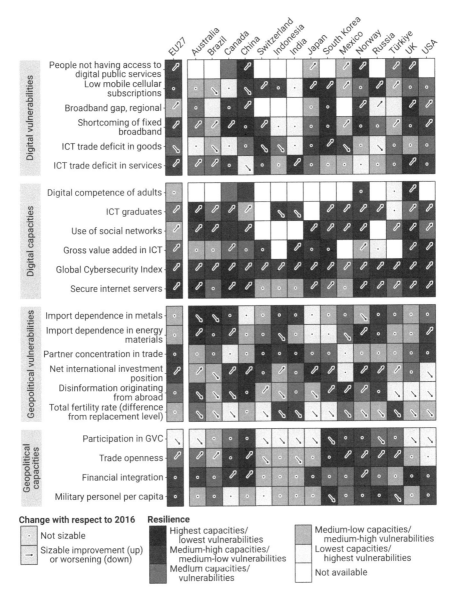

Figure 2.5. Global resilience dashboard for the digital and geo-political dimensions.

Source: Joint Research Centre (2023) "Resilience dashboards".

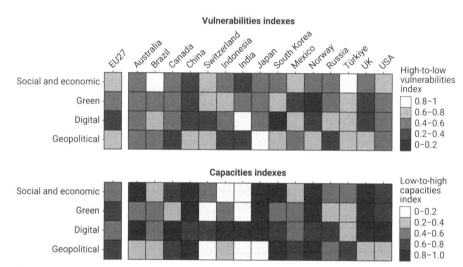

Figure 2.6. Global synthetic indexes for the four dimensions.

Source: Joint Research Centre (2023) "Resilience dashboards". The overall vulnerabilities (capacities) index is obtained for a country by the median value over all the vulnerability (capacity) indicator positions. A high vulnerabilities/capacities index for a country indicates high vulnerabilities/capacities compared with other countries.

Céline Charveriat

3 | A New Global Deal for governing planetary boundaries

The triple planetary crisis of climate change, biodiversity loss and pollution is currently spinning out of control, raising alarms among scientists over humanity's ability to maintain the inhabitability of planet earth for its 8 billion human inhabitants.

According to the latest report of the Intergovernmental Panel on Climate Change (the Sixth Assessment Report), greenhouse gas (GHG) emissions to date have already caused a warming of 1.1 °C above preindustrial levels, and the world is on course for an average 3.2 °C of warming by 2100.[1] At about 1.9 °C of warming, half of the human population could be exposed to periods of life-threatening climatic conditions arising from the coupled impacts of extreme heat and humidity. There is already evidence of instability in many of the earth's major systems, including the Amazon rainforest, the summer ice cover in the Arctic and the West Antarctica ice shelf, suggesting that current climate models might be underestimating the rate of change that the existing concentration of GHG is already driving.[2]

At the heart of the triple planetary crisis lies a terrible injustice: benefits and costs of the plundering of the environment are unequally shared within each country, between countries and across generations. The most vulnerable members of society – such as children, older people and female-headed households living in the most vulnerable countries – will be the hardest hit. Thus, the challenge ahead for humanity is to remain within not only safe but also just planetary boundaries, which minimise

---

1   Intergovernmental Panel on Climate Change (2021) "Sixth Assessment Report" (www.ipcc.ch/assessment-report/ar6/).

2   Whiting, A. (2022) "'Tipping points' lead to irreversible shifts – climate experts". *Horizon*, 10 June (https://ec.europa.eu/research-and-innovation/en/horizon-magazine/tipping-points-lead-irreversible-shifts-climate-experts).

human exposure to significant harm from earth system change (the "no significant harm" principle), enable access to resources for all, and ensure distributional and procedural fairness.[3]

According to the United Nations Environment Programme (UNEP), "none of the SDGs with an environmental dimension will be achieved nor will the main internationally agreed environmental goals (e.g. Paris Agreement, Aichi Targets, etc.)" without a change in the policy and governance framework for the environment.[4] Due to insufficient action since 1995, when United Nations climate talks officially started, evidence also suggests that the window for achieving the 1.5 °C target for global warming has now closed. Even if all production halted today, the existing concentration of GHG in the atmosphere is already too high.[5] According to UNEP's 2023 Emissions Gap Report, current pledges under the Paris Agreement, if they are implemented, will put the world on track for a 2.5–2.9 °C temperature rise above preindustrial levels this century.[6] Instead of moving towards clean energy, oil and gas companies are continuing to invest twice as much they should in fossil fuels, according to the International Energy Agency.[7] Equally worrying is that "adaptation planning and implementation appears to be plateauing" according to UNEP, which estimates the current adaptation finance gap at $194–366 billion per year.[8]

While the biodiversity crisis attracts less attention from the international community, it is equally threatening for present and future human wellbeing. More than half of global GDP depends on high-functioning biodiversity. Australia, Israel and South Africa rank near the top of Swiss Re's index of risk to biodiversity and ecosystem services, with India, Spain and

3   Rockström, J., J. Gupta, D. Qin et al. (2023) "Safe and just Earth system boundaries". *Nature*, 619: 102–111 (www.nature.com/articles/s41586-023-06083-8).

4   United Nations Environment Programme (2022) "Scoping of the seventh edition of the Global Environment Outlook: action for a healthy planet" (www.unep.org/resources/toolkits-manuals-and-guides/scoping-seventh-edition-global-environment-outlook-action).

5   McGrath, M. (2023) "Global warming set to break key 1.5C limit for first time". *BBC*, 17 May (www.bbc.com/news/science-environment-65602293).

6   United Nations Environment Programme (2022) "Emissions Gap Report 2023: broken record" (www.unep.org/resources/emissions-gap-report-2023).

7   Ambrose, J. (2023) "Companies still investing too much in fossil fuels, global energy watchdog says". *The Guardian*, 23 November (www.theguardian.com/business/2023/nov/23/companies-still-investing-too-much-in-fossil-fuels-global-energy-watchdog-says).

8   United Nations Environment Programme (2023) "Adaptation Gap Report 2023: underfinanced; underprepared" (www.unep.org/resources/adaptation-gap-report-2023).

Belgium also highlighted.[9] In terms of the third planetary crisis, which is linked to pollution, almost all of the global population (99%) breathe air that exceeds safe thresholds and contains high levels of pollutants, with low- and middle-income countries suffering from the highest exposures.[10]

As environmental challenges spiral out of control, the international environmental governance system remains incomplete, fragmented and decentralised. Today, there are well over 250 multilateral environmental agreements (MEAs), with different negotiating committees, secretariats and monitoring mechanisms.[11] Environmental norms suffer from a major implementation gap, with only 10% of targets under MEAs signed between 1972 and 2022 having been met.[12] The lack of a hierarchy or relationship between international environmental agreements and other norms – whether related to economics, trade and finance or to health – also creates major policy and governance conflicts, without clear pathways for their resolution. Transboundary governance issues continue to be challenging because of competing sovereignty claims, especially over critical, at-risk or resource-rich ecosystems, such as the Amazon, the Arctic and the Antarctic, not to mention the oceans. While it seems difficult to imagine a fully consolidated system, a greater "orchestration of global environmental governance" that reduces the costs of fragmentation is necessary.[13]

As the world scrambles for solutions and competes for resources, difficult new governance issues are also emerging, such as the governance of geoengineering and other climate-distorting technologies; green mining; land governance; and the scarcity of critical resources (such as water and food, but also critical raw materials). These new challenges are demanding new norms, processes and institutions at the national,

9   Carrington, D. (2020) "Fifth of countries at risk of ecosystem collapse, analysis finds". *The Guardian*, 12 October (www.theguardian.com/environment/2020/oct/12/fifth-of-nations-at-risk-of-ecosystem-collapse-analysis-finds).

10   World Health Organization (2021) "WHO global air quality guidelines" (www.who.int/publications-detail-redirect/9789240034228). See also www.who.int/teams/environment-climate-change-and-health/air-quality-and-health/health-impacts/types-of-pollutants and www.who.int/health-topics/air-pollution.

11   "An Introduction to InforMEA". InforMEA website (www.informea.org/en/article/introduction-informea).

12   Stockholm Environment Institute and the Council on Energy, Environment and Water (2022) "Stockholm+50: unlocking a better future" (www.stockholm50.report/).

13   Abbott, K. W. (2012) "The transnational regime complex for climate change". *Environment and Planning C: Government and Policy*, 30(4): 571–590. DOI: 10.1068/c11127

regional and global levels at a time when the implementation of solutions to existing challenges is still out of reach.

Not all is doom and gloom. Over the last two years the global community has still been able to find consensus around new biodiversity-protection targets, fishery subsidies and the high seas. New negotiations have been started – for instance, to address the challenges linked to plastics pollution – and talks over the implementation of the Paris Agreement are continuing to move forward. In 2023 a high-level conference on water, the first of its kind in a decade, created a voluntary Water Action Agenda with 700 actions registered.[14]

Despite this continued willingness to find cooperative solutions, the world is not moving at the scale and speed required because of five key intertwined challenges.

- The path dependency of current systems and the perceived lack of viable alternatives to extractive growth and mass consumption. Ensuring shared prosperity for all, especially in countries still faced with major demographic growth and widespread poverty, while at the same time drastically reducing the carbon and material intensity of growth, is seen as impossible by most decision-makers, whether politicians or CEOs.

- The complete loss of trust between the Global North and the Global South, due to unmet international obligations and commitments to protect nature and broken promises of redressing fundamental inequities. While the world still has not recovered from the "vaccine apartheid", the North–South tensions created by the wars in Ukraine and in Gaza are leading to further fragmentation, making cooperation both more necessary and difficult.

- Increasing geopolitical rivalry. The systemic rivalry between the United States, China and Europe is fuelling a new race for critical raw materials across the entire world, leading to further degradation and injustice. The world is also witnessing an expensive military build-up, diverting resources away from investments needed to implement the Sustainable Development Goals (SDGs).

---

14   "Water Action Agenda". UN 2023 Water Conference website (https://sdgs.un.org/conferences/water2023/action-agenda).

- The formidable power of fossil fuel interests. The biggest oil- and gas-producing countries, including the United States, Russia, China, Iran and the Gulf States – supported by oil and gas companies and other relevant economic interests (e.g. the petrochemical and banking industries) – are using their influence to create divisions and stonewall progress at the international level. Unsurprisingly, they are also investing into technologies, such as geoengineering, that are unproven, highly costly and not at scale, in the hope of profiteering on both sides of the equation.

- The scale of inequities at the heart of the environmental crisis, between countries, people and generations. This rift is well illustrated by the unwillingness of the richest 1%, who emit as much GHG as two thirds of the rest of humanity,[15] to move away from lucrative fossil-fuel-based investments and to adopt more sustainable ways of living.

Against this backdrop, it is urgent to have a global reset. In the words of UN Secretary-General António Guterres, a New Global Deal is needed "among countries to ensure that power, benefits and opportunities are shared more broadly and fairly".[16] This requires action in five key areas: rebuilding trust, focusing on the drivers of existential risk, completing the global environmental governance system, mobilising means of implementation and putting an end to impunity.

Rebuilding trust

The 2023 review of the SDGs[17] unanimously concluded that the world is not on track to achieve them by 2030. Building on the proposal of the UN secretary-general for an SDG Stimulus, an effective action plan that

15   Morrow, A. (2023) "World's richest 1 percent emit as much carbon as two-thirds of humanity: report". *Radio France Internationale*, 20 November (www.rfi.fr/en/environment/20231120-worlds-richest-1-percent-carbon-two-thirds-of-humanity-report-oxfam-climate).

16   United Nations Regional Information Centre for Western Europe (2021). "UN Secretary-General António Guterres calls for a global reset in 2021". News article, 28 January (https://unric.org/en/un-secretary-general-antonio-guterres-calls-for-a-global-reset-in-2021/).

17   United Nations (2023) "As SDG Summit concludes, Secretary-General urges world leaders to lift political declaration 'off the page', invest in development like never before", Meetings coverage, 19 September (https://press.un.org/en/2023/ga12531.doc.htm).

prioritises the issues and countries left further behind must be spear-headed by the G20 under the leadership of Brazil.

In preparation for the 2024 Summit of the Future, a few proposals for boosting environmental governance have been made by the UN secretary-general's report Our Common Agenda,[18] by the High-Level Advisory Board on Effective Multilateralism[19] and by a diverse set of stakeholders. However, there are concerns on the part of G77 countries that an environmental track as part of the Summit of the Future might distract from existing processes such as the United Nations Framework Convention on Climate Change (UNFCCC) and become a tool to curtail sovereignty, attack G77 solidarity and renege on the principle of common but differentiated responsibilities. This fear must be addressed head-on to avoid a complete demotion of environmental issues within discussions around global governance reform.

As proposed by the UN secretary-general, trust can be rebuilt by announcing a package of support measures for developing countries at the next G7 and G20 summits and at the 29th Conference of the Parties (COP29). Prioritising the issues on the environmental governance agenda for which the poorest countries have demanded action would also be a good place to start, beginning with more effective mechanisms to facilitate access to green technologies and clean energy and to support green industrialisation. To provide highly indebted developing countries with the fiscal space to finance the transition, and building on the vision of the Bridgetown Initiative, next year's G20 should announce a global action plan to mobilise adequate funding for loss and damage, which could be provided through debt restructuring and/or partial cancellation, going beyond the current proposals contained in the Bridgetown Initiative.

Focusing on the drivers of existential risk

A New Global Deal should prioritise action on the following drivers, which create existential risk for all human beings.

Fossil fuels and other high-risk pollutants

A New Global Deal should first borrow from the thinking developed during the Cold War in the context of the nuclear arms race. On the basis of the

---

18   United Nations (2021) "Our Common Agenda" (www.un.org/en/content/common-agenda-report/).

19   See https://highleveladvisoryboard.org.

acknowledgement that the current path is leading the world into mutually assured destruction, rivalry and sovereignty must be constrained by rules meant to protect the inhabitability of our planet and avoid such a scenario. Borrowing from the same domain, and building on the outcomes of COP28, a new framework must also be established to phase out the exploration, production and consumption of fossil fuels.

A new nonproliferation treaty for fossil fuels must be concluded, with the goal of phasing out and eventually banning fossil fuel exploration, extraction, production and use on a timeline that is compatible with the 1.5 °C scenario. In order to create incentives to join this nonproliferation treaty, signatories would have access to a number of benefits, including preferential trade, investment and procurement treatment; solutions and funding for deploying distributed renewable energy at scale; and access to a green technology licensing facility.[20]

Alongside this treaty, the plastics treaty must be concluded expeditiously, as plastics are a fossil-fuel-based material. To support the pathway towards a fossil fuel ban, measures restricting and eventually prohibiting foreign direct investment and equity in fossil-fuel-based projects would have to be put in place. A similar phase-out approach should be followed for all polluting materials, starting with those that pose the highest risk to planetary health and life, including forever chemicals such as per- and polyfluoroalkyl substances (PFAS).

Transforming the broken food and land systems

The global food system is the primary driver of biodiversity loss, with agriculture alone being the identified threat to 86% of the species at risk of extinction. The global food system is a major driver of climate change, accounting for around 30% of total human-produced emissions.[21] The further impoverishment of small-scale farmers, increasing crop failures, rising food prices and innutritious diets are already putting the goal of eliminating hunger by 2030 out of reach.[22] Due to climate

---

20   Ibid.

21   United Nations Environment Programme (2021) "Our global food system is the primary driver of biodiversity loss". Press release, 3 February (www.unep.org/news-and-stories/press-release/our-global-food-system-primary-driver-biodiversity-loss).

22   Independent Group of Scientists appointed by the Secretary-General (2023) "Global Sustainable Development Report 2023: times of crisis, times of change; science for accelerating transformations to sustainable development". United Nations (https://sdgs.un.org/gsdr/gsdr2023).

change and water scarcity, the situation is likely to continue to worsen. In fact, the probability of crop yield failures is projected to be as much as 4.5 times higher by 2030 and up to 25 times higher by 2050 across global breadbaskets.[23]

While there is a legitimate focus on the transformation of the energy and mobility systems in order to combat climate change and pollution, much more attention must be paid to the food system. The current governance system, recently marked by the competition between the model promoted by the Committee on World Food Security and that of the UN Food Systems Summit,[24] is not leading to the development of effective controls (for instance, around climate-distorting and environmentally harmful methods of production, subsidies or unfair marketing and commercial practices). Nor is it producing and diffusing adequate solutions backed by finance to resolve hunger and malnutrition in a changing climate.

A New Global Deal for food systems must support dignified and robust livelihoods for all actors engaged in food systems, promote healthy and sustainable diets, ensure access to affordable and nutritious food and protect future generations' right to food by protecting natural capital and restoring degraded ecosystems. In this context, food security could be one of the first issues to be taken up by the emergency platforms proposed by the UN secretary-general.

Overconsumption and the waste of natural resources

According to the 2019 Global Resources Outlook of the UN International Resource Panel, resource extraction has more than tripled since 1970. Based on historical data, resource use could double by 2060. Moreover, industrial water withdrawals could increase by up to 100% over 2010 levels, and the area of agricultural land could increase by more than 20% in that time, reducing forests, grasslands and savannahs by around 20%.[25]

---

23   Caparas, M., Z. Zobel, A. D. A. Castanho et al. (2021) "Increasing risks of crop failure and water scarcity in global breadbaskets by 2030". *Environmental Research Letters*, 16(10): Paper 104013 (https://iopscience.iop.org/article/10.1088/1748-9326/ac22c1).

24   Canfield, M. C., J. Duncan and P. Claeys (2021) "Reconfiguring food systems governance: the UNFSS and the battle over authority and legitimacy". *Development*, 64: 181–191 (https://link.springer.com/article/10.1057/s41301-021-00312-1).

25   United Nations Environment Programme (2019) "We're gobbling up the Earth's resources at an unsustainable rate". News article, 3 April (www.unep.org/news-and-stories/story/were-gobbling-earths-resources-unsustainable-rate).

Tackling this challenge effectively requires a new paradigm of a regenerative economy and egalitarian eco-sufficiency. Economic systems must be designed to regenerate nature and strengthen human capital. Poorer countries (and poorer populations within countries) who need extra resources to achieve SDGs must be given priority over other, nonessential usage. There should be a gradual convergence of resource use per capita and the definition of economy-wide resource caps, with targets to be agreed for 2030 and 2050. There should also be new mechanisms to address economic or physical scarcity of critical raw materials in order to achieve fair sharing and the development or deployment of alternatives.

Emergent climate- and nature-distorting technologies

Given the risk of private individuals or single governments making research and development decisions that put humanity onto risky pathways, the emergent technological framework proposed by the UN secretary-general must address the difficult issues of climate- and nature-distorting technologies, ensuring a fair and transparent decision-making process. In the case of geoengineering, norms for the global governance of geoengineering and the prevention of unilateral use must be negotiated, building on existing conventions such the Environmental Modification Convention (ENMOD),[26] which prohibits environmental modification techniques for military purposes. Given the large carbon and material footprint of new artificial intelligence technologies, as well as the societal risks associated with them, new technologies must be designed to help humanity stay within planetary boundaries.

Completing the environmental governance system

The world needs an environmental governance system that is fit for purpose. The failure of the past 50 years, since the first Stockholm Conference of 1972, illustrates the need for a completely new approach.

Timely, policy-relevant and actionable scientific information must be generated in order to inform decision-makers but also to create the conditions for greater accountability on the part of duty-bearers. This requires

---

26 Versen, J., Z. Mnatsakanyan and J. Urpelainen (2021) "Preparing the United States for security and governance in a geoengineering future". Brookings Institution, 14 December (www.brookings.edu/articles/preparing-the-united-states-for-security-and-governance-in-a-geoengineering-future/).

the creation of an interconnected science–policy interface mechanism for earth systems governance[27] that would provide recommendations to a UN Global Resilience Council[28] and direct the efforts of a unified environmental agency of the UN and a coherent intergovernmental negotiation process. This integrated system must also ensure that the international community does not focus exclusively on climate change to the detriment of the biodiversity and pollution crises.

The current global governance system is suffering from short-termism and anthropocentrism. This is why we must rebalance representation and ensure equitable decision-making by giving rights to future generations and other species in decision-making processes. The proposed UN declaration on youth and future generations, to be negotiated at the Summit of the Future, should be translated into international law through an amendment to the Universal Declaration of Human Rights. These new rights could then be promoted through a UN high commissioner for future generations, as well as national ombudspeople.[29] To provide other species with rights, countries should borrow from current examples of legal decisions or treaties giving rights to nature (building on the precedent of Mal El Menor in Spain[30]).

As recommended by the High-Level Advisory Board on Effective Multilateralism, economic and financial governance institutions (the WTO, the IMF and other international financial institutions) must become implementation agencies accountable to the environmental governance system. This also means changing their mandate and instruments to ensure greater macroeconomic coordination so that vital decarbonisation, nature restoration and SDG investments can accelerate. This will require preventing too steep a rise in interest rates while avoiding hyperinflation. Criteria for debt sustainability must consider economy-wide climate risk. Sectoral negotiations should also be considered when

---

27 Obura, D. (2022) "The case for an international expert panel on planetary boundaries", Global Challenges Foundation; Jiborn, M. (2022) "The case for an international expert panel on earth systems catastrophic risks", Global Challenges Foundation; "Governing our planetary emergency", statement of the Climate Governance Commission, September 2023.

28 "GRC – Global Resilience Council". Foundation for Global Governance and Sustainability website (www.foggs.org/grc-global-resilience-council/).

29 Vincent, A. (2012) "Ombudspersons for future generations: bringing intergenerational justice into the heart of policymaking". *UN Chronicle*, 49(1–2) (www.un.org/en/chronicle/article/ombudspersons-future-generations-bringing-intergenerational-justice-heart-policymaking).

30 See www.boe.es/diario_boe/txt.php?id=BOE-A-2022-16019.

necessary to address the economic and/or physical scarcity of critical raw materials (such as lithium, sand and phosphorus) or to address particularly vital sectors and materials (as in the case of high-carbon meat production).

The mobilisation of adequate means of implementation

To close the financial gap for the implementation of MEAs, the Summit of the Future could adopt the recommendations of the High-Level Expert Group on Climate Finance, which recommends the mobilisation of $1 trillion per year in external finance by 2030 for emerging markets and developing countries other than China.[31] A key measure would be to move to a demand-driven model of climate and biodiversity finance. Similar principles to those used in the 2002 Education for All Fast-Track Initiative could be adopted (i.e. that no developing country with a solid plan for reaching 1.5 °C, adaptation or nature-restoration targets should be denied financing). Financing might take the form of budgetary support and partial or total debt cancellation. Countries' contributions to the effort must be based on objective criteria (such as GDP per capita or consumption emissions per capita).

A global tax treaty or innovative finance negotiation track encompassing all aspects of taxation (taxing environmental externalities, a wealth tax, corporate tax harmonisation, digitalisation, a financial transaction tax, and an end to fiscal evasion and competition) must be established to generate the trillions needed. The mandate for such negotiations needs to include a financial mobilisation target commensurate with needs – just as 1.5 °C is a target for UNFCCC negotiations.

The "polluter pays" principle must become a key principle that allows for courts but also governments to levy taxes and place exceptional levies on major polluters in order to compensate for loss and damage. At the other end of the spectrum, the failed Yasuni framework[32] for ecosys-

---

31   Songwe, V., N. Stern and A. Bhattacharya (2022) "Finance for climate action: scaling up investment for climate and development". Grantham Research Institute on Climate Change and the Environment, London School of Economics and Political Science (www.lse.ac.uk/granthaminstitute/publication/finance-for-climate-action-scaling-up-investment-for-climate-and-development/).

32   "Ecuador Yasuni ITT Trust Fund: terms of reference", 28 July 2010 (https://mptf.undp.org/sites/default/files/documents/10000/yasuni_fund_tor._english_3_august_2010.pdf).

tem services must be built on to remunerate land stewards and farmers so that they benefit financially from environmental protection.[33]

Green finance must become the norm, rather than a niche. To this end, the international community must agree to a global taxonomy and to mandatory green bond standards (building on Europe's experience so far),[34] on the basis of the most ambitious models to date and by disincentivising brown assets through differential taxation as well as by penalising brown entities through curtailed access to public procurement.[35]

While globalisation contributed to lifting many people out of poverty, it did so at the expense of natural capital because it was not properly regulated. We need to harness trade for sustainability. This requires that all trade and investment negotiations include the achievement of MEAs as an operative goal. To this end, investment and trade agreements must phase out and eliminate environmentally harmful subsidies, and they must include sustainable standards for products and services as well as measures to build green and resilient supply chains and trade infrastructure. Addressing green capacity constraints in developing countries, especially for green industrialisation, is paramount.

A global research and development treaty financed through a share of the GDP of all nations must provide financing for the development of mission-oriented research, innovation and technology that aims at responding to the most important societal challenges (building on the example of European Union Missions). All discoveries must be initially rewarded through secured procurement contracts and then become open access.

---

33   For carbon, see Foucherot, C. (2022) "Remunerating farmers for their stored carbon, Europe's good idea?", blog post, 27 January, Institute for Climate Economics (www.i4ce. org/en/remunerating-farmers-carbon-europes-climate/); for the production of biochar, see Nazaroff, D. (2021) "Biochar: the waste product that could help mitigate climate change", Phys.org, 4 August (https://phys.org/news/2021-08-biochar-product-mitigate-climate.html).

34   Council of the European Union (2023) "European green bonds: Council adopts new regulation to promote sustainable finance", press release, 24 October (www.consilium. europa.eu/en/press/press-releases/2023/10/24/european-green-bonds-council-adopts-new-regulation-to-promote-sustainable-finance/); "EU Taxonomy Navigator", European Commission website (https://ec.europa.eu/sustainable-finance-taxonomy/home).

35   Casier, L., and R. Bechauf (2022) "Advancing green public procurement and low-carbon procurement in Europe: insights". International Institute for Sustainable Development, 2 March (www.iisd.org/articles/deep-dive/advancing-green-public-procurement-and-low-carbon-procurement-europe-insights).

Putting an end to impunity

Too often, perpetrators of environmental destruction, whether individuals, companies or countries, can evade any responsibility. This gross injustice is weakening environmental norms but also eroding trust between countries as well as between citizens and their governments.

Building on the current initiative led by Vanuatu, the advisory role of the International Court of Justice in terms of clarifying state obligations on environmental issues should also be strengthened.[36] In a context of the lack of enforcement of many MEAs, the withdrawal of most-favoured nation treatment or curtailed access to international finance must be explored when countries show no willingness to comply with their obligations. The use of satellite imagery for enforcement and the constitution of a UN Corps of Inspectors, like those monitoring the civil use of nuclear energy, should be explored.

Much progress has been made with the recognition of the right to a healthy environment at the UN Human Rights Council in 2021. To make these new rights a reality, the international community must empower citizens and multilateralise existing accords that facilitate access to environmental information and to justice, such as the South American Escazú Agreement and the Aarhus Convention. Empowering citizens also means having a more effective strategy to protect environmental defenders – in the Global North and the Global South – from imprisonment and murder. In this context, the Aarhus rapid response mechanism is a useful precedent that could be built on further.[37] Three out of the twelve most financially rewarding transnational criminal activities are linked to environmental crime. Overall, the annual value of transnational environmental crime is estimated to be $70–213 billion.[38] This is why there must be more cooperation between governments to fight against environmental crime more effectively. Ecocide, which refers to unlawful or wanton acts committed with knowledge of substantial, widespread

---

36   Tigre, M. A., and J. A. Carrillo Bañuelos "The ICJ's advisory opinion on climate change: what happens now?" *Climate Law*, 29 March, Sabin Center for Climate Change Law, Columbia Law School (https://blogs.law.columbia.edu/climatechange/2023/03/29/the-icjs-advisory-opinion-on-climate-change-what-happens-now/).

37   "'Landmark decision' gives legal teeth to protect environmental defenders". *UN News*, 22 October 2021 (https://news.un.org/en/story/2021/10/1103792).

38   "Environmental crime". Europol website (https://bit.ly/49wbrq7).

or long-term damage to the environment, must be considered a crime, building on precedents in several jurisdictions.[39]

With the rising death toll and increasing destruction from natural disasters, and the irreversibility of some of the environmental damage to date, a process for global restorative justice must be explored, building on the current debate on loss and damage (both economic and non-economic). In addition to sufficient funding and humane solutions for displaced people, formal state apologies should be made to indigenous people or inhabitants of low-lying islands, who are suffering from irreparable economic, health and cultural damage.

Conclusion

To secure a New Global Deal that can deliver wellbeing for present and future generations, global environmental governance must urgently be reformed. The demotion of environmental governance in the proposed scope for the Summit of the Future is cause for serious concern. Environmental protection cannot become a political football in a context of increasing political tensions. Doing so would be tantamount to accepting the mutually assured destruction of humanity. A fit-for-the-future governance system for planetary boundaries cannot be built without restoring trust, which means recognising the severity of the plight faced by developing countries and the necessity of addressing their key demands, starting with access to green energy and green industrialisation.

---

39   Kurmayer, N. J. (2023) "EU strikes deal on new 'ecocide' rules to put polluters in jail". *Euractiv*, 17 Novemeber (www.euractiv.com/section/energy-environment/news/eu-strikes-deal-on-new-ecocide-rules-to-send-polluters-in-jail/).

Azita Berar Awad

4 | A New Social Contract through a New Global Deal

"Social" refers to a vast domain that embraces virtually all aspects of human lives and livelihoods and of societal norms, institutions and outcomes. It is related to most, if not all, goals under the 2030 Agenda for Sustainable Development. Social outcomes are determined or affected by policies in a range of domains, including economic, financial, industrial and trade policies; by education, health and social protection systems; and by the major technological and environmental disruptions that are taking place at present. Interactions and spillovers (positive and negative) between goals and policies are manifold. In addition, social outcomes are heavily affected by conflict, pandemics, natural disasters and other sudden or protracted crises, and social deprivation and inequalities in turn exacerbate conflict.

In spite of this web of interactions, the social dimension, under the mainstream globalisation policies of the last few decades, has rarely been the starting point or the benchmark to guide action at the national or global level. Rather, it has been subjected to the primacy of economic and financial policies. At best, strong social policies or pillars have been put in place to correct and compensate for the negative effects, and particularly the effects on groups identified as "vulnerable" or "disadvantaged".

It is befitting, one could add imperative, that this quest for a New Social Contract – called for by UN Secretary-General António Guterres in Our Common Agenda – sets the right priorities through the lens of the social, first and foremost. And it is equally important that the Pact for the Future provides a vision for a new transformative and systemic perspective on the social question that goes beyond the "vulnerable groups" or "low-income country" lens alone.

In this chapter we will focus on two particular dimensions of the social question: work and employment, and social protection – broad domains that are further broken down into a range of subthemes. We will highlight the main deficits in current policies and institutions, in particular at the level of global governance, and we will single out the most important structural reforms that are urgently needed. We believe and hope that ideas for reform nourished through multiple multilateral processes – chief among them the Sustainable Development Goals Summit (2023), the Summit of the Future (2024) and eventually the World Social Summit (2025) – will mutually strengthen the resolve of the global community and yield tangible results.

In spite of weakened and fragmented multilateralism and heightened conflicts and geopolitical divisions, it is encouraging to see that discussions on these very issues are taking place in other forums in addition to the UN system, including the G20, the BRICS and other regional and sub-regional institutions (such as the European Union and the African Union), with multiple formal and informal channels of communication and cross-fertilisation between these institutions and processes. While there may not yet be agreement on the priorities and content of the reform, there is a growing consensus that business as usual is no longer sustainable, that our global institutions in the area of economic and financial architecture are no longer fit for purpose (or are "morally bankrupt", as the UN secretary-general put it), and that in other areas they are at best ineffective in ensuring implementation of the norms that members of the organisations and parties to treaties have ratified.

At the outset, we need to demystify the belief that social policy is a prerogative of national policy and jurisdiction alone, and that it is the domain least affected by global economic, financial and trade policies and turbulence. In fact, to the contrary, the reform of the global economic financial architecture, as discussed below, will potentially have a greater impact on social outcomes, and in particular on jobs, incomes, and inequalities, than targeted social interventions. The predominant macroeconomic paradigm has shaped and is shaping national policies by determining their limits and their content, with the result of significantly constraining policy space and limiting policy options – in particular, but not only, in developing countries, including medium-income countries. Moreover, the widespread debt distress, along with its unsatisfactory management through existing financial policies and instruments, has severely limited fiscal policy space, the single most important policy area for tackling rising economic and social inequalities.

In the context of major technological and environmental transitions, we highlight the importance for building a New Social Contract and a

New Global Deal of financing and managing "just transition" policies with a focus both on jobs and on social protection. We should bear in mind that, in the current debates, the concepts of economic and social justice, as well as that of climate justice, each have two underlying strains. The first strain and group of ideas deals with interstate or intersovereign entities' demands for rebalancing the global economic and financial order and its governance, so as to achieve more inclusivity and representation and to meet the needs of populations in the Global South. In the area of climate change, the notion of climate justice includes in addition the acknowledgment of historical asymmetrical responsibilities. The second strain of ideas around reform concerns just transitions within countries and societies and a just distribution of losses and gains among different segments of the population.

These two strains underlying the notions of economic, social and environmental justice are interconnected in multiple ways. However, reform within one strain of economic and climate justice does not automatically lead to positive outcomes for the other. Coherent and consistent policy shifts, governance reforms and accountability mechanisms are needed at all levels – local, regional and global. Policies and institutions matter, as do geographical and historical contexts, and policy actors and shapers are continually intervening in both the between-country and within-country arenas.

We believe that, at the present juncture, a paradigmatic and systemic perspective on the social question and the New Social Contract is needed, going beyond a list of policy measures that impact the "social".[1] We argue that the predominant economic paradigm of neoliberal hyperglobalisation is systemically generating economic insecurities, deficits in decent work, social inequalities and informality. Furthermore, the management of sovereign debt crises, an increasing occurrence, is constraining policy and financial space for investment in public goods and in managing just transitions. A proemployment, prodevelopment, proenvironment, proinvestment and prosocial macroeconomic framework is needed to deliver the creation of decent work and universal social protection – key components of a New Social Contract supported by a New Deal at the global level. This framework must be supported by a perspective that

---

1   The European Social Pillar includes no less than 20 principles and action areas. The most recent global negotiations at the International Labour Conferences on Employment Policy (2022) and on Social Security (2021), for example, each contained some 50 measures.

is rights-based and that aims at rebuilding trust in public institutions and policies.

In addition to the paradigm shift in global financial management, this chapter emphasises key areas of policy incoherence among different actors of the global governance system – areas that need to be redressed in order to move towards a New Social Contract and a New Global Deal. In particular, we discuss policy gaps and incoherence in global supply chains, in assessing the investment and business environment, and in the area of debt management and fiscal policy space.

The social dimension in crisis: key issues and challenges

In 2023 several economic and social indicators were in the red and regressing. The 2023 progress report on the Sustainable Development Goals (SDGs), which draws on global institutions' statistical reviews and analyses, depicts a stark picture of the nonachievement of SDG targets at the midpoint of the 2030 Agenda.[2] Most if not all SDG indicators are social indicators, revealing different aspects of the social crisis. In this chapter we highlight only three goals: SDG 1, on poverty; SDG 8, on sustainable growth and decent work; and SDG 10, on inequality.

The combined effects of recent crises – including the lingering impact of the Covid-19 pandemic, inflation, insecurity over food and energy supplies, armed conflict, and natural disasters – have wiped out years of global progress towards the first goal, on the eradication of extreme poverty. SDG 10, on inequality, has been the worst-performing goal even though the indicator of "shared prosperity" used for its monitoring is considered by many to be a weak and inadequate indicator, underestimating the extent of inequalities. The dramatic widening of both income and wealth inequalities within and between countries has reached new levels. In this regard, we support the call for a change of measurement indicator for SDG 10, replacing the World Bank's "shared prosperity" indicator with more accurate indicators such as Gini coefficients and Palma ratios.[3]

---

2   United Nations (2023) "The Sustainable Development Goals report 2023: special edition" (https://unstats.un.org/sdgs/report/2023/The-Sustainable-Development-Goals-Report-2023.pdf).

3   Martin, M. (2023) "A call to action to save SDG10: the world must reverse the explosion in inequality which endangers us all". Policy briefing, June, Development Finance International.

Data show that extreme poverty and extreme wealth have risen sharply and simultaneously for the first time in 25 years. Between 2019 and 2020 global inequality grew more rapidly than at any time since World War II. The richest 10% of the global population currently takes 52% of global income, whereas the poorest half of the population earns 8.5%. Billions of people face high and rising food prices, and hunger and child labour increased in recent years after decades of steady decline, while the number of billionaires has doubled in the last decade.

The world also recorded the largest increase in between-country inequality since World War II. Inequality between countries rose because of the more limited fiscal capacity for responses to protect people, economies and jobs during the pandemic in emerging and developing economies, further exacerbated by inflation and food and energy insecurity. In some parts of the world, private wealth is increasing faster than public wealth, with implications for public spending and tackling crises.[4] Rising and widening inequalities and increasing inaction not only undermine trust in public institutions, eroding democratic governance, but also bring social goals into sharper conflict with environmental goals and the transition to a low-carbon economy.

The objectives set in SDG 8 of "sustained, inclusive and sustainable economic growth, full and productive employment and decent work for all" have also suffered a major setback during the pandemic. In many countries, employment levels have not returned to prepandemic levels. While Covid-19 magnified and exposed preexisting inequalities, including health inequalities and inequalities in the capacity to respond, labour market inequalities had been deeply entrenched for two or more decades prior to that.

The global jobs gap stood at 473 million people in 2022, corresponding to a jobs gap rate of 12.3%. The global jobs gap is a new and better measure of the unmet need for employment in the world. It consists of the 205 million unemployed and the 268 million who have an unmet need for employment but for various reasons, especially a lack of prospects for finding a decent job, remain outside the labour force.[5] The jobs gap is particularly large for women, youth and those in developing countries. Of those working, an estimated 214 million workers were living in extreme

---

4   World Bank (2022) "Poverty and shared prosperity 2022: correcting course" (www.worldbank.org/en/publication/poverty-and-shared-prosperity).

5   All labour market data are from various editions of the International Labour Organization's Global Employment and Social Outlook, unless indicated otherwise.

poverty (earning less than $1.90 per day per person in purchasing power parity terms).

A more important indicator of deficits in access to and in the quality of jobs is the incidence of informal work. Those working and producing in the informal economy today account for over 62% of the global workforce, or around 2 billion people. A majority of workers, small businesses and entrepreneurs around the world have no or limited access to labour protections, social protections and other development opportunities that accrue to formal work and business operations. The phenomenon of informality, which for many decades was associated with the conditions of developing countries, remains today one the most pertinent indicators of the social state in the Global South. However, its incidence is not insignificant in advanced economies, and it has been reemerging in multiple sectors, including the digital gig economy. Informality increased during the Covid-19 crisis, and employment recovery in many countries in the Global South has been driven mainly by informal employment. Overall, 4 billion people, working and nonworking, do not have access to any type of social protection.[6]

As labour income is the main, if not the sole, source of income for most households in the world, what happens in labour markets matters a great deal for overall inequality. The single most critical indicator, characterising jobs and connected social crises, is the labour income share in total income. This share has been on a declining trend everywhere over the last few decades of globalisation and liberalisation policies, in spite of major labour productivity gains accrued in the same period. This declining trend is a major contributor to the rise in extreme income inequalities that we are observing, in contrast to the situation prior to the mid-1970s. It has been undermining the European model of social dialogue, which is based on tripartite negotiations (between employers, workers and governments) to ensure the equitable distribution of economic and productivity growth, and which, by and large, has inspired global systems of social dialogue and collective bargaining, including the International Labour Organization (ILO) system of international norm setting and monitoring.

Across the above indicators, the fault lines of gender, race, ethnicity, education and age (at both extremes, young and old) show large inequalities in the world of work. Overall, for a large number of people, work is not performing – as it did and as it should – its inclusionary and

---

6 For a detailed perspective, including regional and country data, see International Labour Organization (2021) "World social protection report 2020-22: social protection at the crossroads; in pursuit of a better future".

redistributive function, and it is not fulfilling the promise of social upward mobility within and across generations.

Gender equality indicators in labour markets have been particularly stubborn. Globally, women's labour-force participation rate stood at 47.4% in 2022, compared with 72.3% for men. Large gender gaps – including those in relation to pay, pensions and quality of work – persist. The World Inequality Report 2022 estimates that women's share of total income from work (i.e. labour income) is around 35%, when it should be 50% in a gender-equal world, and that it has not changed in the past three decades![7] In addition, disproportionate care responsibilities have a significant impact on women. In 2018, 606 million women globally were unavailable for employment due to unpaid care and domestic work, compared with only 41 million men.

The 2007–8 global financial crisis revealed the extent of the youth employment crisis as a global challenge in the Global North as well as the Global South, and in ageing societies as well as countries undergoing a youth bulge. Numerous studies and surveys undertaken since then have shown how the nature and pathways of school-to-work transitions have changed, becoming more difficult and offering more uncertain outcomes, including for educated youth. Young people (aged 15–24) face severe difficulties in securing decent employment. Their unemployment rate is three times as high as that of adults. More than one in five are neither in education nor in employment or training (NEET), an SDG indicator that has risen; and among working youth, one in four is in informal employment. After only a decade since the global financial crisis, youth were particularly severely hit by the Covid-19 crisis in terms of their education, jobs, incomes and sociopsychological health. There is ample evidence to show that young people who lose their job or fail to obtain one are particularly vulnerable to "scarring", the phenomenon whereby their future labour market outcomes are worse than those of their peers even when macroeconomic conditions improve again. They may end up accepting a job for which they are overqualified, which risks trapping them in an employment trajectory that involves informality and low pay.

Studies and opinion polls on youth transitions that were carried out following the waves of youth-led protests in different regions of the world reveal the extent to which, in youth perceptions and expectations, the issues of work, rights, space for civic engagement and political participation are intertwined. At a time when youth are showing their incredible

---

7   Chancel, L., T. Piketty, E. Saez et al. (2022) "World inequality report 2022". World Inequality Lab (https://wir2022.wid.world/).

power to come together and mobilise for the planet and the environ-mental transition, the Pact for the Future and a renewed social contract should make a larger space for supporting multiple youth transitions, as well as engaging with their critical and constructive thinking in influenc-ing governance reforms and solutions at the local and global levels.

In this stark global picture, there are variations in the form and severity of the deficits and the social crisis, partly explained by historical and geo-graphical structural factors but mostly by policies, institutions, social sys-tems and public funding. However, the scarcity of opportunities to access meaningful, stable and decent work, along with the insecurity of incomes, inadequate conditions of work and limited social protection for large swathes of the population in the Global North and Global South, plays a large part in the overall state of the social crisis and in uncertainty, socio-economic insecurity, and mistrust in policies and institutions. Situations of protracted armed conflicts, forced displacements of populations, and major disruptive technological and environmental transitions are clearly compounding the social crisis and adding to anxieties. These grievances and disappointments are impacting political systems, weakening democ-racies and becoming instrumentalised by populist discourse.

In the face of such compelling evidence, there is a shared diagnosis among social scientists, including economists of all streams (the phe-nomenon is rare and deserves to be underscored), that globalisation policies of the last three decades, by and large, have not delivered jobs, social protections and social cohesion and have failed to generate and distribute the prosperity long promised.

Key measures existing at the national and global levels

Evolving policy strategies and paradigms

The post-World War II recovery and reconstruction policies and eco-nomic plans pursued in Western democracies delivered, by and large, on the triple objectives of full employment, high economic growth and social welfare policies, in tandem and in synergy. For nearly three dec-ades, from 1945 to 1975, this consensus model and paradigm inspired the pathway for economic and social policies in the rest of the world. In retrospect, however, this period described as the "golden age" appears as an exception.

A new policy thinking that advocated privatisation, the liberalisation of trade and finance, a belief in free markets, and a diminishing role for government intervention, regulations, trade unions and social dialogue was consistently deployed across countries. This shift to the neoliberal policy paradigm saw, in particular, a growing disconnect between economic growth and employment, as well as the subordination of the objective of full employment to the primacy of economic and financial liberalisation. A second disconnect, in policy action and in mainstream thinking, opposed economic performance to social progress. As noted above, social norms that were considered by the ILO's founders and constituents to be a means to improve the quality of work and productivity, to increase purchasing power and global demand, and above all to achieve social peace and peace between countries were increasingly portrayed by mainstream policymakers, think tanks and major economic and financial international organisations as "distortions" promoting "rigidities" in the labour market, and as obstacles to job creation and economic growth.

This policy framework – which has, by and large, been disseminated across the globe – structurally weakened the post-World War II governance consensus in the world of work. As mentioned above, this consensus was based on cooperation among the three parties (government, employers and workers' organisations) to negotiate and bargain for the fair sharing of growth and productivity gains, including those accruing from technological innovations. Where the arrangements introduced under this consensus remain in effect, they have proved inadequate and ineffective in governing the tremendous cross-border development that is taking place through global supply chains, capital liberalisation and trade agreements, and the new generation of technological innovations. These tensions have led to different layers of policy contradictions and policy incoherence at the local, national and global governance levels that are also apparent in the current debates on the reform of the global financial architecture and just transitions to digital economies and low-carbon economies.

In highly integrated and volatile financial and capital markets, each wave of regional or global economic and financial crisis has been followed by a cycle of austerity measures. The fiscal consolidation policies enacted in response have taken a great toll, with a long-lasting impact on the social dimension and on labour markets where they have been introduced. Social and labour market recovery has been lagging behind economic recovery, and in many instances the objectives of financial stabilisation have not been sustained over time. Recurring sovereign debt distress has dire consequences for sustainable development, for investment in public goods and for social justice.

The crisis response measures at the global and national levels have also shown the limits, contradictions and deficiencies in national and global policy approaches and instruments. Targeted policies, where they exist, have provided at best partial or temporary relief, without redressing or reversing the structural dynamics of low-quality job creation, informality and limited social protection. The Covid-19 pandemic acted as a dramatic wake-up call, exposing and laying bare multiple layers of social inequalities and vulnerabilities. It shed light on those without proper access to basic health; on workers and businesses in the informal economy who could not isolate themselves without the risk of starvation and of losing the livelihoods on which they and their families depend; on young and old people; and on those workers in the formal economy whose services became essential and lifesaving during the pandemic, in the food and retail sectors and in the care and health system. With this came the realisation that these workers, since labelled "essential workers", are at the bottom of the salary scale, have precarious and difficult conditions of work, and are often migrants.

While in most advanced countries extraordinary public policies and public funding were deployed to cushion the negative impacts, the situation was mixed in developing countries, because of more limited fiscal space but also because of a lack of proper policies and institutions to channel and monitor timely crisis response measures. Although Covid-19's wake-up call failed to generate the level of international solidarity and cooperation needed for vaccine dissemination, it nevertheless increased the moral imperative for a change in policies and a reform of institutions both at the national (local) level and at the international (global) level.

Though there is no agreement on the content and extent of reforms, it is interesting to note that voices of criticism include some of the previously staunch advocates of the neoliberal paradigm in addition to those who all along had advocated for alternative policies. There are growing strains of thought that maintain that business as usual is not socially tenable and that major shifts in policy are needed to build a New Social Contract and a New Global Deal. A key part of this shift has to do with the global institutions responsible for the governance of economic, trade and financial policies, whose structures, mandates and policy instruments are no longer considered fit for purpose.

While a new consensus is yet to emerge on strategies and governance rules that could pursue in tandem sustainable development, full employment, worker protection, welfare provision and improved living standards, as well deliver on global public goods and just transitions, we believe that this is the time for a new systemic vision for building a New Social Contract. This New Social Contract needs to be sustained by new policy approaches and a New Deal at the global level, whereby economic and social priorities are given equal preeminence and resources.

Policies addressing or impacting the social dimension are manifold and cannot be discussed in detail in this chapter. In recent years, however, the crises and response measures have shattered a number of policy taboos in mainstream economic thinking in the Global North and in the Global South, such as those around the role of the state and of fiscal policy, the debt-to-GDP ratio, or the need for industrial policy.

SDGs at their midpoint

The 2030 Agenda remains the (only) overarching consensus platform in the present context. The SDGs and their indicators are the result of long and intense negotiations preceding their adoption in 2015 and prior to the current context of geopolitical tensions and weakened multilateralism. While there is severe disenchantment with the achievements so far at the midpoint of the SDGs' time horizon, the goals have the advantage that they have been embraced by all parties: states in the Global North and Global South, the private sector, and civil society.

The 2019 Global Sustainable Development Report, as well as many other studies, have analyzed SDG interlinkages. The findings highlight that while most "SDGs are synergistic, both social and environmental Goals have systemic impacts that drive overall SDG progress".[8] It is clear that prioritising policies and investments that have multiplier effects across these goals is the way forward. In the run-up to the September 2023 SDG Summit, emphasis was laid, rightly, on the huge financing gap, or to put it in the UN secretary-general's words: "Achieving Goal 8 will require a wholesale reform of our morally bankrupt financial system in order to tackle rising debts, economic uncertainties and trade tensions, while promoting equitable pay and decent work for young people."[9]

---

8   Independent Group of Scientists appointed by the Secretary-General (2019) "Global Sustainable Development Report 2019: the future is now; science for achieving sustainable development". United Nations (https://sdgs.un.org/gsdr/gsdr2019).

9   United Nations (2023) "United Nations Secretary-General's SDG Stimulus to deliver Agenda 2030".

The proposed SDG Stimulus – by massively scaling up financing to at least $500 billion per year through long-term lending at lower interest rates, debt relief, and the creation of a robust and effective sovereign debt resolution mechanism; by expanding contingency financing to countries in need; and by driving both public and private investment towards the SDGs – brings into a coherent whole a range of reform proposals that have emanated from different parts of the governance system. It provides a rich platform for the 2024 Summit of the Future.

New measures to be proposed for a New Global Deal

The financing aspect of a New Global Deal, which, as mentioned, is galvanising most of the policy thinking and discussions, including those in the run-up to the Summit of the Future, is of critical importance for delivery on social objectives, universal social protection, decent job creation, healthcare, quality education, sustainable food systems, infrastructure, renewable energy and digital transformation.

In this section we also highlight other critical policy areas, less debated in the context of summits but with a huge bearing on the social dimension and just as in need of systemic change. Together with the reform of global finance, we need to consider issues of policy (in)coherence, in particular between the governance of economic and financial strategies on the one hand and social and labour policies on the other.

The remaking of the global financial architecture: key for social policy space

The importance of the reform of the global financial architecture for investing in job creation, in public policies and in institutions for better social outcomes cannot be overemphasised. Three issues are particularly highlighted here: debt management, the reform of multilateral development banks and the reform of special drawing rights.

It is a shared diagnosis that the international financial system, designed by and for the industrialised countries of the post-World War II period, at a time when neither climate risks nor social inequalities were considered preeminent development challenges, is unfit for purpose, unfair and unable to respond to today's realities and challenges. Some critics go beyond this, underlining the impact of some existing policy tools and frameworks in further exacerbating inequalities.

We need bold and ambitious reforms, somewhere between what President Lula of Brazil called for at the Paris Financing Summit – a clean slate – and the more incremental fixes that the management of international financial organisations or their current shareholders have introduced or proposed to introduce. Below, we briefly highlight proposals that we consider most pertinent for social investment.

Debt crisis and management

Repeated global financial crises that spread fast in highly integrated and volatile financial markets result in recurring sovereign debt distress, with dire consequences for fiscal space, long-term development financing, climate finance and public expenditures, including spending on education and social protection.

The burden of debt overhang is battering the economies of many developing countries. Currently, nearly 60% of low-income economies are either at high risk of debt distress or already in it, while one in four middle-income countries, which host the majority of the extreme poor, were at high risk of fiscal crisis.[10] There are numerous areas of dysfunction and a great divide among developed and developing countries. Three issues are of particular relevance.

- The higher borrowing costs for developing countries in financial markets. Even prior to the recent rise in interest rates, developing countries that borrowed from international capital markets often paid rates of 5–8%, compared with 1% for many developed countries. More recently, rising investor risk-aversion has pushed the cost of borrowing above what would be warranted by macroeconomic fundamentals in many countries, with some middle-income countries with investment-grade ratings paying between 6 and 7 percentage points above US treasury yields in 2022.[11]

- Vast variation in countries' access to liquidity in times of crisis. Many middle-income countries near debt distress are excluded either

---

10   International Monetary Fund (2022) "Crisis upon crisis: IMF annual report 2022" (www.imf.org/external/pubs/ft/ar/2022/).

11   United Nations (2023) "United Nations Secretary-General's SDG Stimulus to deliver Agenda 2030".

because of eligibility criteria or in practice, for a series of political reasons. The international system, in short, does not have the tools to facilitate debt restructuring effectively, sufficiently and in a timely manner in order to reduce countries' debt burdens and to address a systemic debt crisis. For those who have access, the response is too little and too late.

- Creditor coordination among and between multiple official and private creditors to a single country. The IMF has no mandate to oversee all global transactions and it has had very little ability to influence private creditors into lowering their premiums and actually restructuring debt. The Common Framework for Debt Treatment, established by the G20 for this purpose, failed to conclude a single restructuring in the first one and a half years of its existence. All reform proposals call for the creation of either an independent authority or an effective coordination platform, a solution that would bring the heterogeneous and fragmented community of public creditors and private creditors together to coordinate debt restructurings.[12]

Financing for development: reform of public development banks, including multilateral development banks and special drawing rights

The existing architecture has also been unable to support the mobilisation of stable and long-term financing at scale for the investments that are needed. Several recent reports have highlighted, through substantiated research, the policy and regulatory frameworks that lead to short-termism in capital markets and have called for a positive change in the business models of multilateral development banks (MDBs) and other public development banks (PDBs) in order to focus on their impact on the SDGs and to more effectively leverage private finance so as to advance the SDGs while thoroughly reviewing the terms of blended finance.

In order to massively scale up affordable long-term financing for development, there are several proposals for the reform of PDBs, including MDBs. PDBs, including MDBs, can scale up long-term financing that is "nonconcessional" but still significantly below the market

---

12   An idea promoted by the High-Level Advisory Board on Effective Multilateralism, in its 2023 report "A breakthrough for people and planet: effective and inclusive global governance for today and the future".

rates currently paid by developing countries, including financing to meet investment needs in middle-income countries. Furthermore, as global financial conditions tighten, it is especially important that the MDBs have the capacity to act countercyclically. It is estimated that, with greater financial capacity, MDBs and PDBs have the potential to play a much larger role in development finance. Strengthening MDBs with stronger capital bases and better use of existing capital would allow them to increase lending from $100 billion per year to at least $500 billion. According to other estimates, under more ambitious but still feasible scenarios of capital increase the boost to lending could be between $1 trillion and $3 trillion.[13]

Reform of the special drawing rights (SDRs) is perhaps the more advanced building block of the current reform proposals. The allocation in 2021 of SDRs equivalent to $650 billion, to support recovery in countries struggling to cope with the impact of the Covid-19 pandemic, was a rare incident in the history of SDRs. By far the largest-ever allocation, it raised hopes that a review of the SDR system could enable it to effectively channel much-needed liquidity for long-term or contingency funding without adding to the debt burden of receiving countries or submitting them to austerity conditionalities of the type discussed below. However, for this to materialise, there are important changes that need to be introduced, such as a review of the IMF's Articles of Agreement so as to allow "selective SDR allocation", enabling only those countries most in need to receive SDRs in a general allocation. New mechanisms are also needed to enable countercyclical issuance of SDRs in a more automatic or timely manner in times of crisis, which would avoid protracted political negotiations during crises and provide SDRs for immediate use when most needed.

Massive investment and new approaches for job creation and social protection

It is critical that finance mobilised through domestic and global resources is invested at a much larger scale to create productive employment, universal social protection for all working and nonworking people, and socially just transitions in three key domains: climate change, digital transformation and the transition from the informal to the formal economy.

---

13   United Nations (2023) "SDG Stimulus".

Job creation through a revival of industrial policy

Higher levels of productive employment are essential to reducing ine-quality. Without employment-derived income, no distribution or redis-tribution is possible on a significant scale. Quality education, training and public services are a precondition for successful labour market transitions, equal opportunities in employment, gender equality and social inclusion. The promise that policies liberalising trade and invest-ment accompanied by loosened regulations will lead to job creation has not been borne out, as illustrated above. As an increasing number of both developed and developing countries are reconsidering their growth models and turning – albeit too slowly – to the green and blue economies and to digitalisation as a means of achieving sustainable development, deliberate investment in job creation has become seen as not only desirable but necessary.

A key area in which policy taboos and dogmatism have been rapidly changing in recent years is the area of industrial policy and the role of government interventions and public investments in spearheading the transformation and crowding-in private investment. Whereas indus-trial policy was decried under the neoliberal paradigm for the alleged distortionary effects of picking and choosing sectors, disillusion with trade-liberalisation policies' outcomes for the creation of quality jobs, as well as new research on industrial policy, has shown the critical role of industrial policy for innovation and job creation in the Global North and the Global South.[14] There is a need and a major opportunity for indus-trial policy in the green, blue, digital and care economies. Employment opportunities are expected to arise, in particular, from investments in clean and renewable energy, construction, sustainable agriculture, recy-cling and waste management. While all policies need to be understood within and adapted to their context, national institutions should con-sider such policies and regional and global institutions should support related strategies.

It is important, in the development of a New Social Contract, to rebuild trust in public institutions and in public policies, including through rein-vigoration of public funding and the role of PDBs. While leveraging private sector financing is a must – including financing to meet job creation and social goals – a new approach to blended finance is needed. The expe-rience with blended finance to date has not been convincing overall and

---

14   Notably in various reports and publications by Dani Rodrick and Mariana Mazzucato.

should be reviewed. A strong emphasis on national ownership is necessary to ensure that blended finance projects are aligned with national strategies, and that the public sector can share both risks and rewards fairly.

There is also ample evidence to show that job creation benefits would accrue if the expansion of investments were preceded by massive investments in quality education and skills development for young women and men and accompanied by inclusive and properly funded labour market institutions, such as employment services and lifelong learning opportunities. Numerous empirical analyses and national policy experiences also show that availability and access to increased job opportunities and securing "decent" working conditions are two sides of the same coin. Without massive job creation to close the jobs gap, there will be little progress in reducing the downward pressure on the quality of work and informality. Investments in sectors characterised more often than not by a high incidence of informality and precarity, low pay, and poor conditions of work, such as the care sector, must be accompanied by a focused reform of labour and social protections, including guaranteed freedom of association, the right to collective bargaining and to equal pay for work of equal value, and the prevention and elimination of violence and harassment.

Towards universal social protection

Four billion people do not have access to any type of social protection. The pandemic exposed deep-seated inequalities and significant gaps in social protection coverage, comprehensiveness and adequacy across all countries.[15] In the current context of inflation and food and energy insecurity, countries are displaying significant differences in their responses aimed at preventing hunger and poverty and sustaining the purchasing power of families. This is due both to the gap in fiscal space and to a lack of the right institutions and mechanisms. A recent ILO analysis of adjustment rules for social protection benefits around the world shows that more than half of the schemes have no specific rule to adjust benefit levels according to inflation, real wages or a combination of the two.

These successive shocks reveal a more structural divide, namely the limited range of policy instruments – in particular social automatic

---

15   International Labour Organization (2021) "World social protection report 2020-22".

stabilisers – in the Global South to deal with ordinary lifecycle contingencies or exogenous shocks and crises. There is ample evidence and experience to show that policy approaches relying only on targeted interventions, with respect to social protection and poverty eradication in particular, are insufficient in monetary terms and in outreach, leaving behind many segments of the population. Furthermore, the multiplication of types and sources of endogenous and exogenous shocks that cannot be fully anticipated and planned for, including those induced by climate change, technological innovation or demographic shifts, calls for universal and multipurpose social protection that leaves no one behind.

A renewed social contract requires the institutionalisation of universal social protection systems, for all working and nonworking people, and a significant upscaling of its financing through mobilisation of domestic resources and a more coherent global governance system that supports its establishment and financing. Tax-funded public spending on other social sectors – and, in particular, quality education, training and lifelong learning opportunities, resilient health services, care, housing, water and sanitation – plays a critical role in reducing social inequalities and promoting equality of opportunity.

Just transitions to formality

The high prevalence of jobs and businesses in the informal economy worldwide epitomises the global jobs crisis, the convergence of deficits in job creation and in the quality of jobs, limited social protection, unsafe conditions and low pay. Legislation and compliance enforcement have proved insufficient to promote a just transition to formality, in the Global North as well as elsewhere, and to curtail economic and labour market dynamics that contribute to the informalisation of formal jobs. Among efforts to enable just transitions to formality, the best results have been shown by integrated strategies that promote innovation and productive job creation, ensure comprehensive social protection, and increase financial inclusion in tandem with appropriate and fit-for-purpose regulations and institutions for their delivery.

The Global Accelerator on Jobs and Social Protection for Just Transitions
To promote such policy approaches, in September 2021 the UN secretary-general launched a new scheme with the ambition of

bringing together member states, international financial institutions, social partners, civil society and the private sector, coordinated by the ILO, to help countries create 400 million decent jobs, including jobs in the green, digital and care economies, and to extend social protection coverage to the 4 billion people currently excluded.

The Global Accelerator aims to promote (1) the in-country development of integrated and coordinated employment and social protection policies and strategies that facilitate just transitions; (2) the establishment of integrated national financing frameworks and the mobilisation of public and private domestic and international resources to invest in universal social protection and inclusive, environment- and gender-responsive employment interventions with a view to creating quality jobs; and (3) the improvement of multilateral cooperation on jobs and social protection for just transitions, with international financial institutions among others.

The Global Accelerator aims to use a new tool, Integrated National Financing Frameworks, to support more investments for productive employment and adequate social protection – boosting domestic resources and expanding the tax base as well as mobilising further development cooperation assistance and international support. Complementary interventions will aim to ensure the more effective use and stronger alignment of current financial flows (both public and private) for social investments.

The Global Accelerator aims at strengthening the level and coherence of the multilateral system's support for countries.

This is not the first time that such multistakeholder initiatives have been launched at the global level. In the wake of the Arab Spring uprisings in 2011, followed by continuing youth-led social unrests in various regions, the ILO at the 2012 International Labour Conference issued an urgent Call for Action concerning the global youth employment crisis. The Call for Action was followed in 2016 by the launch at ECOSOC (the UN Economic and Social Council) of a multistakeholder Global Initiative on Decent Jobs for Youth, which brought together 34 UN entities in addition to other public and private stakeholders. Unless the massive upscaling of financial efforts such as those foreseen under the SDG Stimulus are directly and systematically linked to the Global Accelerator, such initiatives will unfortunately remain, at best, pilot schemes supported by selective voluntary contributions.

Financing and managing just transitions

Socially just transitions to low-carbon economies

The interactions of the social agenda with climate change and environmental transitions are multiple, complex and multidirectional. Net carbon neutrality by the middle of this century, the objective of the 2015 Paris Agreement, can be achieved only through a major transformation of energy systems and structural changes to economies. Structural changes of this scale and within a limited time horizon are bound to create major disruptions in employment, livelihoods and social wellbeing too.

A just transition implies the recognition of the significant redistributive impacts of both environmental degradation and environmental transition action, as well as recognising the need for compensatory policies and programmes to bring out a more equitable outcome. The concept embedded in the Paris Agreement of "taking into account the imperatives of a just transition of the workforce and the creation of decent work and quality jobs in accordance with nationally defined development priorities" has been gaining ground and momentum in international policy frameworks and discussions on climate change.

It is estimated that the jobs and livelihoods of more than1.2 billion people and 40% of total world employment depend directly on the ecosystem. Under the "business as usual" scenario, climate change and environmental degradation, through their various manifestations, threaten jobs, businesses and livelihoods, as well as access to water and other resources, especially for the poorest and most vulnerable. Jobs, businesses and livelihoods are particularly vulnerable to the higher incidence of environmental disasters, whether slow-onset events (such as droughts, erosion, soil degradation or sea-level rise) or rapid-onset events (such as extreme weather events or forest fires).

Environmental degradation is also contributing to population displacement and internal and cross-border movements, and it has increased the risk of conflict. Both climate change and environmental policies for transitions to low-carbon economies exacerbate conflicts around the access to and distribution of resources among different population groups – conflicts not only between the big business interests and the more vulnerable, but between the more vulnerable themselves. Large-scale adaptation measures and policies for a just and timely transition are essential to deliver improved livelihoods and enable millions more people to overcome poverty. However, as we know, adaptation measures in the context of the Paris Agreement and since then have not received the same level of policy attention, and the financing mechanisms put in place fall short of achieving their ambition.

Several proposals for the reform of the global financial architecture include proposals and tools for climate finance, addressing primarily climate justice between countries and the need for loss-and-damage and adaptation finance, for instance. As put forward in the Bridgetown Agenda, greater use of state-contingent clauses in MDB lending can also provide breathing room to countries hit by shocks, as they can automatically suspend payments in the case of a disaster, economic or financial crisis, or other exogenous shocks. To finance adaptation and just transitions, recourse to reformed SDRs (another proposal of the Bridgetown Initiative) would upscale funding without adding to the debt burden. The IMF has already operationalised a Resilience and Sustainability Trust, but its scale and ambition are not commensurate with the challenges faced by the world and the growing demand for resources.

Tackling the social and distributional impacts of various policies and the conflicts they give rise to within countries is, however, still a domain in need of innovative thinking and policy engineering. Just transition policies should involve a broader perspective than, for example, only compensating workers and communities affected by the closure of coal mines, as necessary as these measures may be. In the recent past, there have been useful attempts to quantify the impact of environmental transition or greening policies – and particularly mitigation policies – on jobs through various modelling exercises (OECD 2016, ILO 2018).[16] These estimates forecast a net positive impact, meaning that the net job creation potential of green policies will exceed the jobs and livelihood losses in other sectors. However, the win-win scenarios over the medium to long term tend to overlook the social costs of transition in the short term, in particular for the poorest and most vulnerable segments of the society. Such neglect in devising adequate policies and institutions to compensate for and accompany these transitions will not only aggravate the social crisis and social unrest, as we have seen in developed and developing countries, but also jeopardise the adoption and

16 Organisation for Economic Co-operation and Development (2017) "Employment implications of green growth: linking jobs, growth, and green policies", OECD report for the G7 environment ministers, June; International Labour Office (2018) "World employment and social outlook 2018: greening with jobs" (www.ilo.org/global/research/global-reports/weso/greening-with-jobs/lang--en/index.htm).

implementation of such measures. The carbon tax and the yellow vest (*gilets jaunes*) protests in France are a case in point.

Thus, the employment and social effects of transitions to low-carbon economies should be considered within a more comprehensive economic and societal cost–benefit framework. This is essential in order to increase the political buy-in for environmental transition policies and to avoid clashes between sustainability objectives and social objectives. Historically there are few examples of socially successful transition policies based on market-driven approaches, and it is clear that the role of the state and political leadership will be crucial in launching large-scale New Deal efforts at the national and global levels.

Moreover, incremental approaches using single or selected policy instruments such as regulatory frameworks, taxation and incentives structures, or policies focusing on technological innovations have shown their limitations. Incremental policies do not respond to the time horizon of achieving carbon-neutral economies by 2050 on a global scale, and they do not factor in the necessary compensation mechanisms for negative impacts. Integrated strategies, on the other hand, have a better chance of creating the desired coherence of objectives and a fairer level playing field. However, at the national level they face the challenge of political and institutional coherence, coordination and cooperation in planning and implementation. A broader and bolder vision is needed for financing and managing just environmental transition as key components of a New Social Contract and a New Global Deal.

Digitalisation and just transitions

The concept of socially just digital transitions has multiple facets too. The extent of the digital divide between and within countries is well established. A third of the world's population (2.7 billion) still do not use the internet. Many of them are women – or live in rural and remote areas – in the least-developed countries.[17] The Covid-19 pandemic shed new light on the digital divides in access to education, skills and jobs for those who were connected and those who weren't, and for those who could muster digital skills and those who could not.

The extremely unequal distribution of profit and productivity gains from digital technologies (such as robotics and artificial intelligence) and monopsonist market structures are contributing to rising income

---

17 International Telecommunication Union (2022) "Measuring digital development: facts and figures 2022" (www.itu.int/hub/publication/d-ind-ict_mdd-2022/).

inequalities. The introduction of new digital technologies spearheaded in the private sector has often outpaced the establishment of national institutions and regulatory capacity to manage these innovations. The multilateral system trails even further behind. A report by the High-Level Advisory Board on Effective Multilateralism has put forward several proposals to close the digital governance and data governance gaps.[18] Digitalisation is also giving rise to new challenges for the effective governance of labour on digital labour platforms, whether those anchored locally or the crowd-work or microtask platforms that operate across numerous countries. Some of the most common issues raised are the blurring of the line between dependent worker status and self-employment; the use of algorithms, with all their embedded discriminatory biases, in managing human work performance and remuneration; and, generally, low pay and limited social protection. In spite of important court rulings, conventional labour market institutions have proved inadequate to uphold fundamental labour rights on digital platforms, in particular those operating across borders.

Addressing the huge policy, financing and governance gaps for just transitions in the digital era – not least in regard to digital labour platforms, which are adding new layers to present social divides and discrimination – should be a priority concern for the Summit of the Future and for a renewed social contract and a New Global Deal.

Addressing policy (in)coherence in (national and) global governance

Apart from the need for the massive upscaling of finance, policy space is constrained at the national, regional and global levels by the (in) coherence of predominant economic, social and environmental policies. The economic policies pursued have failed to generate a virtuous and automatic dynamic of social progress and upgrading. And the social policy responses to compensate for the pressures of deregulation, social exclusion and inequality have varied in their ambition, policy approaches and effectiveness.

Three examples of policy space and policy coherence at the global level are discussed here. The first concerns the massive expansion of global supply chains through the operations of private sector corporations, as well as the inability of national and global systems

---

18 High-Level Advisory Board on Effective Multilateralism (2023) "A breakthrough for people and planet".

to uphold public labour and social standards, including the body of relevant international labour standards adopted through successive international negotiations at the ILO. The second issue is the use of labour indicators in the assessment of the business and investment environment. The third concerns the constraints on policy space and the social consequences brought about by debt restructuring measures, and specifically by IMF conditionalities.

Global supply chains

The multiple disruptions in global supply chains (GSCs) since the onset of the Covid-19 pandemic, and the implications for the economy, inflation, national security, and other areas of concern, have galvanised policy attention. Yet relatively little is said about the compliance with labour rights and the labour and social governance of GSCs.

It should be recalled that, through a profoundly restructured international division of labour and value distribution, GSCs now form a complex integrated web of businesses for the procurement, production and distribution of goods and services around the world. Corporations, with their increasing power and influence, are shaping international and national strategies across multiple national jurisdictions, with significant implications for employment relationships and industrial relations at the bottom of the chain. This transformation, sustained by the liberalisation of trade and of financial and investment policies, favoured countries with the least taxation and the least labour regulation and protection, which in turn created the dynamics of a race to the bottom.

Violations of human and labour rights in GSCs have been widely documented in various sectors and have regularly become headline news. The operation of the GSC business model clearly shows that risks and the costs of social compliance have continuously devolved to the bottom of the chain, and typically to businesses in developing countries and to the weakest segments of these businesses, such as workers. Workers in supply chains often lack access to social protection, adequate protections that ensure they can perform their work in safe conditions, or a voice to bargain for better conditions. Last year marked the 10th anniversary of the Rana Plaza tragedy in Bangladesh, in which thousands of workers perished or were wounded in a textile factory producing for major brands in the Global North. Continuous pressures from the lowering of prices for final consumers, mostly in the Global North, and from the curtailment of public institutions' capacity and finances, mostly in the Global South, have created a system with asymmetrical and explosive consequences for the quality of jobs and the respect of human and labour rights.[19]

In addition to efforts towards the effective implementation of the International Labour Standards, which are negotiated through the ILO and, when ratified, are translated into national legislation and inspection systems, there has been a proliferation of private standard-setting and monitoring initiatives. A fragmented and incoherent system has developed through a combination of corporate social responsibility (CSR) initiatives on the part of corporations; the adoption of unilateral codes of conduct and social auditing; and NGO-led or multistakeholder initiatives – driven partly by consumers and partly by labour unions – to define standards and audit, monitor and certify compliance. In this sea of the "privatisation of labour standards" developed outside the realm of the ILO's standard-setting and supervisory mechanism, and outside the realm of national public inspection and enforcement mechanisms, coherence, transparency, effectiveness and accountability gaps remain major issues.

In free trade agreements too, clauses or chapters on social and labour rights, when they exist, present the same challenge of a plurality and diversity of approaches, as in the case of unilateral corporations' codes. Both in public initiatives, via free trade agreements, and in private CSR initiatives over the years, there has been increasing convergence and reference to ILO standards, and in particular to the 1998 Declaration on Fundamental Principles and Rights at Work. The enforceability of such rights in practice, however, has been limited. The 1998 declaration is not the first attempt to provide a global framework for GSCs. The ILO Multinational Enterprises (MNE) Declaration of 1977 was adopted a year after the adoption of the OECD Guidelines for Multinational Enterprises. Other initiatives at the global level include the UN Global Compact, which invites enterprises to voluntarily enter into commitments with the UN secretary-general, whereby public and private entities commit to adhere to a certain number of principles. It includes a self-reporting mechanism without a third-party assessment of self-declared goals. Other soft mechanisms include the UN Guiding Principles on Business and Human Rights, which were adopted in 2011 and have gained traction among corporations, and due diligence initiatives at the level of the OECD.

---

19 For a more detailed discussion, see Berar, A. (2022) "The International Labour Organization: social justice in global governance", in *Handbook of Labor, Human Resources and Population Economics* (Berlin: Springer Nature).

Achieving effective cross-border regulation of the employment relationship is vital given the highly integrated and globalised economy. In a global governance system where enforcement of labour protection essentially and *theoretically* remains within the realm and responsibility of individual national jurisdictions, transnational companies operating across multiple borders retain substantial leeway around respect for labour standards. The multiplication and diversity of global public and private initiatives have neither fully addressed the challenge nor created the necessary global adherence by all concerned actors. The reform of social and labour governance in GSCs needs be considered urgently as a key part of global governance reforms under the New Global Deal. There is a need for out-of-the-box proposals that bring together public authorities, private corporations, employers' and workers' organisations, and concerned civil society groups under a binding and coordinated governance structure.

Redressing global policy (in)coherence through a social lens

As highlighted in the Addis Ababa Action Agenda, financing sustainable development is about more than the availability of financial resources. National and global policy frameworks and institutions (such as rating agencies) influence risks, shape incentives, impact financing needs and help determine the cost of financing. They can also constrain fiscal policy space and determine, to a large extent, its content. It is well established that the current paradigm has given rise to policy conflicts and contradictions between economic, trade and financial institutions and governmental and private sector priorities for labour and social policy. Rising policy (in)coherence has also been generated by differences between parts of the global governance system, such as differences between policy frameworks (i.e. for policy assessment and recommendation) used by intergovernmental international organisations in the UN system, or between those used by international financial institutions (such as the World Bank and the IMF), the WTO and other, specialised agencies (such as the ILO and the UNCTAD). Two examples are discussed below.

Assessing investment climates and business environments

A notorious example of interagency policy incoherence around job creation and regulation was the World Bank's influential Doing Business report, which started in 2004 and was only interrupted in 2021. The report, which

---

ranked 190 countries on the "ease of doing business", played a critical role in orienting global investment and in driving policy and regulatory changes that were favourable to businesses and corporations.

Over the years, the report has received criticism from different quarters for its selection of the performance criteria and indicators used to rank countries and for pushing them into a race to the bottom in terms of deregulation and liberalisation. The ILO has been particularly concerned with the "employing workers" indicator. Through research, interagency dialogue and public statements, it has consistently demonstrated the "dismantling" effect of the ranking criteria on workers' rights and on other social and environmental safeguards. Although the use of workers' rights among the ranking criteria stopped in 2010 as a result of persistent criticism and pressure from unions and civil society groups, the recently launched successor framework – the World Bank's B-Ready index, which aims to measure annually the business and investment climates in 180 economies worldwide – has met with equal scepticism from the International Trade Union Congress and civil society. The critics have once again highlighted methodological biases in the index, undermining labour rights and social protection across employment sectors.

Fiscal policy for crisis response: turning current conditionalities into positive conditionalities

The "great divergence" between poorer and richer countries in their capacity to cope with recurring crises and contingencies through fiscal policy became even more obvious in the recovery from the Covid-19 pandemic. Constrained by economic slowdown, rising debt burdens and shrinking fiscal space, many countries now face an even more daunting policy landscape, with few policy tools to tackle the social impact of financial, food and energy shocks.

These episodes reveal an endemic policy incoherence among global institutions in the management of debt crises. As discussed earlier, the rise in debt stress and debt crises due to the highly integrated and volatile nature of financial markets vulnerable to cross-border contagion has generated a recurring (and for some countries, never-ending) cycle of debt management. Debt relief measures are often conditional on austerity measures that curtail fiscal space and cut essential public spending, including social spending. In particular, fiscal consolidation policies advocated by the IMF in the process of Article IV reviews and in the management of debt crises have regularly come under increasing criticism across countries. The impact of austerity measures on the contraction of public spending, of public institutions providing essential services, of food and energy subsidies, and of social assistance programmes is exacerbating economic and social crises.

The primary aim of the conditionalities imposed by the IMF, and supported by major economic powers as a condition of further technical and financial support, is to secure the debtor country's capacity to repay creditors. However, there are many instances in which, amid widespread socioeconomic insecurity, the primary objective of financial stability is not achieved either. In spite of evolutions in the social-spending frameworks used by the IMF in the Article IV review process, the nature of measures remains procyclical at a time when countercyclical strategies are needed. Moreover, the IMF's approach to social spending, where it exists, is limited to short-term targeted social assistance. Such programmes suffer from major exclusions, in contrast to the systemic expansion of social protection, which would have a broader social impact.

In the process of financial and budget stabilisation, a critical yet underemphasised step is to revitalise state institutions while at the same time holding them accountable for development and social spending. An approach totally different from the current paradigm is proposed here: a complete turnaround of conditionality by seeking to secure more ambitious social and equality goals and by making debt restructuring measures conditional on spending on social SDGs and just transitions. In general, social indicators should be used more systematically in processes for accessing contingency and development finance and in accountability frameworks for public expenditures.

Towards a New Social Contract through a New Global Deal?

The previous sections have identified the main global actors in each area of reform. Initiatives are not lacking. There are those launched by the secretariats of global intergovernmental institutions themselves, chief among them that of UN Secretary-General António Guterres. Proposals are prepared by these secretariats as well as through independent expert bodies and high-level commissions set up for the purpose. Civil society and think tanks are weighing in in those debates. The UN secretary-general's proposal for a SDG Stimulus plan, mentioned earlier, sums up the main issues of reform. These proposals are put forward for adoption through intergovernmental negotiations – and in particular will be on the agenda of the forthcoming UN summits – and/or (current) shareholder agreements in the case of international financial institutions.

There are several other processes initiated by other state groupings and regional bodies, such as the G20 and the BRICS, that are focusing on the same issues, and in particular on the reform of global financial architecture, climate finance, security and a fairer sharing of decision-making power in global governance. It should be borne in mind that members of these institutions are also all members of the UN; however, they play by different rules, and these processes are governed by different dynamics. Individual countries are also launching initiatives, such as the Paris Financing Summit convened by France in July 2023. Private sector institutions, after having initially bought into the SDG framework, are rather absent from the debate, and this in spite of their weight in determining economic and social outcomes around the world.

Though most parties accept the need for a New Social Contract based on different policy approaches and a major overhaul in the post-World War II global governance system, there are several competing and evolving narratives on the priorities for reform and the nature of reform. No agreement has been reached so far in the specific context of G20,[20] which brings together a select group of countries in the Global North and Global South, but these discussions are a useful way to clear the ground, to have all parties express their positions, and to build new dynamics and momentum, even if there may be a long way to go before cooperation based on common platform. And while the Global South and Global North clearly have distinct views or sensibilities as to the reform of global governance, neither group has a monolithic position. There is a wide diversity of conditions, objectives, and interests within each group. The current context is increasingly characterised by patterns of coalitions that change according to the issues, which makes the path forward less predictable but at the same time leaves the door open to opportunities.

A Pact for the Future embracing a New Global Deal that is supportive of a New Social Contract needs to draw on these narratives in order to tackle the rebalancing of representation and decision-making in global governance between the Global North and Global South and to ensure a significant increase in the mobilisation of domestic and international

---

20   The global Debt Roundtable – initiated by the G20 under the Indian presidency with the participation of finance ministers, the IMF and the World Bank – met three times in 2023 without notable progress to date.

resources, a larger policy and fiscal space for tackling inequalities and enabling just transitions, and a major shift in rebalancing economic and social priorities and in the policy coherence between them. Trust and dialogue at all levels need to be revitalised. Social Europe, with its strong social model, can be a key player in this new vision, which responds to the new realities and the needs of future generations.

Francesco Lapenta

5 | An alternative model and vision for our tech-driven AI future

This chapter attempts to establish some key concepts that may position the United Nations as a key diplomatic player and global platform in promoting an alternative and inclusive socioeconomic model and vision for humanity's technological and digital future, and it attempts to address the following questions. What global regulations should digital economies promote to favour sustainable growth, fairness and economic stability? What global incentives can promote the development and adoption of sustainable technology across sectors and regions? How can sustainable development and digital inclusivity be supported by international digital infrastructure standards? How can a global economic governance framework help to redistribute technological innovation fairly between developed and developing nations? How can technological innovation, especially around digital platforms and artificial intelligence (AI), better support the Sustainable Development Goals (SDGs)? What alternative socioeconomic models can be used to promote technology transfer and knowledge sharing so that all nations benefit? How can global policies ensure that AI and digital technologies promote digital cultural inclusion? What supports are needed to boost digital technology and AI education, research, innovation and development in developing countries?

The long view and state of play of technology-driven social innovation

In 1930, despite the early steps of two industrial revolutions, much of the world faced economic hardship, struggling to meet basic needs. That year, amid the Great Depression, economist John Maynard Keynes optimistically predicted that "technological advances and increased productivity" would eventually end poverty and lead to economic growth, shorter working hours and improved wellbeing for future generations in industrialised countries.

Unforeseen by Keynes, the predicted transformative impact of technology emerged at a high cost from World War II and the military–industrial complex.[1] The war increased competition and government intervention, hastened innovation and expedited international cooperation among a host of allied countries. The imperative of technological innovation as a key strategic advantage shaped postwar economies' significant transformations. Following the war, a number of industrialised societies realised some Keynesian ideals by increasing government control and spending, by investing in public infrastructure, housing, manufacturing, mobility, education, research and innovation, and by fostering a growing open market supported by strengthened international laws and financial institutions (the Bretton Woods system).

These strategies established a technologically dependent economic model that allowed high economic growth and social progress based on a number of factors: energy dependence, permanent cycles of technological innovation and adoption, increased efficiency and increased productivity, increased centralisation of innovation cycles in dominant tech hubs, competitive dominance in standardisation processes and intellectual property protection, and leadership in emerging technological innovation as a strategic and competitive advantage for socioeconomic expansion and global geopolitical influence. The legacy of these drivers of technological innovation can be systematically felt today in at least three major outcomes, all of which are interconnected.

The winner-takes-all business model

Financial markets have prioritised investment in cutting-edge technologies and leading technological research and companies, exacerbating the winner-takes-all business model, widening the global technological and socioeconomic gap, and allowing big tech to grow, remain undertaxed and consolidate mostly unregulated in the early stages of the development of emerging technologies. This self-reinforcing cycle of innovation and capital concentration gives technologically developed nations, dominant economies and companies a compounding advantage, because technological baselines allow them to maintain their dominance. Dominant

---

1   Brynjolfsson, E., and A. McAfee (2014) *The Second Machine Age: Work, Progress, and Prosperity in a Time of Brilliant Technologies* (New York/London: W. W. Norton).

economies have little incentive to regulate too early and prefer to inter-vene slowly or only when market or geopolitical conditions change.

Growing inequality between and within nations

While bringing socioeconomic gains to some regions, this model simul-taneously widened disparities between nations in terms of technological adoption and wealth, and it enabled the greatest disparity in per capita consumption of resources and natural ecosystems in history. Importantly, it also exacerbated inequalities within nations over time, creating unprec-edented imbalances in access to capital and contributing to increasing domestic economic divides.

Permanent geopolitical competition for technological leadership

This socioeconomic model strengthened the notion of technological innovation as a form of permanent geopolitical competition – whether military, industrial, economic or political – in which technological lead-ership and innovation are not always viewed as a collective shared path towards the improvement of the human condition, but rather as instru-ments of a permanent confrontation of ideologies, values and social and economic systems in constant competition or conflict for economic growth and cultural and geopolitical influence.

A century of growth, increasing inequality and the centralisation of technological innovation

Exceptional human progress has occurred over the last century, signal-ling a departure from *Homo sapiens's* 250,000-year history. There have been three significant interconnected shifts: a demographic surge, urban-isation and the exponential rise of the role of science and technology. The global population surged remarkably, going from 1 billion to 8 bil-lion in just a century. This surge, which has been largely attributed to agricultural, scientific, medical and healthcare advancements, has meant that sustaining the planet's 8 billion inhabitants is now heavily reliant on technology, putting the planet under increasing strain and exacerbating unequal resource consumption and access disparities.

Part of the challenge lies in the inherent nature of the adoption cycles of early analogue technological innovations themselves. The very dynamics of modern technological innovations created an uneven distribution, granting certain communities first access to technological advancements and greater benefits than others.[2] These dynamics were correlated to urbanisation. As large urban conglomerates emerged, they became powerful catalysts for innovation, early technological adoption and economic growth.[3] They also resulted in the formation of high-innovation echo chambers, where high demand was combined with increasingly high barriers to wider participation (as exemplified by increasingly complex administrative aspects, including patent claims and intellectual property protection, and the ability to secure financing and safeguard innovations). Technological innovation cycles exhibited increasingly centralising socioeconomic tendencies that embodied and inherently limited equitable access to their designs and benefits. These divergent dynamics have resulted in growing inequality in all areas over the past century: in advanced economies, the mostly urban majorities (representing 15% of the global population) have full access to the latest technological affordances and socioeconomic benefits, while in developing regions and rural areas (where 50% of the global population reside), 1 billion people lack or lag behind in basic infrastructure, or even access to water and electricity.[4]

These dynamics, gatekeepers and institutional controls have created barriers for broader and more diverse cultural groups seeking to influence technological development trajectories, reinforcing the cultural influence and dominance of a small minority. This is clearly understood and clearly stated when, for example, a technology or product is labelled as being "designed in country X and assembled in country Y", highlighting the cultural origin of the design.

The impact of the original designers' cultural contexts and values has grown exponentially with the spread of digital platforms as more people adopt global communication technologies and platforms designed by dominant minorities. As AI systems advance, this influence will become more socially and culturally significant, and more problematic. The persistent disparity in accessing, and designing, emerging and dominant

---

2   Piketty, T. (2013) *Capital in the Twenty-First Century* (Cambridge, MA: Harvard University Press); Piketty, T. (2019) *Capital and Ideology* (Cambridge, MA: Harvard University Press).

3   Weiner, E. (2016) *The Geography of Genius: A Search for the World's Most Creative Places from Ancient Athens to Silicon Valley* (New York: Simon and Schuster).

4   Stiglitz, J. (2013) *The Price of Inequality: How Today's Divided Society Endangers Our Future* (London: Penguin).

digital and AI technologies will remain a significant challenge for global development, for equal participation and representation and, fundamentally, for sustainability. To understand the historical challenges that await in the current era of technological evolution in data and AI, one must recognise first and foremost that all technologies, and especially digital technologies and AI, are cultural phenomena with strong cultural and innovation biases. As such, they tend to privilege the needs of certain cultures and groups, and in the current socioeconomic model they will perpetuate and amplify existing inequalities while potentially hindering the realisation of equitable, sustainable and inclusive global progress.

A new model for innovation and sustainable economic growth for the 21st century

In the third decade of the 21st century, several global crises have highlighted the urgent need to reevaluate and renegotiate the goals, benefits and existential risks of technological innovations that have increasingly impacted human existence and the planet. Although technologies, energy systems, the digital realm and AI are all systematically interconnected by science, they do not exist outside of a human agenda. They are incredibly powerful tools designed by humans to achieve set goals, whether increased efficiency and economic growth for the few or systemic resilience and sustainability for all. Regardless of the tool, its actual development and use reflect human agendas, goals, narratives and visions.

Existing UN initiatives such as the 2030 Agenda for Sustainable Development and the 2020 Roadmap for Digital Cooperation have laid some important groundwork. Other efforts, such as the Digital Cooperation initiative and the similarly oriented AI for Good initiative, have also made valuable contributions to promoting inclusive technological development while respecting human rights. However, the scale of the transformations underway calls for an even more ambitious and unifying vision. The call for the UN to evolve and meet 21st-century challenges is growing.[5] The new UN proposal for a global Pact for the Future could unify these efforts, forging a new mission for the UN and a forum for the collective development and implementation of a comprehensive social contract for a shared vision of humanity's future.

This new Pact for the Future must directly address the function of science and technology, and most importantly of AI, for the future of

---

5   Lopez-Claros, A., A. L. Dahl and M. Groff (2020) *Global Governance and the Emergence of Global Institutions for the 21st Century* (Cambridge: Cambridge University Press).

humanity. It must first and foremost recognise and strongly reaffirm the principle that, despite the significance of technological innovation, it is human leadership, vision and social innovations that have transformed the course of human history. Those who assert that humanity and current socioeconomic systems and dynamics cannot change overlook all the historical evidence to the contrary – or have an interest in maintaining the status quo.[6] Developing the complex, systemic thinking required to conceive and, incrementally, realise global large-scale change is a key responsibility of 21st-century leaders.[7] In the case of science and technology, and specifically the digital realm and AI, what is needed is an interconnected, long-term vision of their function for the 21st century and the future of humanity – a vision of how to harnesses their potential for diversity, decentralisation of innovation, and technological solutions that support diverse, micro, locally developed social innovations within new models of global sustainable development and resilience.

Decentralising innovation: a necessary novel approach for global technological transformation and sustainability

The disparity in living standards and access to education and technological solutions between certain mostly urban areas of the world and the majority of the world's other regions demonstrates the need for those interested in rebalancing the existing gaps to reconsider development and innovation on a global scale. As certain urban areas flourish, a significant portion of the world's population in developing countries and rural areas lag behind or lack access to basic necessities. Most countries do not decide their technological future but are left to pick among existing options designed by a dominant minority. Resolving this disparity is critical not only for equity and social justice but also for realising the vast majority of humanity's untapped creativity and innovation potential. Having a global strategy to support diverse education patterns and to promote innovation on a local scale can help to unlock latent and local creativity. This creativity can be used to develop new solutions and new standards of excellence, and to experiment with alternative and parallel paths to innovation – going beyond the model of increasingly problematic and

---

6   Lapenta, F. (2021) *Our Common AI Future: A Geopolitical Analysis and Road Map for AI Driven Sustainable Development, Science and Data Diplomacy* (Rome: Institute of Future and Innovation Studies, John Cabot University).

7   Schwab, K. (2016) *The Fourth Industrial Revolution* (Geneva: World Economic Forum).

unsustainable processes of urbanisation as the precondition for socioeconomic growth, or plans for technological adoption that are impossible to implement. Sustainability is based on technological innovation, decentralisation and diversity.[8]

Diversity provides significant opportunities for innovation, problem solving, social transformation and sustainability. Bringing the same technological solutions and innovation models to all underserved regions of the world is not only impossible but also culturally, strategically and economically problematic. It increases the likelihood that existing cultural and economic gaps will be exacerbated by the providers of these premade solutions. Furthermore, it lacks fundamental sustainability. The dominant model that has emerged and been culturally and geopolitically fostered is a top-down model of imitation, global adoption and dependency on technologies developed by a dominant minority in specific socioeconomic contexts. In the energy sector, for example, the assumption of universal dependence on fossil fuels has precluded the participation of many developing regions in technological advancement; and atomic energy, fundamentally a military technology, is rightly heavily supervised, regulated and guarded, and is not available to all. This strategy and the complex technological and infrastructural ecosystem required to support such forms of energy, as well as their dependencies, left many nations behind. Nations in Africa, for example, would have been much better served by controlled foreign investments and research partnerships focused on alternative technologies and solutions, such as solar energy, which is abundant in the region, scalable and less dependent on complex infrastructures and the geopolitics associated with them, and which could have transformed certain African countries into leaders in the sector.

In order to achieve sustainable development objectives, it is necessary to decentralise elements of innovation, and to combine macrosustainability goals with locally developed microsolutions. Establishing overarching sustainability goals and governance for new technologies is an important and necessary component of macrostrategies. All countries should participate in setting these goals. Globally effective macrostrategies, however, require scalability and adaptability to diverse local

---

8   Rifkin, J. (2013) *The Third Industrial Revolution: How Lateral Power is Transforming Energy, the Economy, and the World* (New York: Palgrave Macmillan); Russell, S. (2019) *Human Compatible: AI and the Problem of Control* (London: Allen Lane); Sachs, J. D. (2015) *The Age of Sustainable Development* (New York: Columbia University Press); Sachs, J. D. (2005) *The End of Poverty: Economic Possibilities for Our Time* (London: Penguin).

conditions. Differentiating solutions' deployment scales – macro versus micro – acknowledges profound regional differences.

The energy sector's shift towards decentralisation and local solutions exemplifies the evolution from macro- to microsolutions. Emerging technologies such as AI present systemic decentralisation opportunities: microsolutions could use AI to connect intangible data to local data, cultures and communities, and AI systems could be trained with locally relevant data to develop local solutions. The digital realm's affordances create alternatives to urban social proximity and communication and could be crucial for the creation of alternative innovation ecosystems. The postpandemic adaptation to working from home provides important insight into alternative paths for education, work, collaboration and community building. Microsustainability involves the transformational actions of individuals, organisations and communities at the local level that are connected differently than in urban environments, with different limitations but also different affordances. But if global governance, dictated by the agenda of a handful of leading countries that control the innovation cycles, continues along its current trajectory, then digital platforms and AI will most likely exacerbate existing disparities.

Developing nations should ideally embrace SDG 9, which aims to promote sustainable and inclusive industrialisation and foster local innovation and demand. By doing so, they can fully participate in the regulation of technology, and of digital technologies specifically, in order to ensure equal opportunities and reduce inequalities of outcomes, and to move towards a dual macro–micro strategy that balances global and local considerations. This approach entails cultivating a global supply chain and fostering exchanges and scientific collaborations that leverage existing global structures, while also strongly promoting the decentralisation, diversification and cultural specificity of innovation, nurturing local competitive advantages, and making strategic investments in independent sustainability and resilience.

This parallel global strategy could balance important top-down global trends by fostering alternative education systems; local innovation, talent and creative enterprises; local resources; diverse technological ecosystems; and localised solutions. While not expected to entirely eliminate socioeconomic disparities, this strategy holds the potential to reduce dependencies, enhance resilience and challenge existing models that often favour established entities controlling the dominant innovation cycles. Fostering local innovation models has a higher likelihood of disrupting entrenched economic models and dependencies, as it nurtures local excellences unique to each region. This, in turn, broadens the spectrum of feasible avenues for social innovation, introduces fresh innovation paradigms and more sustainable solutions and nurtures a more inclusive and diverse environment for innovation.

The unique opportunities of the digital and AI era

To support decentralised microstrategies, we need globally effective macrostrategies that promote scalability and sensitivity to local conditions. AIs could play a key role, combining macro global solution scales with micro community-specific ones, and analysing and integrating profound global and regional differences. AI-enabled microsolutions could connect abstract data to on-the-ground local cultures, resources and communities. Exploring alternative routes that decentralise innovation, cultivate local talent and make use of local resources and knowledge can challenge entrenched models that favour established players in terms of control over the direction of innovation cycles. In this way, AI and other emerging technologies, when guided by inclusive global governance, could help to bridge top-down and bottom-up approaches. AI's data-integration capabilities could contextualise global knowledge and innovations for local needs. And its decentralisation potential, via local data training, could empower communities to drive grassroots change rather than rely on distant centralised systems and solutions.[9] Locally developed solutions are better positioned to capitalise on regional excellence and expand social innovation avenues through the exploration of entirely new paradigms.

If global governance can embrace a truly inclusive vision, the novel digital era of AI systems could present unprecedented opportunities to reimagine education, growth and technology-adoption patterns. Rather than exacerbating inequality, AI and automation could distribute capabilities more equitably across regions if guided by a globally agreed sustainability goal. A micro–macro approach that is well balanced would combine the advantages of global collaboration, exchanges and knowledge flows with diverse, resilient local innovation networks that are tailored to community contexts. Although a part of, and interconnected with, the technological innovations of the past, the digital realm and emerging AI systems offer historically unique opportunities to steer this social,

---

9   Markoff, J. (2015) *Machines of Loving Grace: The Quest for Common Ground Between Humans and Robots* (New York: HarperCollins).

cultural, economic and technological change. As other general-purpose technologies have in the past, AI advancements will result in a systemic transformation of societies. This presents a rare opportunity.

Digital technologies and AI exhibit unique economic properties, as well as unparalleled accessibility and scalability potential compared with previous technologies. The general-purpose and industrial technologies of the past require massive investments, with a high cost for supply chains and physical infrastructures. Digital and AI solutions have a much lower economic barrier in terms of energy and infrastructure, and they can spread through software alone, potentially reaching in real time vast communities cut out from other technological advancements and solutions. This ability to diffuse to end users swiftly and at low cost uniquely positions digital and AI solutions as possible tools to bridge economic and geographic divides, potentially powering a knowledge, service and innovation economy that far exceeds the global reach and investment/return required by other, more costly, investments.

They also have the potential to be uniquely designed so as to provide diversity and local solutions for local cultures and economic contexts with different strategies, transforming innovation processes in fundamental ways: from centralisation to decentralisation, and from a winners-take-all model to socioeconomic diversity and scalability. However, this is highly unlikely right now. Reaping the potential benefits of these emerging technologies requires systematic and globally coordinated investments and regulations, guided by a truly global governance approach and vision that limits and redirects the default trajectory of digital technologies and AI. This trajectory will most likely entrench inequalities instead of bridging divides, both among nations and within nations, and it seems set to exacerbate possible risks around privacy, surveillance, disinformation, biases and a number of other threats to democracy, the environment and humanity.

Ultimately, the only reason to develop AI should be to help humanity solve planet earth's sustainability problem, and to help us totally reengineer our social, technological and economic infrastructures from the ground up in order to achieve global standards and sustainable socioeconomic resilience for 10 billion people – not 1 billion or fewer. To be effective, such a strategy would need to articulate a vision that goes beyond just another timely agenda on the global geopolitical table and instead provides a more long-term strategy of multiple actions and permanent operations to reshape existing social, scientific, technological and innovation models. The UN is in a unique position to lead the urgent establishment of an inclusive (in line with SDG 16) international super-vising organisation for AI and digital technology, or a similar mechanism or institution (following the example of the International Civil Aviation Organization) to regulate global innovation and adoption processes for AI and digital technology while ensuring equitable representation. This essential global governance mechanism would enable participation in the shaping of technological standards and norms for AI, incorporating the values of justice, inclusion and shared prosperity, and it would promote the strong international laws that are essential for regulating the global development and adoption of AI for ethical and sustainable purposes.

Informed by the considerations presented above, the synthetic and nonexhaustive map of concepts below has been selected to provide a meaningful agenda for reimagining the existing innovation models and fostering a parallel path for an alternative, decentralised model. The agenda will draw attention to a number of key and potentially powerful concepts that have the potential to be included in a multistakeholder foresight exercise aimed at reimagining a globally coordinated model and strategy centred around technological, digital and AI diversity. These concepts are

- a shared future narrative;
- a shared human-centric definition of AI that emphasises its mission and goals, and not its technical dimensions;
- working towards the recognition and regulation of the digital realm and AI as global commons;
- supporting open data as sustainable data based on FAIR data principles and tools;
- building an equitable global framework for data and AI.

A shared future narrative

The ability to anticipate and shape future scenarios through narratives has yielded significant geopolitical, economic and social benefits for the leading postwar societies. After World War II, influencing the future emerged as a crucial geopolitical strategy. The narratives guiding future development became key instruments for asserting control and influence. For decades, this understanding was the basis for competition among diverse national and economic actors to define the future and secure strategic advantages across societal, economic, technological and political domains. Shaping societal visions grew as important as controlling innovation cycles and global production in the arena of geo-political, economic and ideological competition. In this high-stakes environment, the capability to direct future trajectories took on a comparable significance to the regulation of technological and industrial predominance globally. Recent innovations such as renewed space exploration, advanced microchips, AI, robotics and autonomous transportation have rekindled more than just public interest in technology; they have also reignited international competition to control the narrative and direction of our technological future. As nations race to lead in areas from supercomputing and next-generation microchips to AI algorithms and driverless cars, a new era of rivalry over whose vision of progress will prevail has reemerged. Significant achievements in cutting-edge fields such AI have reignited an ambition among superpowers to dominate the trajectory of technological progress and dominate influential narratives about humanity's technological future.

In this context, the UN's proposal of a Pact for the Future could be seen as a significant countereffort and achievement in global politics. The global impact of such a pact could ease technological divisions in key innovation areas and facilitate scientific and technological diplomacy, providing a platform for negotiation beyond any one ideology while focusing on containing common risks and achieving common goals. By organising collective action according to a long-term vision of the future, despite unavoidable competition, the UN could offer a vital forum for aligning international cooperation and stand as a formidable endeavour and geopolitical force, capable of harmonising the collective actions of countless globally distributed stakeholders that have an interest in moving towards the accomplishment of the SDGs and beyond individual national interests, winner-takes-all strategies, the further unequal distribution of competitive advantages, increased strain on earthly nonrenewable resources, and a lack of true social innovations such as those that could be ushered in by a new generation of truly sustainable, diverse and transversal sociotechnical innovations.

A shared human-centric definition of AI that emphasises its mission and goals, and not its technical dimensions

Few things will be more consequential than the dominant and officially adopted definitions of AI. These will have long-term consequences not only for national and international law but also for all possible treaties in which AI is involved. Both will be based on a set of emerging definitions that delimit the realm of AI from several angles. These definitions will also reverberate through all the business memos, applications for funding, cultural explorations and tropes, and incredibly complex sets of standards and regulations that will naturally emerge over time. A fight for the definition of AI has already emerged, with the voices of certain key actors and institutions having greater resonance – some of the dominant definitions being those of the European AI High-Level Expert Group, the NIST (National Institute of Standards and Technology), the IEEE (Institute of Electrical and Electronics Engineers), the World Economic Forum, OpenAI, Google the OECD and even the World Health Organization. Each definition, while sharing some elements with all the others, has subtle variations that clearly define an agenda. All these definition have in common some elements that resonate with the early definition first used by John McCarthy, Marvin Minsky, Nathan Rochester and Claude Shannon in a proposal to the Rockefeller Foundation for funding the 1956 Dartmouth Workshop. The proposal defined AI as "an attempt [...] to find how to make machines use language, form abstractions and concepts, solve kinds of problems now reserved for humans, and improve themselves".

However, none of the officially more dominant definitions adopt a truly human-centric definition of AI. A critical discussion of the possible versus desirable future developments of AI, and hence its definition, cannot be separated from the larger ethical and philosophical issues raised by the question: "Why do we need AI?" Is the goal of AI development simply to replace humans with automated machines (replacing labour, decisions or interactions)? And what should the scope of this evolution be? The hypothesis of "human-like identity" for AIs raises not only fundamental ethical quandaries (what is the legal status of intelligent machines and artificial moral agents, for example, or of cloning?) but also calls into question the possibility, desirability and necessity of human-like AIs. The idea of AIs having a second "superhuman" identity (as seen in notions of strong AI, artificial general intelligence and the "singularity") is perhaps the most fraught with ethical quandaries and existential risks. The UN would be in a very strong position to contribute to a long-term future-orienting definition if it generated another, more holistic and human-centric definition that, instead of focusing on the technical definition of AI, placed humanity (the moral primacy of humans in the human–machine relation) squarely at the centre of this agenda for the future evolution of AI. This would clearly define machine learning applications, and AI systems first and foremost, as tools that must be designed for the emancipation of humanity, the enhancement of human values and the enrichment of our individual and collective cognitive and collaborative abilities and qualities.

According to this alternative interpretation, AI systems should be defined not on the basis of their technical qualities but on the basis of their mission and goals. Their human-like qualities should be defined and designed to function as rich and empathic interfaces that do not replace but rather expand and enhance the realm of possibilities for human interactions, empathy, individual and collective creativity and intelligence, problem solving, individual expertise and crowd wisdom, and human agency and values. Building on the unique qualities and ability of machines to process and analyse real world big data, as well as their ability to project complex augmented and virtual worlds, a truly human-centric definition of AI systems should be conceived with an emphasis on their ability to operate "as powerful tools and interfaces designed to interact and collaborate with humans, in cognitively deep and rich ways in order to enhance humans' ability, to process complex data systems, or to empower humanity to explore alternative logic systems that support human development, creativity, innovation, emancipation and transfor-mations".[10] Few things will be more consequential and future-defining than a truly human-centric dominant definition of AI.[11]

Working towards the recognition and regulation of the digital realm and AI as global commons

The history of global commons goes back centuries and describes a long historical evolution through which different communities came to recognise certain resources and spaces as shared resources that tran-scend concepts of national or individual ownership. Over time, these nat-ural resources – such as rivers, seas, the deep ocean, outer space, deep space, Antarctica, and the atmosphere – were eventually recognised as shared global commons, characterised by principles of open access, the equitable distribution of benefits and shared collaborative governance and control. These global commons have over time become regulated by convention, treaties and protocols, such as the UN convention on the law of the sea, which establish global norms to protect and regulate the shared and equitable use of these shared resources. The important principle established by the concept of global commons is that there are

---

10   Lapenta, F. (2021) *Our Common AI Future.*

11   Taleb, N. N. (2007) *The Black Swan: The Impact of the Highly Improbable* (London: Allen Lane).

resources that belong to all of humanity, and that as such they have to be protected and equally shared.[12] In the last few years there has been increasing debate over the potential recognition of the digital domain as a global commons.[13] The concept of the digital commons doesn't contest the intellectual property rights connected to individual digital applications; instead, it asserts that the digital realm in which they operate as a whole is a shared global commons, and that as such it requires a set of protocols, treaties or conventions to guarantee the fair, safe and shared use of its resources. Given the global nature of these technologies, it is argued, the UN should have the responsibility to lead these negotiations for the fair and shared use of these digital resources, just as it has with the governance of resources such as the oceans.

While the goal of recognising the digital realm as a global commons is rather arduous, the underlying diplomatic discussions and negotiations around science, technology, data and AI in order to articulate such a concept are needed and necessary.[14] Science and technology diplomacy have historically been a very contentious and tumultuous area of geopolitical relations, diplomatic practices and international agendas. And given the current geopolitical dynamics, it seems that these difficulties are deepening rather than easing. However, the concept of science and technology diplomacy has recently gained new momentum, despite the geopolitical crises, as all governments have been reminded that some major global crises transcend national boundaries and present common social, scientific and technological challenges. Emerging fields such as AI are recognised on all sides of the geopolitical spectrum as having great potential, but also posing great existential risks. Hence, demand has recently increased, especially from developing countries, for the UN to provide a formalised forum for open confrontation around science, technology, data and AI diplomacy. One possible outcome of these scientific and technological talks could be the designation of a number of internationally agreed "scientific green zones", which would represent collective scientific quests and challenges that transcend global geopolitical disputes or even major confrontations, and whose resolution would benefit all communities and humanity.

---

12   Hardin, G. (1968) "The tragedy of the commons". *Science,* n.s. 162(3859): 1243–1248.

13   Gill, A. S. (2021) "Aligning AI governance globally: lessons from current practice". Stiftung Entwicklung und Frieden/Development and Peace Foundation.

14   Nye Jr, J. S. (2011) *The Future of Power* (New York: PublicAffairs).

Supporting open data as sustainable data based on FAIR data principles and tools

Fundamental to this quest for a shared green scientific agenda for the common good and the fair use of the digital domain is the complex balance that needs to be achieved in the process of sharing the results of scientific discovery and the data sets that could lead to such discovery. With data-driven technologies such as machine learning and AI becoming more important drivers of growth in the global economy, intangible assets such as data and metadata are becoming increasingly valuable. As a result, it is critical for data diplomacy to focus on promoting international governance frameworks[15] that ensure data is deployed legally, ethically and safely, while maintaining a balance between intellectual property protection, national sovereignty and a negotiated strategy for sharing data for the common good.

The effective management of global data exchanges will require strong multilateral organisations or institutions that can manage data trade agreements, host data trade talks, and serve as potential platforms for multilateral global governance to bring common rules to data exchanges amid wildly different data regimes. Enlisting the UN in this mission will place scrutiny on the crucial aspects of the burgeoning data disparity between the Global North and the Global South and its ensuing socioeconomic repercussions. This approach will also serve to ensure diversity, incorporate various perspectives, mitigate inequality, guarantee equitable data access, emphasise the cultural relevance of data and foster a multifaceted and inclusive global landscape for data governance.[16]

The scientific and societal benefits of open data exchanges and open science are difficult to argue against, as are the costs of not sharing scientific data, particularly when it comes to publicly funded research data. Large amounts of scientific data produced at great public expense are never used again. This "data waste", as well as the cost of reproducing overlapping and duplicate data, has quantifiable scientific, social and economic costs for society and the planet, and it is in every way equivalent to other types of energy waste. From this perspective, we can consider "open data as sustainable data" to describe data that can significantly contribute to the goals of resource organisation, waste reduction,

---

15   Raworth, K. (2017) *Doughnut Economics: Seven Ways to Think Like a 21st-Century Economist* (New York: Random House)

16   Schneier, B. (2015) *Data and Goliath: The Hidden Battles to Collect Your Data and Control Your World* (New York/London: W. W. Norton).

optimising and expediting scientific discovery, increasing social benefits and contributing to sustainability and economic growth.

The main problem with open data is that it is, by definition, fully open, available and accessible to everyone for use, reuse, and redistribution – subject, at most, to attribution and/or sharealike licenses. This definition runs counter to the competing global political and legislative drive to protect intellectual property rights, fair economic competition and the government's role in guaranteeing a balance between publicly funded research and fair business investments and interests. There are, of course, numerous reasons to strike a balance when it comes to intellectual property protection. And the first step is to establish strong forms of data diplomacy, to internationally coordinate data and metadata exchanges, and to establish globally recognised institutions that can negotiate data and AI practices and shared rules.

To solve these tensions, the European Commission has supported and adopted the "FAIR data principles model" for their newly launched EOSC platform (the European Open Science Cloud), which has the potential to have a global impact as a best practice and strategy for balancing the legitimate protection of intellectual property and private data while allowing their controlled use and sharing for the benefit of all.[17] The FAIR data principles – an acronym for Findable, Accessible, Interoperable and Reusable data – was created at the Lorentz conference in 2014 and could become the underlying principle governing the operations of data trusts and data stewards for both businesses and individuals. In practice, this means that the openness of FAIR-compliant data is determined by who created it. The creator and owner of the data decide who can access it, when they can access it and under what conditions. Under the FAIR license system, data can be closed, open to a select few, or open and accessible to all at different stages of its lifecycle. Data owners can also impose stricter restrictions, limiting the specific data that can be used, how it can be used and what purposes it can be used for. It can be made available to select partners if certain conditions are met, or it can be made open and accessible to everyone.

The global adoption of this or an equivalent model, and the creation of globally interconnected data-sharing platforms under the same model, would open a variety of opportunities for AI training, development and scientific discovery, allowing access to open and trustworthy high-quality data that would otherwise remain an economic, scientific and cultural

---

17   European Commission Expert Group on FAIR Data (2018) "Turning FAIR into reality".

advantage for the leading economies that could afford the "pay for access and use" models most likely to emerge.

Building an equitable global framework for data and AI

Understanding the challenge of macro–micro sustainability and the role of AI

Discussion around sustainable development focuses mostly on the macrotrends of emerging technologies that might offer possible solutions to existing problems, often disregarding the complex social and economic contexts in which these technologies and sustainable solutions will have to operate. A realistic assessment must be based on the microconditions and pervasive social and economic disparities that form the context in which these hypothetical solutions will have to be implemented. To make real progress, as discussed above, the two strategies must be combined. The macrosustainability goals set by states and international entities must define goals at a global scale and establish governance structures to guide the transition to sustainable emerging technologies; and at the same time, at the local level, microstrategies for local implementation have to be created so as to offer and make use of a range of available micro low-tech alternatives. These should create two tracks for innovation, allowing decentralisation away from the macrotrends created by a leading minority, and localisation based on accessibility and the creation of local solutions. Microsustainability encompasses the actions taken by individuals, organisations, cities, neighbourhoods, regions and local rural communities to transform their activities and social environments through local solutions within the broader context of sustainable development. Since the scalability of these strategies, along with their adaptability to a variety of local socioeconomic conditions, is essential to their effectiveness on a global scale, AI systems could play a key role in this transition.

The global data challenge and the need for a new global data governance system

Few things will be more consequential in the new AI era than the new global data order that will emerge to feed the heavily data-dependent AI system. Any AI system can only be as strong as the data that it is trained on. This, in time, will make the access to and use of a variety of scientific, industrial and personal data sets the most contentious area of global governance and competition, as geopolitical actors will try to control to their advantage the competitive affordances of AI. A sharp dichotomy will emerge between AI systems trained with publicly available data and closed-access AI systems trained on a variety of data not subject to the same limitations as public AIs. As the world evolves and adapts to these new AI and data systems, several challenges will emerge for global legislation and regulation around data mining, data training, and the use and limitations of AI output. These dynamics will create "data and AI regimes", in which different models for data use will compete for national and global adoption. For any global governing body or global standards organisation tasked with creating and governing a global reference legal framework, one of the most important tasks will be to organise these data regimes for the interoperability and compliance of civil and global use on the open market.

AI's role in bridging global and local solutions

The homogenisation of these local, national and international data regimes will be most unlikely, as different geopolitical forces will compete for the dominance or protection of their data sets and models, which will be measured on their ability to power different AI systems. Private (whether military or not) and public AIs will operate very differently. Despite the competition, however, a shared model should emerge to allow some level of global interoperability and exchange, and most importantly to guarantee the global safety of these emerging AI systems. One important area of contention will be the ability of developing data economies to train these AI systems, and specifically to train them with a focus on diversity so as to support locally designed solutions and avoid data exploitation, concentration and gatekeeping, which would further increase an unprecedented socioeconomic gap that will most certainly extend to data sets. If a model of "pay for use" emerges globally, as is most likely, then developing economies that are unable to afford the same access to data will be once again set at a disadvantage.

Towards equitable and sustainable AI development

A globally coordinated ecosystem for data and AI that guarantees equitable access to AI systems' training and data sets would be a precondition for guaranteeing shared human rights frameworks and shared possibilities and benefits, since it would enable the use of local data sets to train AIs in order to solve local problems and offer locally tailored solutions. Data diversity, access to AI training, and the availability and use of AI output will be an incredibly contentious area of global governance in the future. Establishing the digital realm as a global commons would help a great deal in achieving the systemic transformation needed for sustainability and equal opportunities. But it will take time, and it is not easy to predict how likely it will be in the next 20 years.

*

To address the pervasive societal transformation envisioned by the SDGs, the UN should engage in a range of transformational activities and initiatives for moving towards the equitable development of AI systems globally, and this should start with data regimes and the regulation of how AIs and digital platforms use data. Existing digital platforms and emerging AI applications could prove to be crucial and effective means of supporting the implementation of the SDGs, as could scalable dual strategies that bridge the gap between cutting-edge high-tech solutions and low-tech alternatives for different socioeconomic conditions. AI systems have the capability, if developed in the right global legal framework, to function as mediators between these micro–macro dynamics, combining the high-level perspectives and domains of global scientific data sets and other forms of global knowledge with the specific cultures, knowledge and conditions represented by the local and personal data of an existing community. AI trained with global scientific data can be fine-tuned through training with local data. The adoption of FAIR data principles and globally standardised FAIR data policies could broaden and empower these diverse data regimes while providing micro–macro scalability opportunities with the potential to reshape the global data economy over time. This decentralised and diversified approach would enable governments to negotiate global data-sharing collaborations that can support important global challenges, such as the training of AIs for multiple shared crisis domains, including weather-disaster planning and crisis response, or responses to health crises, for which AI could help by combining global strategies and data with locally collected data and adapted solutions. Or AI systems could be used for neighbourhoods – both local and extended – for which it could combine general scientific data with local data to solve local problems, showcasing the potential of this model.

However, before the full potential of this model can be opened up, there is a need to agree on shared standards and operational guidelines for data-sharing approaches that can be applied to diverse domains. This will soon require an open international negotiation process for the clear regulation of open data exchanges and the use of their data for AI training. Diplomacy to find these shared solutions should be a key investment for both governments and the UN, as we need to collaborate to shape a shared vision and an equitable model for a sustainable AI-driven future.

In conclusion, this chapter advocates for the UN to lead and coordinate a long-term, multistakeholder initiative to create a global data and AI governance framework, or Digital Compact, in collaboration with other key global institutions such as the WTO, the World Economic Forum, the International Telecommunication Union and UNESCO, as well as with national governments and various civil society organisations. Alongside international standard-setting bodies such as the International Organization for Standardization and the IEEE, this initiative would aim to develop open technical standards and protocols. To ensure a fair and sustainable AI future, the UN needs to champion a coordinated strategy that emphasises ethical and human-centric AI and data practices, fosters and supports digital advancement in developing countries, and motivates private sector involvement, aiming for digital inclusion and global equity with targets that go beyond the 2030 SDGs. This initiative demands long-term, ongoing collaboration and adaptability to evolving scenarios for effective and inclusive AI and data governance. Therefore, a dedicated, permanent UN body should be established to oversee and coordinate these efforts, navigating the forthcoming tumultuous global policy landscape towards a common vision for the function of technology, data and the digital and AI realms for the future of humanity.

Gerhard Stahl

6 | Development of supply chains in a multipolar world

Well-functioning global supply chains are the backbone of the international economy. They are shaped by the political and economic decisions of governments as well as by the investment decisions of companies. Which rules and strategies are needed to ensure that global supply chains will contribute to, rather than hinder, achievement of the Sustainable Development Goals (SDGs) in developing and developed economies?

The high point of globalisation is over. During the period from 1980 to 2007, the integration of the international economy made great progress. Dominant economic thinking favoured the reduction of customs duties, free capital movements and a liberal market economy. The cross-border flows of goods, services and finance as a percentage of global GDP rose from 26% in 1980 to 53% in 2007.[1] International supply chains developed that benefitted from the opening up of China, making this country the factory of the world.

The international financial crisis in 2007–8 was the first serious setback for this globalised economy. Concerns about international financial stability and the social and environmental costs of the globalised economy became more prominent. The "America first" policy under US President Donald Trump led to a fundamental change in American trade policy. Instead of the promotion of open international markets, the protection of key industrial sectors of American industry became a political priority. Protectionist measures were introduced, and bilateral trade agreements were favoured over international agreements. Furthermore, geopolitical conflicts (such as those linked to Iran, Venezuela, China and Russia) motivated the United States and its allies to implement economic sanctions against companies, countries and

---

1   McKinsey & Company (2016) "Digital globalization: a new era of global flows". April, p. 1.

even individuals. Over the years the US–China rivalry has increased, and exchanges of high-tech products and services have, in particular, become more and more restricted.

The temporary breakdown of supply chains during the Covid pandemic showed the risks of a highly integrated international economy. Governments and companies discovered the importance of resilient supply chains. Furthermore, there are the negative social and environmental consequences of free trade that needs to be addressed.

Currently, the international economy is at a crossroads. Proponents of the benefits of free trade are finding themselves on the defensive. Some governmental reports and studies come to the conclusion that differences in political and economic systems undermine fair economic competition. Decoupling, derisking and friendshoring are keywords for the new economic policy orientations. The fact that numerous key technologies can be used for civilian as well as military purposes is increasingly becoming a barrier to the free flow of goods and services and increasingly curtailing technological and research cooperation. The Stockholm International Peace Research Institute estimated that the global trade in dual-use goods and technologies was worth approximately $1 trillion in 2017. This figure includes a wide range of goods and technologies, such as electronics, chemicals and machinery that can be used for both civilian and military purposes.[2] Countries such as the United States, China, India, Russia, Japan, South Korea and some European states have developed export control measures that have a significant impact on global trade. The use of financial sanctions against companies and individuals as a way to react to security threats and military actions is also undermining further global exchanges.

New supply chain laws in Western countries require companies to monitor environmental and human rights issues in their supply chains. Companies have started to reshape and relocate supply chains in order to take into account new legislation and geopolitical risks. These reactions have already changed trade and investment flows. A reallocation of supply chains is taking place, integrating new countries and reducing supply from traditional economic partners. This can be seen in the US–China economic relationship. Despite the growth in absolute levels, US imports from China witnessed a significant reduction in market share of around 5 percentage points from 2017 to 2022, whereas imports from Vietnam

---

2   Stockholm International Peace Research Institute Yearbook (2017) "Dual-use and arms trade controls", Chapter 15 of *SIPRI Yearbook 2017*, p. 471.

and Mexico in particular gained in market share.[3] The United States has implemented a comprehensive set of policies aimed at restricting Chinese firms' access to critical technologies, most prominently semiconductors. These developments have led to a situation in which the world is confronted with the development of two technological ecosystems, one centred on the United States and the other on China. Both powers are attempting to build the largest possible cohesive bloc, a process that may lead to increased technological bifurcation.

*

Concluding, we have to admit that the new trade barriers and conflicts indicate that the international consensus around the old rules-based trading system is broken. The Global South complains that existing rules benefit the United States, especially by favouring the US dollar as the international reserve currency and by giving American and European governments a dominant role in the Bretton Woods financial institutions. China and developing countries argue that the current global order is unjust and inequitable. They call for a new or at least reformed global order that is based on the principles of multilateralism, equality and mutual respect.[4] A multilateral system that is fit for the 21st century.[5]

The US government and developed economies complain that some developing countries and especially China distort fair competition via subsidies, barriers to market entry and state interventions. China is criticised for forced technology transfers, insufficient intellectual property protection and preferential treatment of state-owned enterprises, providing unfair advantages over foreign companies.[6]

Despite the different positions, the Global South and Western developed economies have a common interest in keeping an open rules-based international trading system. This interest is stronger in small countries than in the big economies that could better succeed in big-power

---

3   Alfaro, L., and D. Chor (2023) "Global supply chains: the looming 'Great Reallocation'". Paper prepared for the Jackson Hole Symposium, 24–6 August, organised by the Federal Reserve Bank of Kansas City, p. 16.

4   See the statements of China (https://gadebate.un.org/en/77/china) and India (https://gadebate.un.org/en/77/india) at the 77th session of the UN General Assembly, in 2022.

5   See South Africa's statement: https://gadebate.un.org/en/77/south-africa.

6   US Trade Representative (2022) "2022 national trade estimate report on foreign trade barriers"; European Commission (2022) "Trade barriers report 2022".

competition. Therefore, international organisations such as the United Nations, the WTO and the OECD must support negotiations to achieve a common understanding of the new rules needed for a sustainable international economic system. A renewed future trading system could be based on the following widely shared principles:

- the need for a rules-based international trading system;
- the importance of trade and investment for economic growth and development;
- the need to support developing countries;
- the obligation to develop a sustainable international trading system taking into account social and environmental concerns.[7]

There are already some positive developments around a more sustainable business model for companies, as a result of new legislation that obliges companies to consider the social and environmental impact of their supply chains. The OECD, the International Labour Organization and the UN support some of these initiatives promoting responsible business behaviour in supply chains.[8] The UN is actively involved in discussions around building more sustainable international supply chains – with the UN Global Compact, for example, having a number of working groups on sustainable supply chain issues.[9] The UN Human Rights Council adopted a resolution that called for the development of a new international instrument on business and human rights, which would include provisions on due diligence and sustainable supply chains.[10]

There is an international consensus that climate change is an existential threat for mankind demanding common actions on the part of

---

7   United Nations Conference on Trade and Development (2022) "Trade and development report 2022: bridging the trade gap".

8   International Labour Organization (2021) "Improving the sustainability of global supply chains: a framework for action"; Organisation for Economic Co-operation and Development (2022) "Due diligence for responsible business conduct: a guide for multinational enterprises".

9   The UN Global Compact is a voluntary initiative for businesses that are committed to aligning their operations and strategies with 10 universally accepted principles in the areas of human rights, labour, the environment and anticorruption. It is the world's largest corporate sustainability initiative, with more than 15,000 companies and organisations participating from more than 160 countries and territories.

10   See UN Human Rights Council Resolution 47/10 on business and human rights, 47th session, 24 March 2021, paragraph 12.

developed and developing economies. To achieve progress, the financing of climate policy and the social consequences of climate policy measures must be addressed simultaneously. This demands not only national policy measures but also international cooperation and international financial assistance. Free flows of technologies facilitating green transitions are, in this context, important for an efficient and affordable climate policy. In contrast, the financing of the transition is threatened by increased military expenditures as a result of geopolitical conflicts.

All these elements have to be taken into account for the establishment of sustainable supply chain policy.

Supply chains and SDGs

The global economic integration that has taken place over the past three decades has helped millions of people become wealthier, healthier and more productive. The globalisation process established sophisticated international supply chains that are helping countries to implement the SDGs. But there have also been setbacks, as can be seen by looking at three SDGs in particular.

SDG 1: end poverty in all its forms everywhere. The globalisation process lifted millions of people out of poverty, but since 2015 global poverty reduction has been slowing down.

SDG 2: end hunger, achieve food security and improved nutrition and promote sustainable agriculture. Progress achieved over the years has been reversed. Disruptions of supply chains because of the pandemic and especially because of the war in Ukraine have increased hunger and undermined food security. The number of people facing hunger and food insecurity has been on the rise since 2015.

SDG 8: promote sustained, inclusive and sustainable economic growth, full and productive employment and decent work for all. The progress achieved during the last four decades is being undermined by war, trade conflicts and technological rivalry.

The IMF has calculated that the number of new trade barriers introduced annually has nearly tripled since 2019 to almost 3,000 in 2022. Protectionism and the costs of technological decoupling could reduce the GDP of some countries by up to 12% over the long term.[11] Fragmentation can also lead to severe disruption in commodity markets and create food and energy insecurity, notably in low-income countries. Finally, the fragmentation of capital flows, which would see investors and countries diverting investments and financial transactions to like-minded countries, would constitute another blow to global growth. The destruction of efficient supply chains due to fragmentation is hard to quantify, but it is obvious that it will lead to lower economic growth, reduced living standards, increased poverty and less investment in health and education. These economic consequences will undermine progress towards achieving the SDGs.

Proposed measures

Sustainable supply chains are essential for achieving the Sustainable Development Goals. The UN, in cooperation with other international organisation such as the WTO, the OECD and the European Union, should develop common guidelines for governments and companies for sustainable supply chain management. These guidelines could be based on the work of the WTO and the UN Global Compact.[12] The following issues should be addressed.

Transparency and traceability. This is the basis for addressing sustainability risks.

Labour. This includes ensuring that workers in supply chains have safe and healthy working conditions, are paid a fair wage and are free from forced and child labour.

Environment. This includes reducing the environmental impact of supply chains, e.g. by reducing greenhouse gas emissions, water pollution and waste generation.

---

11   Kristalina Georgieva (2022) "Speech by Managing Director Kristalina Georgieva at the Brookings Institution", IMF website; Aiyar, S., J. Chen, C. Ebeke et al. (2022) "The global economic outlook: geopolitical fragmentation and the future of multilateralism", IMF Staff Dicussion Note 2023/001.

12   World Trade Organization (2022) "The role of trade in promoting sustainable supply chains".

Human rights. This includes ensuring that human rights are respected throughout supply chains, e.g. by preventing discrimination and violence against workers.

Anticorruption. This includes preventing corruption in supply chains, e.g. by promoting transparency and accountability.

Procurement. This would involve governments and businesses giving preference to suppliers that are committed to sustainability. This could be done through public procurement policies and private sector initiatives such as supplier codes of conduct.

Export control instruments. Common rules for these instruments should be developed, taking into account the discussion in WTO and OECD committees and working groups.

To achieve sustainable supply chains, multilevel governance and close cooperation is needed. All levels of government, businesses and other stakeholders must work together. This includes sharing best practices, developing standards and providing financial and technical assistance. The UN Global Compact can play an important role in promoting sustainable supply chains. It can do this by providing a platform for collaboration, developing resources and tools and advocating for policies that support sustainable supply chain management.

The UN should invite member states, in cooperation with other international organisations, to develop scenarios for geopolitical risks. Based on a common understanding of these scenarios, guidelines for appropriate policy measures to minimise risks should be developed. These efforts could contribute to increased trust in the stability of supply chains by making geopolitical interferences more predictable.

Economic sanctions pose enormous problems for the organisation of supply chains. The extraterritorial consequences of some sanctions decided by national governments force even companies working in third countries to reshape supply. The UN should promote an agreement that UN member states will apply economic sanctions to countries only on the basis of a UN mandate.

Lastly, international trade and investment that translate into reliable supply chains need not only common rules but also trust that countries are committed to solving conflicts peacefully. The International Criminal Court (ICC) plays an important role in the global rule of law. The court has jurisdiction over genocide, war crimes, crimes against humanity and crimes of aggression. The best way to show the commitment to a multilateral order is to accept international jurisdiction. The UN should undertake renewed initiatives to convince all UN member countries to become party to the ICC.[13] The EU should support this initiative with all available means. The acceptance of the rulings of the ICC by powerful countries such as the United States and China would increase trust in international relations and reduce geopolitical tensions.[14]

---

13   At its 52nd session the UN General Assembly decided to convene a diplomatic conference on the establishment of an International Criminal Court. This conference was held in Rome, and in July 1998 it decided the statute of the ICC. The ICC was established in 2002 in The Hague. Currently more than 120 countries are party to the court.

14   The United States, China, India, Russia and Israel, in contrast to EU member states, are not party to the court.

Robert Sweeney

7 | Industrial policy and sustainable development

The state of play for industrial policy

The Sustainable Development Goals (SDGs) cover a wide range of different social, economic and environmental targets. From no poverty to zero hunger, from quality education to clean water and sanitation, many of them address symptoms of a common, underlying cause. Implicit in the "D" in SDG, the problem is one of underdevelopment. For an individual country, a key component of addressing underdevelopment is economic growth. For the world at large, the goal is for countries to grow in an environmentally and ecologically sustainable manner.

The precise conditions that gave rise to industrialisation among the rich countries of today continue to be the subject of debate. It is clear, however, that industrial policies have been key. This has included infant industry promotion using tariff protection, export subsidies, quotas, industrial espionage, restrictions on foreign ownership and foreign direct investment (FDI), local content requirements, preferential credit for key industries, capital controls, state-owned enterprises and more.[1]

To take some examples, during the early stages of industrialisation the highest tariff rates on manufacturing goods were implemented by the United Kingdom (45–55%) and the United States (35–45%). These rates surpassed the highest levels used by Japan (30%), Germany (26%) and other high-income countries at any stage during their development processes. Germany, aside from having tariff protection somewhat lower than UK and US rates, copied British-made goods by circumventing the comparatively weak intellectual property (IP) rules of the day. Japan, unlike Western countries, did not have particularly high tariffs during its

---

1 Chang, H. J. (2008) *Bad Samaritans: The Guilty Secrets of Rich Nations and the Threat to Global Prosperity* (New York: Random House).

rapid growth period post-World War II. It did, however, use export subsidies, exercise control over foreign exchange, restrict or ban foreign ownership in key industries and use local content requirements.[2]

While the heyday of industrial policy for today's developing countries – the middle part of the 20th century – produced rates of economic growth higher than those of the subsequent period of trade liberalisation,[3] the strategy of industrialisation through import substitution faced limits. This included overly ambitious catch-up plans, financial constraints, domestic market limitations and political-economy factors. A more outward orientation proved successful in some countries, such as India, where infant industry promotion prior to its liberalisation in the 1990s produced some results, though these were comparatively disappointing. It was unable to strike the correct balance between state involvement and markets, with excessive amounts of regulation and inappropriate use of state-owned enterprises. Similarly, Ireland's attempt at infant industry promotion in the 1930s must ultimately be deemed a failure. A poor innovation system led to inappropriate sectoral policies given its market size. Still, it is almost a law of economic history that economic development requires promotion of indigenous industry and extensive industrial policies.

Contemporary industrial policy in developed countries takes a different form. It is less coordinated and less concerned with "picking winners", instead focusing on funding and derisking research, which then spills over into private sector entrepreneurship. Many of the major technological breakthroughs of the modern era, such as computers and the internet, were first incubated under military procurement programmes in the United States. The United States also funds research through universities and the National Institutes of Health.[4] Similarly, Japanese industrial policy shifted from industry promotion to technology promotion. In Germany, publicly funded research institutes and training are oriented towards the needs of its strategically important small and medium-sized enterprises, which are mainly financed by municipal and cooperative banks.

An exception to the trend away from sector-specific policies is agriculture. The United States, the European Union and other entities provide

---

2   Ibid.

3   Weisbrot, M., and R. Ray (2011) "The scorecard on development, 1960–2010: closing the gap?" DESA Working Paper 106, June, United Nations (www.un.org/esa/desa/papers/2011/wp106_2011.pdf).

4   Mazzucato, M. (2013) *The Entrepreneurial State: Debunking Public vs Private Sector Myths* (London: Anthem Press).

extensive subsidies to their agricultural industries. The EU also subsidises and provides incentives to businesses under the banner of reducing regional inequalities.

For developing countries, industrial policy varies depending on the level of income. Their ability or willingness to use industrial policy has been constrained by international rules and domestic political developments. To give an easily quantifiable metric, the average tariff level on manufacturing goods in the BRIC countries is currently only 9.7%. This is considerably lower than one would expect given how far behind developed countries they are. The ratio of R&D expenditure to GDP is also significantly below that of high-income countries.[5]

There exists, however, considerable heterogeneity between countries. R&D expenditure as a share of GDP in China (2.4%) exceeds the EU's (2.3%) whereas in Latin America it is considerably lower (just 0.7%). Naturally, many other industrial policy tools are leveraged by middle-income countries, including ones already discussed. China, for instance, has been very successful in inducing multinational corporations to share technology as a precondition for accessing its market. China, India and Brazil have also used different forms of local content requirements to grow their renewable energy sectors, though a number of cases have been brought against them for violating WTO rules.[6]

The context in low-income countries is distinct from that in middle-income countries. Challenges include very high poverty, low literacy, political instability, civil wars, malnutrition and food insecurity, an excessive number of microenterprises, high dependence on agricultural and rural activities, weak manufacturing and premature tertiarisation. Accordingly, the developmental toolkit is likely to be different. An average tariff level of 12.1% among sub-Saharan African countries indicates at first blush a willingness to promote indigenous enterprises. But while this is higher than tariffs in BRIC and high-income countries, here too the global economic distance between the national haves and have-nots is much greater than in the past. R&D spending is very low in low-income countries, and many have little to no strategy for industrial upgrading.[7]

---

5 "Research and development expenditure (% of GDP)". World Bank website (https://data.worldbank.org/indicator/GB.XPD.RSDV.GD.ZS) (accessed 2023).

6 Mathews, J. A. (2017) *Global Green Shift: When Ceres Meets Gaia* (London: Anthem Press).

7 Chang, H. J., J. Hauge and M. Irfan (2016) "Transformative industrial policy for Africa". United Nations Economic Commission for Africa.

Modern developments and implications for sustainable growth

The rise of services and the digital economy

As is recognised by the SDGs, the major challenge for developed and developing countries alike is to pursue a socioeconomic model that is in balance with the constraints imposed by the environment. On a state level, the largest emitter of CO_2 is China, followed by the United States and the EU. On a per capita or cumulative level, it is the United States and the EU that bear most responsibility for climate breakdown.

The industrial policy tools described above are usually geared towards the developmental potential of a growing manufacturing sector. The manufacturing sector has historically demonstrated the greatest ability to generate sustained increases in productivity through automation and economies of scale. The difficulty is that it is also the most energy-intensive sector when compared with services and agriculture. In addition, the poorer a country is, the less likely it is to have access to clean technologies. Global climate change has therefore narrowed the ecological space available to developing countries to follow the industrialisation path originally pursued by today's rich countries.

It might be argued that the move towards a service-based economy mitigates the economic and environmental challenges of manufacturing-based development. Services are less energy intensive, whereas low fixed and marginal costs mean that barriers to entry are lower and scale can be more easily realised. It is true that the modern service sector can yield long-term productivity increases that are more economically sustainable than those of the service sectors of the past, and more environmentally sustainable than those of the manufacturing of the past.

A number of qualifications, however, need to be borne in mind. Some of the growth in services is statistical reclassification. For instance, firms whose main outputs are physical goods might not be classified as manufacturing depending on how many workers are directly employed in the underlying administrative and service component wings. Furthermore, much of today's service economy is dependent on the manufacturing sector. Manufacturing tends to generate more backward linkages to the economy than services do, so the overall contribution to the economy will be greater than the number of people directly employed.[8]

---

8 Hauge, J. (2023) *The Future of the Factory: How Megatrends Are Changing Industrialization* (Oxford: Oxford University Press).

The digital economy, being service-based, is less energy intensive than manufacturing, while also having lower fixed-capital investment costs. Some of the policy tools have been similar, though with regional variation. Both the United States and China, the two leading countries, have used publicly-funded programmes within universities and research institutes that have been spun off or used by private companies. Standard setting and public procurement can and have also been used. Both countries rely on IP protection, though enforcement of IP is weak in China, as is the commercialisation of patents. China's Great Firewall, which blocks its citizens from consuming a range of US and Western-originated tech services, functions as an extreme form of protection for Chinese tech companies. The United States, in turn, is embargoing a number of Chinese tech products and slowing China's technological development.[9] The EU has an underdeveloped digital industrial policy and relies largely on US – and to a lesser extent Chinese – technology.[10]

The two technologies now leading the way are artificial intelligence (AI) and cloud computing.[11] AI relies on extensive mining of data using machine-learning-based algorithms. The larger a company is, and the more data it gathers and processes, the better its AI technologies are. Moreover, tech giants benefit significantly from network effects, wherein the greater the number of users of a service, the more likely others are to use it (as with Meta/Facebook). Cloud computing requires considerable investment in infrastructure such as data centres. While countries such as India have been successful in inserting themselves into the IT supply chain, there are still significant advantages to company size, making it difficult for firms to break into the top tier.

Global value chains

The dependence of different sectors on each other touches on another important change in the global economy: the rise of global value chains. The fragmentation of production across countries and regions creates both opportunities and challenges for development, and it changes how industrial policy is pursued. It constitutes an opportunity because an individual country no longer needs to build a domestic supply chain

9   Rikap, C., and B. Å. Lundvall (2021) *The Digital Innovation Race: Conceptualizing the Emerging New World Order* (Cham: Springer International).

10   Timmers, P. (2022) "Digital industrial policy for Europe". Centre on Regulation in Europe, December.

11   Rikap, C., and B. Å. Lundvall (2021) *The Digital Innovation Race*.

from scratch in order to develop. Rather, countries can strategically insert themselves into segments of global value chains so as to build industrial capabilities without all upstream activities in place. They can therefore begin exporting sophisticated products more quickly.[12]

At the same time, the processes with the highest value added are still undertaken in the developed countries. This includes highly productive and profitable activities such as design, marketing and manufacturing but excludes assembling and transporting the end product. For instance, China has been the leading exporter of electronics since 2004 but its profit share of electronics exports is only 3%, compared with 25% in Taiwan and 33% in the United States.[13]

From an industrial policy perspective, the fragmentation of production means that countries need not promote or shield all inputs that comprise a finished product but can instead specialise in components. Keun Lee argues that the case for integration into global value chains is stronger for low-income countries than for middle-income countries.[14] Countries can learn and can improve productivity by manufacturing or assembling products according to the specifications and guidelines of the home country. This can help in achieving middle-income status. For middle-income countries, the arrival of FDI provides a boost to employment and income in the short term. That said, unless it is combined with policies to link foreign investment to the indigenous economy or otherwise upgrade local technology, rising wages subsequently render the host country uncompetitive in the low-value goods in which it specialises. Global value chains require the judicious use of industrial policies to promote strategic segments, though these have become more difficult to pursue in recent years.[15]

---

12   Hauge, J. (2023) *The Future of the Factory*.

13   Wade, R. H. (2019) "Catch-up and constraints in the twentieth and twenty-first centuries", in A. Oqubay and K. Ohno (eds), *How Nations Learn: Technological Learning, Industrial Policy, and Catch-Up* (Oxford: Oxford University Press).

14   Lee, K. (2019) *The Art of Economic Catch-Up: Barriers, Detours and Leapfrogging in Innovation Systems* (Cambridge: Cambridge University Press).

15   As a complement to industrial policy, middle-income countries can also capitalise on propitious international conditions to advance their technological capabilities. This includes making use of opportunities to enter new markets due to regulatory changes, focusing on sectors in which technological change is frequent and purchasing technologies at lower prices during downturns. See Lee, K. (2019) *The Art of Economic Catch-Up*.

The narrowing of policy space

The policy space within which developing countries can pursue industrial policy is much narrower today. WTO rules in conjunction with various regional and bilateral trade agreements have committed to lowering trade and other barriers to cross-border commerce. Other multilateral agencies such as the IMF and the World Bank may provide financial assistance only on the condition that countries remove FDI and trade barriers. Countries may also have decided to liberalise their domestic markets unilaterally. For reasons of space and scope, we will focus on multilateral trade and investment rules.

The WTO is committed to the reduction of trade barriers, and tariff levels have duly continued to fall over the last 30 years or so since the WTO came into existence. Members are required to "bind" or set maximum tariff levels so that members have discretion as to what tariff level is actually applied. A gradual reduction in the upper limits is planned for both developed and developing countries, though low-income countries can avail of exceptions. Quotas and export subsidies are eliminated under WTO rules, though again some exceptions are allowed. In the case of quotas, this includes agricultural standards and measures to safeguard countries' balance of payments. Low-income countries are permitted to use export subsidies and are generally allowed other subsidies too. This includes R&D subsidies and those aimed at reducing regional inequalities.

This raises an important point about the regulation of FDI. The agreement on Trade Related Investment Measures (TRIMS) prohibits the use of local content requirements. It does not prevent the use of other forms of FDI regulation, such as imposing conditions on joint ventures with local firms, technology transfer arrangements between foreign and local firms or limitations on foreign equity ownership. Temporary exceptions to the WTO TRIMS agreement are once again permitted for low-income countries and countries addressing balance-of-payments issues.[16] Bilateral and regional trade agreements have used local content rules, including EU antidumping measures.[17]

While trade barriers have fallen, international rules also provide protection in some areas. The agreement on Trade Related Intellectual Property Rights (TRIPS) strengthens protection of patents and other IP rights. Though patent protection is one way of financing innovation in areas

---

16   Chang, H. J., J. Hauge and M. Irfan (2016) "Transformative industrial policy for Africa".

17   Ibid.

---

where it would not otherwise be undertaken, the IP protection afforded to companies under TRIPS goes significantly beyond previous levels. In many industries, copying technology is not straightforward, so innovation naturally gives the inventor temporary monopoly profits. The TRIPS agreement, though, has expanded the items subject to protection, lengthened the protection period and narrowed the allowable exceptions. Coupled with bilateral trade agreements that have further strengthened IP protection, the international regime on IP rights is ill-suited to the needs of developing countries.[18]

It should be pointed out that there is more leeway to pursue environmentally sustainable industrial policies. As renewable energy technologies are still young, patents and IP rights do not constitute, as of yet, a major stumbling block to their diffusion. Rather, developing countries are not incentivised to adopt them given the absence of regulatory, fiscal and other measures that promote clean energy, as in developed countries.[19] Similarly, so-called feed-in tariffs are not precluded under WTO or other international rulesets. These are arrangements whereby the state requires energy providers to purchase a certain amount of energy from renewable energy generators. The cost is typically borne by the consumer. These have been used extensively by the EU and across the world to promote the renewable energy sector. While the name implies that they are a form of tariff, they could equally be termed a form of subsidy or, indeed, local content requirement. Under WTO rules, members have a right to implement policies to protect the environment or health. Other green policies that could be used, if there was the inclination and/or legal-institutional context to support them, include public investment, green bonds, public banking and environmental performance standards.

When it comes to the actual negotiating process, representatives of developing countries may be disadvantaged by being excluded from high-level meetings, assuming they have the appropriately qualified personnel to take part. In instances in which it is the developing country that may bring action for violation of rules, it might not have the resources to do so. While beneficial for firms and consumers in developed countries, the removal of trade and investment barriers is, in many cases, developmentally inappropriate for middle- and low-income countries.

---

18   Baker, D., A. Jayadev and J. Stiglitz (2017) "Innovation, intellectual property, and development". AccessIBSA.

19   United Nations Conference on Trade and Development (2021) "Trade and development report 2021".

Available policies and recommendations

Though the available policy space has narrowed, it has not closed. As discussed, developing countries have unused policy space at their disposal in the form of tariffs, special dispensations based on the level of development or on extenuating circumstances, and permitted tools such as the promotion of R&D and regional equality.[20]

Low-income countries ought to be more competitive than middle-income countries due to their lower cost base. Because of infrastructural deficiencies, they are not. Upgrading infrastructure can enable low-income countries to gain a foothold in global value chains. Combined with industrial policy tools, it can lead to technological upgrading. Middle-income countries also need infrastructural upgrading in line with their evolving economic structure. They likewise, if not to a greater extent, require industrial policy tools to graduate from middle-income to high-income status. A challenge for both sets of countries is fiscal capacity, which has come under pressure of late from rising indebtedness.[21]

The following recommendations, however, are based not on working within existing constraints but on expanding the policy space available to developing countries, particularly in relation to multilateral trade rules.

Exempt renewable industrial policies from multilateral rules

Countries should be allowed to use industrial policy to build their capacity for renewable energy generation. While derogations from international trading rules are available for environmental purposes, these are not strong enough. For large developing countries, local content requirements have been one of the most important types of internationally restricted industrial policy for promoting renewables. Exemptions could come in a number of different forms, such as a rule change on local content requirements specifically, reestablishment of previously permitted "green light" subsidies or a broader declaration of renewable energy as a global public good.

---

20   With R&D, an additional challenge for developing countries is aligning public spending with the needs of firms. See Lee, K. (2019) *The Art of Economic Catch-Up*.

21   Fischer, A. M., and S. T. H. Storm (2023) "The return of debt crisis in developing countries: shifting or maintaining dominant development paradigms?" *Development and Change*, 54(5): 954–993.

Commit a share of high- and middle-income GDP to international open-source research

Certain forms of research, such as basic research, are most suitably done through public funding or provision. Translating basic research into practical applications is the job of the private sector. International rules on patents and IP increasingly block the undertaking and diffusion of important research. A global fund to address technological bottlenecks by making findings available to all has the potential to address many of the important challenges society faces. This could be done under the aegis of organisations such as the International Energy Agency that contract private sector and other entities to undertake and publish research.

Encourage developing countries to use the industrial policy space available to them

Though the industrial policy space for developing countries has been considerably curtailed, it has not been eliminated. Many countries are not using the space available to them. This can be seen in the large difference that often exists between the binding or ceiling tariffs countries have agreed under WTO rules and the actual levels countries choose to implement.[22] This difference is a testament to the fact that a large part of the unused space is owed to pressures emanating from outside the WTO, including domestic-led liberalisation. Instead of promoting liberalisation as a precondition for assistance, international and supranational regional institutions should encourage the use of industrial policy tools for long-term sustainable development purposes.

Address anomalies in multilateral economic governance

In a sense, core aspects of multilateral governance are anomalous in that they prevent or restrict developing countries from leveraging the industrial policy tools that today's rich countries used in the past. While an overhaul of global economic governance is unlikely, a number of anomalies exist that could be addressed. For instance, R&D subsidies are allowed but export subsidies are not. This is despite the fact that the international markets in which developed-country multinational corporations operate can be considered oligopolistic. Allowing developing countries to use

---

22   Chang, H. J., J. Hauge and M. Irfan (2016) "Transformative industrial policy for Africa".

export subsidies would therefore level the playing field.[23] Similarly, developed and developing countries have considerable latitude to subsidise the agricultural sector, despite its role in global emissions. While policies to pursue a secure and stable food supply should be permitted, similar policies should be allowed to ensure a stable and secure environment. A review of anomalies is therefore warranted.

---

23   Lee, K. (2019) *The Art of Economic Catch-Up*.

Arancha González Laya

8 | Making trade work for prosperity, people and planet

Guiding questions

International trade has been fundamental to growth, innovation and jobs over the last few decades. Open markets coupled with strong domestic reforms have also allowed millions to exit poverty, particularly in Asia. But in certain countries open markets and the competitive pressure that they generate – coupled with technological progress – have also contributed to job losses and workers' displacement from sectors and even entire regions. In countries with weak social safety nets, trade has been the lightning rod for growing inequalities and worker disaffection. During the same period, climate change has arisen as our common existential threat, and questions have been asked about how the global economy and international trade should be repurposed to help fight against it, and against environmental degradation more broadly. The spread of unilateral approaches to trade and growing geopolitical rivalries have weakened the multilateral rules-based international trading system. Three essential questions face international trade today. First, how to restore confidence in the value of open trade. Second, how to ensure that trade works for prosperity, people and planet. Third, how to restore trust in the rules-based multilateral trading system.

How did we get here?

The fall of the Berlin Wall ushered in a new era with a clear hegemon: the United States. Trade openness and a rules-based multilateral trading system helped foster global economic welfare and development, with more than 1 billion people exiting extreme poverty over the last three decades. Since 1990, extreme poverty declined from around

40% of the global population to around 8% in 2019, and this is no small achievement.

The post-Cold War trade consensus was composed of four essential principles. First, "openness" was seen as the default option. Trade opening was accompanied by a set of rules to ensure stability, predictability, fairness in international exchanges and transparency. Governments could also adopt trade-restrictive measures to protect legitimate interests such as health, the environment, natural resources, public morals or national security. But those rules had conditions attached to them to prevent potential abuses by other members.

Second, there was a strong belief in the integration of all countries into a single system: the WTO. This was combined with deeper trade integration happening in parallel bilaterally or regionally, through which many countries opened their markets to each other beyond WTO terms. The opening of markets also took the form of unilateral measures adopted by many countries who sought to improve their competitiveness by making their imports cheaper. But the WTO remained central to the governance of international trade. As a result, the organisation grew gradually to its current size of 164 members. China, Chinese Taipei, Vietnam, Ukraine, Russia, Kazakhstan and many more members all seriously adjusted their trade and economic framework to accede to the WTO.

The third principle meant that markets had the upper hand over state intervention. This did not prevent WTO members from making public investments too. In many constituencies, such as the European Union or Canada, solid investments were made into social safety nets, particularly when compared with the United States. But there was a broad consensus on ensuring a certain hands-off approach on economic matters and trade.

Finally, economics were considered the dominant force. The period saw serious conflicts, with the Gulf Wars, the 9/11 terror attacks, the invasion of Iraq, turmoil in Afghanistan and much more, but economics trumped geopolitics. There is no doubt that, following the fall of the Berlin Wall, the economy became the major source of political attention, over security or defence.

The era of a relatively unchallenged openness doctrine suffered a severe blow with the 2008 financial crisis and the ensuing turbulence in the global economy. The opening of the financial sector had not been accompanied by commensurate efforts on the regulatory side – in particular in the United States. Overexposure to risky financial products triggered a crisis in the United States that quickly spread around the globe and morphed into an economic crisis. In the EU the lack of convergence on fiscal and financial management frameworks was also a source of instability, particularly among the eurozone countries. What could have been an even worse economic depression was averted partly because countries maintained open markets – particularly China – and did not engage in widespread protectionism. The WTO helped avert beggar-thy-neighbour policies by introducing a mechanism to monitor trade-restrictive measures and foster responsible behaviour among its members.

The 2008 crisis also left severe scars that pointed to the insufficient attention paid by national governments to the distributional impact of the crisis and of the recovery. The result was growing inequalities in many parts of the world. Just as we know that closing markets does not help solve inequalities, persistent inequalities undermine political support for open markets.

During the same period, we have seen growing concerns about the impact of open markets on the sustainability of the planet. After several unsuccessful attempts, the international community finally converged around the Paris Agreement on climate change. The goal of the Paris Agreement is to keep the rise in global temperatures to well below 2 °C above preindustrial levels, and preferably to limit the increase to 1.5 °C, recognising that this would substantially reduce the impact of climate change. This objective is to be achieved through nationally determined contributions, leaving each member free to decide on the pace and the means of achieving the mitigation. Measures taken by members to cut emissions have had spillover effects on other members, including negative effects in the form of unfair competition.

Since 2016 these forces have accelerated. The rise of China brought with it a raft of trade-distorting policies. The arrival of US President Donald Trump to the White House marked a turning point for trade: the hegemon of the system, the country that had inspired the rules-based trading order, abandoned its basic tenets and engaged in trade protectionism vis-à-vis its main trading partners. Tariffs were significantly increased on solar panels, washing machines, and steel and aluminium from many countries, as well on many a wide range from China. The argument of "national security" was extensively invoked to protect domestic sectors against competition rather than to address existential security threats.

The Covid pandemic exposed the risks around the security of essential supplies – from masks and medical equipment to medicines and essential ingredients – and it triggered moves to derisk value chains for essential products. Russia's invasion of Ukraine has led to the imposition of a raft of trade sanctions and reinforced the need to build resilience in value chains.

The growing rivalry between China and the United States is fuelling calls to decouple, friendshore and expand the remit of national security exceptions to rules-based trade, especially around technology.

As a result of these changes, global trade is shifting towards a different set of principles.

Closing is becoming the default option, in particular regarding technology. The United States and other countries have introduced measures to restrict China's access to advanced technologies (and China has followed suit) – such as semiconductors, artificial intelligence, quantum information technology and silicon-chip-making technology – by restricting exports of these products or investments in these sectors, with a focus on technology for military applications in order to safeguard national security. Consideration is also being given to introducing outbound investment restrictions. Given the porous borders between civil and military uses, it is unclear how large the scope of these measures will end up being.

We are also seeing the risk of fragmentation of the trade playing field, with the creation of trade alliances and regulatory systems outside the WTO or simply disregarding WTO principles or rules. The IMF and the WTO have both analysed the costs of trade fragmentation. According to the IMF, greater international trade restrictions could reduce global economic output by as much as 7% over the long term, or about $7.4 trillion. Significant additional costs could come from technological decoupling and disrupted capital flows. According to the WTO, if the world economy decouples into two self-contained trading blocs, it would lower the long-run global GDP by at least 5%, with some developing economies facing double-digit welfare losses.

Greater state intervention in the economy and in trade is becoming more prevalent. While it is understandable that the digital and ecological transitions require significant public investments, the manner in which these investments will be articulated will matter to the maintenance of fair trading conditions in areas such as green technologies.

Finally, geopolitics have taken the upper hand over economics, with a growing number of trade restrictions being introduced in the name of national security or protection of strategic interests.

At the same time, it is also important to note that in the last five years there has been a flurry of trade agreements in many parts of the world, showing a commitment to more open trade. In 2018, African countries concluded the African Continental Free Trade Agreement, seeking to boost intra-African trade through the gradual reductions of tariffs and nontariff barriers between them. This is a significant move, as many African countries had previously displayed a relatively defensive approach to international trade. Also in 2018, the original proponents of the Trans-Pacific Partnership, with the exception of the United States, concluded the Comprehensive and Progressive Agreement for Trans-Pacific Partnership. This highly ambitious trade agreement signalled the commitment by 11 nations across the Pacific to open trade even after US President Trump decided to exit the negotiations. In 2020, 15 nations across the Asia-Pacific region, including members of the Association of Southeast Asian Nations, Australia, New Zealand, Korea, Japan and China, signed the Regional Comprehensive Economic Partnership agreement. India, which was an original participant, ultimately declined to sign it. The EU has also signed important trade agreements with Japan (2018) and with Vietnam (2020).

The proposed way forward: making trade work for prosperity, people and planet

Trade has a clear record in raising living standards and increasing prosperity in advanced and developing economies alike. Trading partners throughout the world stand to benefit from each other's respective strengths in the production of certain goods and services, following the principles of comparative advantage, specialisation, economies of scale and economic efficiency. The utilisation of these principles, along with globalisation and technological advancements, has built a global trade and economic integration system that is becoming more interconnected and intricate by the day. This system, however, has also been subject to legitimate concerns that must be remedied. Trade-related environmental harm, distributional aspects relating to unemployment or income, a decreased quality of certain goods, potential increases in prices and lower resilience to shocks due to excessive dependence on trade partners are some of the main critiques that must be addressed.

Despite its outstanding significance, trade must not be viewed in isolation. The challenge for policymakers lies in approaching trade with a comprehensive perspective, connecting the dots to adjacent policy areas. For promoting a greener, more inclusive and prosperous economy in the coming decades, adopting a trade-only lens is inadequate. Any path forward must imply a holistic approach. Seizing economic opportunities must be done in concert with supporting development and addressing social and environmental pressures.

The way forward must combine the following four interlinked ingredients.

Make trade possible within a reformed multilateral trading system

Trade policies must focus on better leveraging global value chains, services and digitalisation. They should include technical measures to protect the health of citizens while refraining from disguised protectionism. They should also leverage policy tools and trade in green goods and services to make trade more sustainable and inclusive.

While it is understood that countries will continue to conclude bilateral and regional trade agreements, investments are needed in a new trade multilateralism. There is much value in protecting the existence of a single system, given the efficiency, inclusiveness and security it provides. Trade policy fragmentation will be costly, inflationary and exclusionary of smaller and weaker countries. But the existing WTO system is in need of reforms, in particular on four issues that are critical for guaranteeing equal conditions for all WTO members:

- the use of state subsidies,
- a binding dispute settlement mechanism,
- the definition of a new framework for national security,
- measures to support the inclusion of the smaller and weaker members.

In all four cases, we need to find a new balance that recognises the legitimate needs of members while ensuring there are controls against predatory unilateral behaviour.

The WTO needs to develop a framework to support the protection of global public goods – such as the mitigation of climate change and the protection of biodiversity – by limiting the spillover effects of national measures, as has been done with the recent agreement to curb subsidies that support overfishing. Absent a common framework, national measures may end up undermining the objectives of protecting global public goods through beggar-thy-neighbour policies. To generate much-needed progress on the regulatory side, members could make greater use of variable geometry in order to develop new rules under the WTO framework in areas such as e-commerce, investment facilitation or environmental sustainability.

Invest in making trade happen

It is not enough to make trade possible by concluding trade agreements. It is also important for countries to take national measures that ensure trade happens by helping with access to trade credit, trade intelligence and a conducive infrastructure environment.

Investments will be required in order to build a trade-facilitating and welfare-enhancing environment. Trade players need to harness available intelligence tools on trade and markets to help them make sound trade and market choices. Emphasis must be especially placed on how smaller businesses and developing countries can leverage these tools to increase their participation and tap into the benefits of global trade. Trade cannot happen without available resources to finance it. Inclusive access to trade finance is crucial, especially given the fact that up to 80% of trade is financed by credit or credit insurance, often of a short-term nature due to the inherent risks linked to international trade. Around the world, trade finance gaps remain for smaller businesses and women entrepreneurs, as well as for smaller and poorer countries. It is also more difficult for trade to happen if adequate infrastructure is not in place, and if that infrastructure does not leverage digital tools. Making trade happen also requires adequate policy-enforcement mechanisms. In addition, a protective environment must allow for the use of trade-defence instruments against unfair trade practices that hurt businesses. Protecting innovators and their innovations should remain a top priority, especially as intellectual property rights protect and enable micro, small and medium-sized enterprises to grow. Foreign direct investment is key for fostering innovation and competitiveness, but today it is also important to maintain a approach of "strategic conditional openness" to protect vital domestic security interests.

Invest in a new legitimacy framework for trade by focusing on making trade work for all

It is clear by now that the market will not take care of "lifting all boats". One should not forget about the "losers" of globalisation, technological innovation, trade and economic integration, notwithstanding the unique contribution of these processes to development and poverty reduction. The legitimacy of trade opening rests on making trade work for all. Concrete policies are needed to help manage various transition costs and to ensure that trade contributes to a wider agenda on social inclusion and the environment. A transition towards broad societal improvements is a multifaceted, multidomain, multiactor and multilevel process.

Fair domestic tax policies and enhanced fiscal and budgetary capacity contribute to reducing inequalities. Empirical evidence shows that inequality spikes have not been uniform across the globe, even among regions comparably exposed to the forces of globalisation and technology. Governments have leverage to correct the downsides of trade, including via active labour market policies. International cooperation on corporate income taxation will be essential to address the loss of government revenue associated with profit-shifting practices. In this respect, the Base Erosion and Profit Shifting (BEPS) initiative of the OECD and the G20 is a tangible example of international efforts towards better globalisation; its outcome must be fully implemented.

Ambitious and meaningful action on trade and the environment is required in order to limit global warming and adhere to the objectives and principles set out in multilateral environmental agreements. The importance of trade as a stepping stone for peace and as a driver for development and enhanced welfare the world over should be recalled. At the same time, adopting an environmental lens in trade and domestic policy is crucial to meet the environmental challenges of our time. International climate and trade diplomacy provides a vehicle to address issues of the global commons. But it will also be essential to ensure greater coherence with policies on agriculture, transportation, energy, value chain due diligence, circularity and competition, to name but a few.

Finally, for those who have found themselves on the wrong side of gaping economic inequality, skills and education policies must concentrate on leaving no one behind. There is a strong connection between trade, skills and employment.

In a nutshell, a progressive approach requires putting equal effort into making trade possible, making it happen and ensuring it works for the benefit of all.

Build a greater coherence agenda in and around international trade

Traditionally, the "coherence agenda" on trade focused on ensuring an effective articulation between the WTO, the World Bank and the IMF. This agenda is far too narrow. Trade cannot operate in isolation from other areas of international governance such as workers' rights, women's rights, the environment, health or taxation, to name a few. All these are

---

areas that need to be brought together under the WTO umbrella to ensure coherence. The same coherence should be displayed by countries at home.

*

Making trade possible within a reformed WTO, making trade happen by investing in broad infrastructure tools and policies, making trade work for all by strengthening social safety nets, and, finally, building a greater coherence agenda in and around trade both domestically and internationally are the ingredients needed to make trade work for prosperity, people and planet.

Paolo Guerrieri and Pier Carlo Padoan

9 | Global economic governance in a polycrisis scenario

Guiding questions for a New Global Deal

What does a global economic governance framework that strikes a fair balance between developed and developing countries look like? How to design a balanced macroeconomic regime and an appropriate exchange rate mechanism that is supported by sustainable and fair burden-sharing to distribute countries' current surpluses and deficits? How can the current global financial architecture be reformed to help implement the climate agenda and to achieve the Sustainable Development Goals (SDGs)? How can massive investments in global public goods – such as the environment, healthcare, education, infrastructure and digitalisation – be mobilised? How can the global tax system be reformed and strengthened to ensure that the global governance architecture is equitable and effective? How to ensure that developing countries are properly represented in the governance of international financial institutions (the IMF, the World Bank and other multilateral development banks)? How can those international institutions be reformed and strengthened to better address current and future challenges? How can the G20 be given a key role in the new global governance regime?

The state of play

How we got here

In the three decades after the end of World War II, multilateralism was the key feature of the liberal world order established in 1945. Global economic governance was embodied by a set of institutional norms and rules ("international regimes"), which countries committed to abide by in the implementation of their economic policy strategies, although they had a high degree of autonomy in their economic decision-making.[1] This type of international cooperation was crucial to maintaining growth and stability.

From the 1990s to the 2008 global financial crisis, during the so-called golden age of globalisation, the centre of gravity of the world economy shifted from the United States and Europe to the Asia-Pacific region. The configuration of the global economic system therefore moved from a bipolar to a tripolar model, China and East Asia being the additional third pole. The world economy and its power structure therefore evolved significantly over the past decade, but multilateral institutions such as the IMF and the World Bank have not changed their organisational and representational structures accordingly.[2]

Over the past decade, multilateralism entered a period of crisis in major high-income economies. The rules, norms and institutions that had governed the world economy for decades, well beyond the collapse of the Bretton Woods system, were no longer fit for purpose.[3] The economic confrontation between the United States and China is a symptom of this crisis; its roots, however, can be found in the decades-long failure of global governance to address global issues that globalisation and technological progress (i.e. automation) brought about, such as slow growth, rising inequality, social fragmentation and intensified migratory movements.[4]

The current state of the world economy

At the beginning of this decade, the global economy was hit by the Covid-19 shock; and the Russian war of aggression against Ukraine and, more recently, the Israel–Hamas war introduced security threats to the global system. Institutional responses to these shocks have been inadequate. The risk of an escalating geopolitical conflict is today greater than it has been since the end of the Cold War. If not reverted, these tensions

---

1   Kindleberger, C. P. (1986) "International public goods without international government". *American Economic Review*, 76 (1): 1–13.

2   Padoan, P. C. (2020) "International economic crisis and multilateral institutions", in M. Telò (ed.), *Reforming Multilateralism in Post-Covid Times* (Brussels: FEPS).

3   El-Erian, M. A. (2016) *The Only Game in Town: Central Banks, Instability and Avoiding the Next Collapse* (New York: Random House).

4   Stiglitz, J. (2010) *Freefall: Free Markets and the Sinking of the Global Economy* (London: Penguin).

may generate additional sources of instability and crisis, such as a return to nationalism in both developed and developing countries.

As a result, the world economy today is characterised by two main features: the presence of several, heterogeneous and interlocking crises, a so-called polycrisis (including Covid-19, the invasion of Ukraine, energy supply shocks, stagflation and food insecurity); and the tendency towards fragmentation across practically all domains – geopolitical, economic and social – with each reinforcing the other.

The most likely scenario for the world economy is a prolonged transitional phase, characterised by a multipolar system without any effective leadership and a growing global governance vacuum. The spectre of powerful centrifugal forces could lead to global fragmentation into rival economic blocs, the economic costs of which are project to be significant.[5] According to the IMF, trade fragmentation could reduce global output by between 0.2% and 7%. If technological fragmentation is added, some countries could see losses of up to 12% of GDP.[6]

Instead of catching up with high-income countries, low- and middle-income countries in this scenario are bound to stagnate or recede in their economic development path, which would translate into deeper levels of global inequality.[7] The Covid-19 pandemic and the Russian war of aggression against Ukraine have hit countries differently. Higher prices for energy and food staples have affected the lowest-income countries the most. While high-income countries have been able to borrow and spend trillions to support their economies, lower-income ones had little fiscal capacity to offset these shocks, which in some cases hit them on top of increasingly frequent and deadly climate disasters. Consequently, about 15% of low-income countries are already in debt distress, and an additional 45% are at considerable risk of debt distress, based on IMF data. These fiscal situations put pressure on low-income countries' governments, which are often called on to compromise social spending on education and healthcare in order to repay sovereign debt. As a result, there is now a real prospect of losing the economic and social benefits that many low-income countries have achieved over the past decades.

---

5   Guerrieri, P. (2020) "A new multilateral agenda after Covid 19: the role of the EU", in *Reforming Multilateralism in Post-Covid Times*.

6   Georgieva, K., G. Gopinath and C. Pazarbasioglu (2022) "Why we must resist geo-economic fragmentation and how". *IMF Blog*, 22 May (www.imf.org/en/Blogs/Articles/2022/05/22/blog-why-we-must-resist-geoeconomic-fragmentation).

7   Aiyar, S., J. Chen, C. Ebeke et al. (2022) "The global economic outlook: geopolitical fragmentation and the future of multilateralism". IMF Staff Dicussion Note 2023/001.

Global governance today

As previously mentioned, a tectonic shift is occurring in the international order, which is moving from an international economic system based on multilateral rules and institutions to a (dis)order based on the balance of power between countries, dominated by the conflict between the two largest economies: the United States and China. This shift also makes it difficult for countries to convene and adopt a multilateral approach to manage common risks. The current configuration of global economic governance is fragmented, loosely defined and lacks an effective regulatory framework. It is thus poorly equipped to respond to the interlocking crises that have characterised the early 2020s.[8]

Such a deficient form of global governance and international cooperation could also weaken the ability of the international system to supply the public goods that are needed to address the most pressing global challenges, such as equal access to healthcare, water scarcity, digital wars, financial stability, cybersecurity and, the most urgent of them all, climate change.[9]

These vital global issues can be tackled only through multilateral agreements and a global deal between governments and other stakeholders, at both a global and a local level. It is true that international cooperation is declining just when it is needed most. Nevertheless, reverting to an old-fashioned multilateral system like the one that was created at Bretton Woods after World War II is neither possible nor desirable, since the powers that shaped it (the United States and Europe) are no longer the unchallenged hegemons of the world economy.[10]

Effective global governance activates collective action – that is, it allows nation states to interact and reach shared outcomes.[11] For collective action to be activated, a set of rules, norms and institutions (also termed international regimes) need to be established. This would allow the fragmentation that derives from the absence of a global government

8   International Monetary Fund (2022) "Geo-economic puzzle: policy making in a more fragmented world". *Finance and Development* 59(2).

9   Buchholz, W., and T. Sandler (2021) "Global public goods: a survey". *Journal of Economic Literature*, 59(2): 488–545.

10   Guerrieri, P. (2020) "A new multilateral agenda after Covid 19".

11   Olson, M. (1965) *The Logic of Collective Action* (Cambridge, MA: Harvard University Press). Sandler, T. (2004) *Global Collective Action* (Cambridge: Cambridge University Press).

to be overcome. For these regimes to work, however, institutions that provide resources and define and enforce rules are needed.[12]

Three specific conditions can be identified as necessary for international regime building. First, nation states must be willing to cooperate and capable of doing so. This in turn depends on the distribution of power among countries.[13] Second, the issues that a regime will address – such as finance and monetary policy, trade, security, technology and health – must be clearly defined. The multiplicity of issues makes regime building more complicated, but it also allows for cross-sector cooperation. Issue linkages may thus play a positive role in providing stronger incentives for cooperation (e.g. around economy and security). Third, a regime should be resilient to crises so as to foster domestic political support. Regime resilience requires two additional conditions: an adjustment mechanism to redress the build-up of imbalances, as is the case for the existing exchange rate regime; and a financing safety net mechanism (based on the public sector and/or the market) to allow for temporary deviations from equilibriums, such as the current mechanism for balance-of-payments financing.[14]

New measures to be proposed for a New Global Deal

To satisfy the principles and requirements of collective action and international regimes, a global governance approach for today should be effective and pragmatic. In other words, global governance must strike the right balance between existing multilateral agreements that address global collective action problems and the many regional and plurilateral agreements that offer more flexible solutions when global deals cannot or need not be achieved. This means both retaining valuable features of the past multilateral order and creating new arrangements that are fairer and more aligned to the reality of the early 2020s. It also means focusing on areas where cooperation is essential by finding new ways to achieve common goals.

One of the issues that must be addressed in establishing a reformed global economic governance structure is the relationship between the

---

12   Keohane, N. O. (1984) *After Hegemony: Cooperation and Discord in the World Political Economy* (Princeton, NJ: Princeton University Press).

13   Gilpin, R. (2001) *Global Political Economy: Understanding the International Economic Order* (Princeton, NJ: Princeton University Press).

14   Kindleberger, C. P. (1986) "International public goods without international government".

---

economy and security, which are increasingly interrelated. Currently, there is a risk that strategic military confrontation, with its zero-sum logic, will dominate the entire spectrum of international economic relations, leading to confrontation in the economic field too.[15] Economic relations would end up being fragmented and reconfigured within groups of military alliances, which would significantly undermine the possibility of collectively managing the supply of global public goods, such as the environment, which necessarily requires multilateral cooperation agreements.

Instead, military-strategic issues in which zero-sum games prevail should be addressed through deterrence and diplomacy, keeping them separate from economic and social issues. Economic cooperation and competition should be fostered, and collaboration should be sought on global issues such as climate change and financial stability. The following subsections outline the areas that a reformed global economic governance framework should address.

Macroeconomic policies and international monetary relations

A key condition for a sustainable growth environment is a strong and credible framework for macroeconomic and monetary (exchange rate) policies. Historically, when such a framework was absent, the interaction of national macroeconomic policies produced, in turn, deflation, monetary and exchange rate instability, and high inflation.[16] This scenario has been perpetuated by the "mercantilist" approach followed by a number of countries, which have held back internal demand to support their export-led growth model. In such a scenario, the costs of adjustment fall squarely on the weakest economies, which are often running persistent current account deficits.[17]

A desirable scenario requires a balanced macroeconomic adjustment mechanism, with sustainable burden-sharing that allows surpluses and deficits to be better distributed and avoids excessive debt accumulation. A sustainable adjustment mechanism is especially needed in a scenario

---

15   Bergsten, C. F. (2022) *The United States vs China: the Quest for Global Economic Leadership* (New York: Polity Books).

16   Eichengreen, B. (2011) "Exorbitant privilege: the rise and fall of the dollar and the future of the international monetary system" (Oxford: Oxford University Press).

17   Guerrieri, P., and P. C. Padoan, (1986) "Neomercantilism and international economic stability". *International Organization*, 40(1): 29–42.

that involves several key currencies and could lead to high instability and volatility.

The role of the IMF should change. The IMF was created to assist countries in need of domestic policy adjustments to overcome balance-of-payments difficulties. However, as the crisis has shown, liquidity provision was inadequate to the needs of lower-income countries. The IMF must be given the mandate to manage a stronger and more effective global financial safety net. It should behave like a lender of last resort when needed, the way a central bank supports its local banks in a crisis. To this end, it should activate a specific facility to provide adequate liquidity during crises. In addition, new emergency financial instruments, including debt instruments, should be introduced (see the next subsection).

The deterioration of the geopolitical environment may lead to fragmentation in financial and trade relations. From this perspective, a global system that includes different currency areas may be effective, provided it does not lead to aggressive regional protectionism.[18] Making progress in this respect requires a strong collective action approach.

The post-Bretton Woods experience has shown that – in a environment of free capital movement – fixed exchange rates and independent monetary policies are unsustainable.[19] The alternatives are fully flexible rates or a full monetary union. The latter case implies a process of deep integration. Free floaters can instead manage their monetary policies themselves, but they may be exposed to high and volatile inflation and financial fragility, for which capital controls can provide only temporary relief. An alternative route has been dollarisation, which in many cases, however, generated strong deflationary pressures.

The choice of exchange rate regime implies a choice with respect to trade policies. Historically, a fixed exchange rate regime, and ultimately a monetary union, often lead to a protectionist policy and full exchange rate flexibility vis-à-vis nonmembers. A liberal trade policy, instead, implies flexible exchange rates between domestic currencies. This then implies that rebuilding global governance requires a joint approach to trade and monetary regimes.

---

18 Arslanalp, S., B. Eichengreen and C. Simpson-Bell (2022) "The stealth erosion of dollar dominance: active diversifiers and the rise of nontraditional reserve currencies". IMF Working Paper WP/22/58.

19 Padoa-Schioppa, T. (2004) *The Euro and Its Central Bank: Getting United after the Union* (Cambridge, MA: MIT Press).

The global financial architecture and debt financing

The current global financial architecture is undersized with respect to its goals. Radical changes are needed to boost long-term financing so as to meet the SDGs and climate goals, relieve lower-income countries' debt burden and improve access to funding.[20] The scale of the reforms should be in line with the scale of the crises that many lower-income countries are already experiencing. Lower- and higher-income countries share an interest in implementing such radical reforms if major instability is to be avoided. In this regard, a new financial contract between the Global North and Global South is needed that covers the following three interrelated areas.

First is finance for development. In the fight against climate change alone, developing countries' needs are estimated to amount to a minimum of $2.4 trillion per year, while the SDG financing gap has increased from $2.5 trillion annually before the Covid-19 pandemic to $4.5 trillion today. The same is true if extreme poverty is to be eliminated. An estimated 120 million people have been pushed into extreme poverty in the last three years. And the two priorities – the fights against climate change and against poverty – are complementary rather than mutually exclusive.

Financing these goals will require new sources of revenue, and we need to mobilise all sources of finance, including official development assistance, domestic resources and private investment.[21] Part of the needed investment will not yield financial returns; hence, it must be financed through official development assistance. In this regard, there should be broader support for the United Nations secretary-general's proposal for an SDG stimulus plan to scale up long-term financing for all countries in need, by at least $500 billion a year.[22] Another important and complementary proposal to be considered is Kenyan President William Ruto's recent call to establish a new "Global Green Bank" that would assist developing

20   World Bank (2022) "Concept note: maximizing finance for development for the water sector and climate impacts".

21   OECD (2022) *Multilateral Development Finance 2022* (Paris: OECD Publishing). DOI: 10.1787/9fea4cf2-en

22   United Nations (2023) "Secretary-general's SDG Stimulus to deliver Agenda 2030" (www.un.org/sustainabledevelopment/wp-content/uploads/2023/02/SDG-Stimulus-to-Deliver-Agenda-2030.pdf).

countries in financing their climate change measures and policies.[23] The funding of this new institution could be based on aviation and shipping emission taxes (see below in this chapter).

The largest part of the needed investment, however, takes the form of potentially profitable projects that could be privately financed.[24] The private sector currently funds around 80% of green investment in high-income countries, but only 15% in developing countries. Higher financing and interest costs for private lending to emerging and developing countries hinder private investment. Private sector financing should be more significantly leveraged, and the operations of the multilateral development banks (MDBs) should be radically transformed to address these new financial challenges (see below in this chapter).

The second area is debt distress and the increasing debt burden for countries in the Global South.[25] Debt vulnerabilities must be addressed through a combination of debt management and growth restoration measures. Debt resolution in lower-income countries, however, has often been prolonged and disorderly, partly due to changes in the creditor landscape, with resulting economic costs. The entire international debt architecture should therefore be urgently reformed along the following lines.

- Debtors and creditors should continue to strengthen those contractual provisions that help minimise economic disruptions when debtors encounter difficulties.
- The suspension of debt service obligations for countries facing catastrophic climate events should be made permanent and be extended, similarly to what was agreed at the height of the Covid-19 pandemic.
- Private creditors should be encouraged to participate alongside official creditors in debt restructuring processes through adequate mechanisms.
- Official bilateral creditors should agree on a common approach to restructuring official bilateral debts that is accepted by both Paris Club members and nonmembers (e.g. China).

23   Bryan, K., and A. Mooney (2023) "Kenya's William Ruto: 'We are not running away from our debt'". *Financial Times*, 10 August.

24   Government of Barbados (2022) "The 2022 Bridgetown agenda for the reform of the global financial architecture" (www.foreign.gov.bb/the-2022-barbados-agenda/).

25   "Debt sustainability analysis low-income countries". International Monetary Fund website (www.imf.org/en/Publications/DSA) (accessed 2022).

- An ambitious debt relief initiative should be launched to allow countries in distress to exchange short-term debt for longer-term instruments at lower interest rates.
- Debt transparency should be increased, ensuring more reliable and comparable information and data.

Third, contingency financing is not working well for many lower-income countries. It must be significantly expanded to allow lower-income countries to deal with unforeseen and unexpected expenses. In this regard, the rules and governance system for special drawing rights (SDRs) based on current IMF quotas should be radically reformed.[26] SDRs should be issued more promptly and automatically, and they should be channelled to the countries that need them most, to provide a countercyclical liquidity boost that contributes to a global safety net. In fact, the recent issuance of SDRs has opened up significant resources to help vulnerable countries, but of the $650 billion issued, higher-income countries received 25 times more than lowest-income countries. In addition, of the $100 billion that G20 countries pledged to redistribute in 2021, only 80% could be reallocated through the IMF. To close the 20% gap, the option of rechannelling SDRs through MDBs, as proposed by the African Development Bank, should be seriously considered, since it would also help expand the constrained available capital of MDBs' through a leverage factor of three to four (see below in this chapter).

Investment and global public goods

Exiting or at least addressing the polycrisis requires massive investment in a wide range of critical areas – environment, healthcare, education, infrastructure and digitalisation. This requires the collaboration of public bodies, institutions and the private sector as part of an innovative approach to public–private partnerships (PPPs). After years of underinvestment, public finance must be significantly redirected towards the provision of global public goods.[27]

Nevertheless, public finance alone will not be adequate to the scale of the financial needs – private investment must be mobilised too. The impetus provided by green finance and the ESG (environmental, social and governance) paradigm can bring about important outcomes, but they

---

26   "Special drawing rights". International Monetary Fund website (www.imf.org/en/Topics/special-drawing-right).

27   World Bank (2022) "Concept note".

can also concurrently generate new challenges in terms of social sustainability and climate transitions. However, protecting global commons has massive potential social returns, which will be much higher than private returns. This fully justifies public sector intervention.[28]

While the case for public–private investment in global commons is clear, there are several challenges facing its implementation. The provision of public goods requires a very long-term commitment, but private sector incentives for investment may fall short of that horizon. However, incentives for private investment can be made stronger by policy measures such as fiscal incentives, better and simplified regulation, and structural reforms that, in combination, can increase investment and employment opportunities. In addition, while there are positive cases of increased private investment in public goods, as exemplified by the development of green finance over the past few years, it is important that greenwashing practices and incentive distortion are monitored closely.

A public good that is regularly underfunded and discussed in multilateral forums, in particular at the G20 level, is financing for infrastructure development, especially in lower-income countries.[29] It was first included in the 2010 Seoul Multi-Year Action Plan on Development, which called on MDBs to work on procurement rules, data provision for investors, assistance for PPPs, project preparation and facilities to attract private investment. Long-term investment financing was later added to the equation, with the development in 2013 of the High-Level Principles of Long-Term Investment Financing by Institutional Investors. The Global Infrastructure Initiative was then launched in 2014 to support quality infrastructure investment, followed by the creation of the Global Infrastructure Hub, and complemented by the World Bank's Global Infrastructure Facility. A Global Infrastructure Connectivity Alliance came next, and the Principles for Quality Infrastructure Investment were released in 2019. Together with the Roadmap to Infrastructure as an Asset Class and the G20 Principles for the Infrastructure Project Preparation Phase, these initiatives all aim to foster private sector investment in infrastructure, catalysed by public/ MDB resources. Nevertheless, the global infrastructure gap continues to stand in the range of trillions of US dollars.

A more recent strand of action within the G20's work on public goods is global health. The Covid-19 pandemic exposed the insufficient levels of preparedness and response capacity among health systems worldwide.

---

28   Buchholz, W., and T. Sandler. (2021) "Global public goods".

29   Bertoldi, M., H. Scherrer and G. Stanoeva (2023) "The G20@15: can it still deliver?" Economic Brief 76, November, European Commission.

G20 leaders first introduced the concept of large-scale immunisation against Covid-19 as a global public good in 2020 and urged MDBs to support the global vaccination agenda. In 2021 a Joint Health and Finance Task Force was created to further highlight the importance of proper financing for global health systems, looking at pandemic preparedness and response too. Private sector sources of finance have been included among the tools to achieve these goals, but instruments to leverage them have not yet been identified.[30]

Finally, the introduction of new technologies such as artificial intelligence and blockchain may require public action through appropriate instruments that can direct investment to cover expensive fixed costs. This may lead to the emergence of nationalistic policy strategies and instruments (such as the US Inflation Reduction Act), which may prompt the proliferation of conflicting scenarios that compress rather than support overall investment. International collaboration and effective collective action are therefore needed. This raises the question of the interaction between global institutions and governments. In some issue areas, such as excludable public goods, it might be appropriate to establish club-type agreements, allowing groups of countries to share collective action when broad or full participation is impossible.

Global tax system

The global tax system is flawed, lower-income countries being the most negatively affected by it. Tax policy, however, is the area in which international cooperation has advanced the most, especially considering the absence of major international agreements and institutions addressing taxation. The G20 was an instrumental forum for achieving global coordination. The initial step was the acceleration in information exchange and the elimination of bank secrecy. Information exchange is a key prerequisite for the fight against tax evasion, which is necessary to finance development and global public goods. Bank secrecy provides a shelter to money laundering and terrorism financing and represents a threat to healthy global governance.

The 9/11 terrorist attacks marked a significant shift in information exchange, with the number of bilateral information exchange agreements rising from a few dozen to several hundred. This eventually evolved into a multilateral structure, which further increased the effectiveness of

---

30   Organisation for Economic Cooperation and Development (2022) *Multilateral Development Finance*.

screening measures. The Global Forum on Transparency and Exchange of Information for Tax Purposes was expanded to include lower-income countries, and it later developed an information exchange mechanism. A framework for cooperation was also established through the Multilateral Convention on Mutual Administrative Assistance in Tax Matters, although several jurisdictions do not yet participate, thus lowering its potential.

Another major step was the launch of the Base Erosion and Profit Shifting (BEPS) Project by the G20 with the support of the OECD.[31] The aim of the project is to provide a platform for the monitoring of profit flows and transfers by multinational corporations. This project has found more difficulty in building consensus, but it still remains a highly ambitious and potentially effective project.

As of June 2023, 137 countries representing 95% of the world's GDP have agreed to rewrite the international taxation rules to impose a global minimum tax on large multinational enterprises and to partially reallocate taxation rights from countries where companies are headquartered to those where they sell goods and services. This tax deal is needed to reduce a race to the bottom in global tax competition and to reform profit-reallocation rules that no longer reflect current economic activity. Another policy advancement is the agreement on a new global minimum corporate tax, an essential instrument in the construction of a resource base to fund global public goods. While the European Union and other OECD members have started to implement the global minimum tax, the US Congress rejected the original agreement and opted for an alternative minimum tax that applies only to a smaller number of US multinationals.

In addition, middle- and low-income countries claim that the global tax deal does not represent a "fair solution" for reallocating taxing rights at the global level,[32] so much so that less than half of all African countries have decided to implement the agreement. African countries have also called for the UN, rather than the OECD, to take the initiative in negotiations to reform the international tax system. Indeed, there is a compelling case for high- and low-income countries to agree on a new, more inclusive round of negotiations at the UN level to achieve more equitable and sustainable global tax reform. It is also important to mention that, while

---

31   Organisation for Economic Cooperation and Development and Group of 20 (2021) "Statement on a two-pillar solution to address the tax challenges arising from the digitalisation of the economy". OECD/G20 Base Erosion and Profit Shifting Project, 8 October.

32   McCarthy, J. (2022) "A bad deal for development assessing the impacts of the new inclusive framework tax deal on low- and middle-income countries". Brookings Global Working Paper 174, May.

significant improvements can still be made around tax cooperation, "tax clubs" may provide limited collective action benefits as long as agreement on global tax policies is lacking.

Besides issues of fairness, international taxes should be considered in order to raise funds to address global problems, such as those related to carbon emissions from the shipping industry, aviation or international financial transactions. Putting a price on carbon in shipping alone could raise $40 billion to $60 billion each year up to 2050. Beyond accelerating decarbonisation in the shipping industry, revenues from this tax could be used to facilitate climate change mitigation and adaptation, especially in the most vulnerable countries.

Entities in charge and the necessary global governance reforms

The reform of international organisations

The IMF and the World Bank (the Bretton Woods institutions) were established in 1944 to safeguard the stability of the international financial system and support postwar reconstruction. Nevertheless, as previously illustrated, their rules and norms are no longer fit for purpose and should be reformed. We do not need a new institutional architecture, but we do need to enable these institutions to address future challenges. Their missions must be updated for a context in which geopolitical factors will pose an increasing economic challenge to the global monetary and financial system.[33]

A fundamental move is the reform of the quota distribution formula and voting shares of these institutions, which currently disproportionately benefit higher-income countries, in particular those in Europe. Developing and emerging countries are playing an ever-more significant role in the world economy today and their representation in the governance of these international financial institutions should be strengthened. In the case of the IMF, following the completion of the Sixteenth General Review of Quotas on 15 December 2023, a new round of quota reviews should be initiated and concluded as soon as possible. As multiple stakeholders have suggested on several occasions, it is particularly urgent to create

---

33   Fettah, N. (2022) "The multilateral development bank for the future". CGD Notes, 30 November, Center for Global Development (www.cgdev.org/publication/multilateral-development-bank-future).

a new African chair on the IMF board, as well as an increase in quota distributions in favour of African countries.

Second, the IMF, the World Bank and the other MDBs must be better resourced and more empowered to make larger and more relevant interventions in this new global era. The MDBs continue to represent important financial hubs, and in addition to the current goals of boosting development and eliminating extreme poverty their spending must be directed at programmes that deliver global public goods, such as climate mitigation and adaptation, pandemic preparedness and water security.

MDBs, however, are currently facing severe constraints on their ability to perform this role. In 2021 they spent around $50 billion on climate finance, which is much less than they should and could spend. Their annual investments in climate action need to triple to $150 billion. This will require reforms of the goals, incentive structures, operating models and financial capacity of these institutional investors. They must also play a much stronger role in mobilising private capital and make greater use of risk guarantees and other credit-enhancement tools. The World Bank Group's Evolution Roadmap has indeed started a conversation on how to optimise existing resources through new instruments, such as hybrid capital and a portfolio guarantee mechanism, with the broader view of making the World Bank more responsive to the current polycrisis. The debate should extend to other MDBs.

Among major reforms, the capital of the World Bank and other (regional) MDBs should significantly increase, and especially the share of their deployable risk capital. They could then use their larger effective risk capital to promote conditions for private sector investment, while preserving their ratings and financial sustainability. In this regard, it is important to remember that macroeconomic risk makes climate projects mostly nonfinanceable in lower-income countries, and that financial markets very often exaggerate these risks. One proposal (Bridgetown 2.0) calls for a joint agency of MDBs, the World Bank and the IMF to offer foreign exchange guarantees and pool currency risks in order to reduce the cost of hedging for investors. Projects with the highest positive impact on climate change and SDG achievement could be then prioritised thanks to the guarantee agency of the MDBs. This proposal estimates that a facility with $100 billion to offer in such guarantees could unlock an additional $1.5 trillion in annual spending on clean energy in lower-income countries.

In addition, the World Bank the other MDBs should expand the use of so-called debt repayment "pause clauses", which offer debt service suspension following an extreme climate event so as to curb debt accumulation during a crisis. These clauses, which have been recently piloted in Jamaica and Peru, can make a dramatic difference for lower-income countries' public finances. The same positive influence can be exercised by expanding eligibility criteria for concessional financing to vulnerable middle-income countries and the least-developed economies.

Finally, GDP growth and macroeconomic stability are still the main metrics that international financial institutions use to measure progress. Alongside these, other indicators should be used when allocating aid, such as a multidimensional vulnerability index.

The key role of the G20 in the future global economic governance regime

From the perspective of rebuilding a global governance regime, a key role should be attributed to the G20 and its member countries, which represent more than 80% of world GDP. At the outbreak of the 2008 global financial crisis, the G20 brought together a limited (though variable) number of high- and middle-income countries, as well as major international organisations (the IMF, the World Bank, the WTO, the International Labour Organization, the OECD, the Financial Stability Board and regional development banks), to function as an informal secretariat. The goal was to provide global leadership in order to manage the impacts of the crisis.

The G20 did not achieve much in terms of deliverables. The most visible results are progress in financial regulation and the kick-off of measures related to international taxation. Other ambitious measures, such as those related to the establishment of a "strong sustainable and balanced growth" path, did not lead to significant policy changes.[34] The group has been showing increasing fatigue, and many doubts have emerged as to the G20's capacity to provide effective governance. It comes as no surprise that today the group is facing a fundamental crisis of legitimacy, as the Russian aggression of Ukraine generated a deep divide in the group that made it impossible to draft a meaningful 2022 communiqué. Nevertheless, the role of the G20 should be strengthened in the future since it is the prime forum for multilateral cooperation. G20 countries represent

---

34   International Monetary Fund and Organisation for Economic Cooperation and Development (2017) "Quantifying the implementation and impact of G-20 members' growth strategies" (www.oecd.org/g20/topics/framework-strong-sustainable-balanced-growth/ Quantifying-the-Implementation-of-Growth-Strategies-2017.pdf).

both industrialised and emerging economies, and they should continue to coordinate their policies while keeping multilateralism as their core principle guiding dialogue and actions.[35]

The G20's experience can provide useful lessons for its future direction. Agenda inflation should be avoided, and policy should focus on a limited number of issues on which there is the greatest chance of reaching an agreement. For example, as part of the global effort to find solutions to the debt crisis, the G20 made great progress with its Debt Service Suspension Initiative (DSSI), which has helped countries by suspending their debt repayments. The Common Framework for Debt Treatment beyond the DSSI also proved useful in some cases in supporting debt restructuring processes. Given the new wave of potential debt insolvency, the G20 should do more and actively engage in bilateral efforts and other multilateral initiatives to prevent severe debt crises.

In times of crisis, such as the current one, the G20 can play a key role as a promoter of multilateral solutions to crises, based on leaders' consensus. High expectations, however, should be avoided if political capital is not mobilised. The forum is not a substitute for high-level diplomacy and the creation of consensus. It provides a forum for the exchange of views and repeated interaction. It could facilitate the alignment of preferences and collective action, including through issue linkage.[36]

In terms of its organisation, there have been multiple calls for reforms of the Group, to increase its legitimacy and effectiveness. These calls have been put forward since the Group was revitalised in the immediate aftermath of the 2008 global financial crisis, and they have highlighted how G20 member countries do not accurately represent the diversity and actual distribution of global economic power in the 21st century. In addition, it is currently not clear what the G20 accession requirements are, or on what basis certain countries are invited to take part in the summits.

As a result, nonmember countries and stakeholders have called for an expansion of the Group, since the current membership overrepresents certain geographical regions, such as Europe, to the detriment of others, which are the object of deliberations but not necessarily the decision-makers. There are increasing calls for countries in the Global South to have a meaningful seat at the decision-making table. This is the case of the African continent, currently only represented by South

---

35   Bery, S., and S. Brekelmans (2020) "The revived centrality of the G20". *Bruegel Blog*, 28 April (www.bruegel.org/blog-post/revived-centrality-g20).

36   Kirton, J. (2023) "The G20's promising past, present and potential". G20 Research Group, 26 January, University of Toronto.

Africa. Establishing a permanent African Union seat at the G20, which many countries already support, would send an important signal about the Group's intention to reform and adapt to a different world.

With regard to its organisational structure, the absence of a formal G20 secretariat has been variously debated. The informal nature of the Group is recognised by some as essential for making meaningful progress on policy issues, since it allows dialogue to continue while also avoiding the legitimacy concerns associated with other, more formal and less representative institutions. Informality, however, also implies lower commitment levels. In this sense, the creation of a more stable secretariat could help address this drawback. One could advocate for a permanent body, as with other institutions. A more institutionalised G20, with a formal, permanent secretariat, could better fulfil the role of "network focal point" that it has acquired in recent years, consulting with other international institutions and "connecting the dots" so as to truly address global crises.

Together with a structural/organisational update, the G20 should seek greater coordination with the UN system, Bretton Woods institutions and other international bodies. Reforms could also include closer coordination of country policy reviews and adaptation plans between the OECD, the World Bank and the United Nations Framework Convention on Climate Change. Interaction with other informal groups such as the G7 or (what used to be) the BRICS may also facilitate collective action.

Regional agreements: the case of Europe

Regionalism could be a building block, not necessarily a stumbling block, on the way towards global and multilateral cooperation (a New Global Deal). Regional and interregional arrangements, rather than being part of the problem, could be part of the solution in paving the way to new forms of multilateral convergence. Regional efforts should therefore be promoted to tackle systemic risks across regions of the world, using regional safety nets to address the many exogenous shocks, and thereby complementing the global safety nets provided by multilateral institutions.[37]

In this context, the EU and European integration are an example of the type of cooperative regionalism that has positively contributed and could positively contribute to global governance by avoiding a drift towards conflicting regionalism. In the post-World War II economic system, the

---

37   Guerrieri, P. (2020) "A new multilateral agenda after Covid 19".

global governance regime and the European regional regime interacted. Europe was therefore active in two interconnected regimes, and European integration, on that basis, has facilitated (and been facilitated by) the evolution of the global regime.

In the case of trade policy, for example, the EU experience shows that the defence of a multilateral trading system does not in any way exclude – and could, on the contrary, be complementary to – more effective policies and strategies in bilateral and plurilateral negotiations. In this regard, the EU has maintained and should continue to maintain a special position, having put in place over the years a complex system of bilateral and regional trade agreements that has never conflicted with multilateral approaches. On the contrary, the interaction between the two has in most cases facilitated the liberalisation of the EU's overall trade relations. In this regard, the ongoing process of trade integration in the Asia-Pacific region, characterised by bilateral and regional agreements, makes Europe's experience even more strategically important.

One should add that in this age of multipolarity, rebuilding global economic governance is a key principle for the European agenda. As the largest and most open trade bloc in the world, the EU has a strategic interest in preserving the global rules-based order. Waiting to see the outcome of the current US–China confrontation risks decreasing Europe's global influence and threatening its commercial interests. Strengthening a new multilateral framework – one that can promote economic integration and cooperation between countries – is therefore vital to European interests.

Stefan Collignon

10 | The global governance of global public goods

If every country fulfilled its obligations under the Charter, the right to peace would be guaranteed. When countries break those pledges, they create a world of insecurity for everyone. So, it is time to transform our approach to peace by recommitting to the Charter – putting human rights and dignity first, with prevention at the heart.

António Guterres[1]

Preserving the survival of humanity is the greatest global public good. No one has expressed the need for improving the governance of global public goods more clearly than UN Secretary-General António Guterres when he warned that "humanity faces 'collective suicide' over climate crisis". In 2015 the United Nations adopted 17 Sustainable Development Goals (SDGs) as a universal call to action to end poverty, protect the planet and ensure that by 2030 all people enjoy peace and prosperity. It was a road map to more inclusive growth and development that respects the limits of nature. These SDGs are one of the most condensed descriptions of global public goods. They set an agenda for 2030 with 17 goals, 169 targets and 232 indicators to monitor progress in pursuit of this end. The 17 SDGs are integrated – they recognise that action in one area will affect outcomes in others. In other words, they generate externalities that define them as global public goods. While there was initially enthusiasm for the agenda, it has now stalled, and in some areas it has even

---

1   Guterres, A. (2023) "Secretary-general's briefing to the General Assembly on priorities for 2023". United Nations, 6 February (www.un.org/sg/en/content/sg/speeches/2023-02-06/secretary-generals-briefing-the-general-assembly-priorities-for-2023).

gone backwards.[2] The evidence is clear: we know what needs to be done, but the actions to reach sustainable development are insufficient. This requires new ideas for improving the governance of global public goods.

According to Inge Kaul, Isabelle Grunberg and Marc Stern, there are three key weaknesses in the current arrangement for providing global public goods:

- a jurisdictional gap is created by states emphasising national sovereignty;
- a participation gap prevents citizens and civil society institutions from monitoring the implementation of international agreements;
- an incentive gap is created by temptations to free ride on others.[3]

I will concentrate on the incentive gap. To understand the governance failure in relation to realising common global goals, we must clarify the nature of global public goods. The incentive gap is intrinsic to the collective action problems generated by public goods.[4] Because everyone can freely access the benefits of these goods, there is no mechanism to ensure that the resources for their creation are provided in sufficient quantity. On the basis of this clarification, we can then design strategies for better policy implementation with global effects.

The nature of global public goods

Global public goods encompass many aspects of ordinary life, from peace and security to natural environments, technological progress, human-made regulations (such as the metric system or international treatises) and even changes in history and cultures. They are all defined by their externalities. As the world becomes increasingly connected, what happens in one corner of the planet can have consequences in many other regions. These interconnections and the resulting spillover effects and

---

2   United Nations (2023) "Progress towards the Sustainable Development Goals: towards a rescue plan for people and planet; report of the secretary-general (special edition". Economic and Social Council, session of 25–6 July 2023 (https://hlpf.un.org/sites/default/files/2023-04/SDG%20Progress%20Report%20Special%20Edition.pdf).

3   Kaul, I., I. Grunberg and M. Stern (1999) *Global Public Goods: International Cooperation in the 21st Century* (Oxford: Oxford University Press).

4   Olson, M. (1971) *The Logic of Collective Action: Public Goods and the Theory of Groups* (Cambridge, MA: MIT Press).

externalities are particularly evident in crises, such as wars, pandemics, climate change, financial breakdowns, and refugee and migration crises; but they also play a positive role in economic development, technological advances, peacekeeping and international aid.

Economics textbooks typically speak of public goods in the context of nation states. Sometimes the analysis is extended to regional public goods, or narrowed to municipal public goods. However, as a result of globalisation a growing number of global public goods have emerged. These goods potentially affect all people living on the planet. The Covid-19 pandemic, refugee crises and climate change, to mention only the most urgent ones, are global problems that have made the existence of global public goods tangible. What is the nature of these public goods? How do they differ from local and national public goods? How can they be supplied globally and efficiently?

The answer lies in the concept of externalities. The difference between public and private benefits (or costs) is an externality that is caused by positive and negative spillover effects from specific actions by third parties. For public goods the externalities are usually large and the benefits diffuse. The mismatch between public benefits and private costs prevents the efficient allocation of resources that markets ensure for private goods.

This mismatch results from the specific characteristics of public goods: they are nonexcludable and nonrivalrous. "Nonexcludable" means that no one can be barred from consuming the good and accessing its benefits, or be immune to the negative consequences of such goods. A classic example is a lighthouse that signals the dangers of rocks to passing ships, or air pollution that affects everyone. "Nonrivalrous" means that the benefits or costs of such goods can be accessed repeatedly by anyone without diminishing the benefits and costs they deliver for others. A classic example is a concert where all people jointly enjoy the music, or the protection of citizens through national defence deterrence.

Public goods are distinct from private goods, because these are excludable and rivalrous. Private goods can be traded on markets, where the price mechanism excludes anyone not willing to pay the price and establishes rivalry between suppliers. Private goods are therefore efficiently allocated by markets because the only way to access privately offered commodities is by paying the price that covers its cost of production. But for public goods there are no markets (i.e. there is market failure). The costs for public goods must be covered by the collective. Local or national public goods are usually financed by taxes. International public goods require cooperation between states, and this cooperation can be strengthened by international organisations such as the UN and the IMF. Producing public goods therefore requires a joint (nonrivalrous) effort. This causes the risk of an undersupply of public goods when people are unwilling to pay for something that has small benefits for themselves but large effects in aggregate. This logic will generate incentives to refuse paying the contributions required and to free ride on others.

The literature distinguishes between pure public goods, which are both nonrivalrous and nonexcludable, and partial public goods, for which the conditions of nonrivalrousness and nonexcludability do not hold jointly. This is shown in Table 10.1.

Table 10.1. Public goods.

	Excludable	Nonexcludable
Rivalrous	Private goods	Common resource goods
Nonrivalrous	Club goods	Pure public goods

When goods are nonrivalrous but excludable (such as toll roads, theatres and the internet, or customs unions, monetary unions and similar institutions) they are called club goods. Club goods generate positive-sum gains. Often, such gains are generated by economies of scale. These joint gains create incentives to cooperate. Asymmetric information (not trusting that the others will do what they promised) can be an obstacle to cooperation, but it can be overcome by setting up independent organisations that ensure the flow of information to all group members. Noncooperative behaviour can also be avoided when potential losers from negative externalities are compensated out of the gains. By contrast, when goods are rivalrous but nonexcludable, they are called common resource goods (such as preserving natural resources, combating climate change and alleviating conditions that generate mass migration). Access to these goods is free and unrestricted, but the more people use them, the more the benefits for each user will diminish. The nonexcludability of common resource goods therefore generates zero-sum or even diminishing benefits, and this impedes cooperation and the efficient allocation of rivalrous benefits. When the benefits from a public good are small for a national government, or if they only occur in the distant future, short-sighted policymakers may seek to free ride on others.

The scope of public goods

Governance theories such as the subsidiarity principle often treat public goods as if they formed a hierarchy from the most specific to the most general, with local public goods at the bottom and national, regional or global public goods on a higher level. Local public goods are often dominated by material conditions, such as the construction of schools, hospitals, streets or power stations. National public goods are sometimes more value-driven and prone to governmental policies that affect all citizens. Regional public goods emerge with regional integration, as in the European Union. Global public goods generate spillover effects from national and regional public goods that potentially affect all humankind.

For the reasons discussed below, it is useful to give up this hierarchical view. A more appropriate approach focuses on the *scope* of public goods. The scope describes the size of the group of people affected by the externalities and by the intensity of their costs and benefits. For example, a hospital mainly affects local people, and so does a nuclear power station that provides electricity for a local community – but if there is an accident, the negative spillover of the nuclear disaster is large and global.

The literature on SDGs has shown that there are crosscutting issues and synergies between the different goals; for example, for SDG 13, on climate action, the Intergovernmental Panel on Climate Change sees positive externalities for SDGs 3 (health), 7 (clean energy), 11 (cities and communities), 12 (responsible consumption and production) and 14 (oceans).[5] Conversely, there also exist trade-offs between the goals, such as between ending hunger and promoting environmental sustainability.

Yet the larger the geographical scale of the potential externalities, the greater is the heterogeneity with respect to the willingness of contributing to the good's efficient provision. Traditionally, spillovers on a narrow geographical scale were managed by foreign policy, but with the expansion of the scope of public goods resulting from technological progress, demographic changes and economic globalisation, institutions of global reach have become a necessity.

---

5   Intergovernmental Panel on Climate Change (2018) "Global warming of 1.5 °C: an IPCC special report on the impacts of global warming of 1.5 °C above pre-industrial levels and related global greenhouse gas emission" (www.ipcc.ch/site/assets/uploads/sites/2/2019/06/SR15_Full_Report_High_Res.pdf).

The governance of global public goods requires cooperation between governments. However, the incentives for cooperation diverge with the increasing scope of public goods. Some of these divergences result from the inherent incentive structure of public goods, as discussed in the previous section. Others result from cultural diversities among countries, or from the narrow interests of dominant elites. This is a fundamental difference between global public goods and national (or European) public goods, for which collective preferences and cultural values are more homogeneous. A crucial but often neglected factor is economic and political regimes. In democratic societies, civil society organisations monitor, and citizens decide. Citizens are the owners of public goods; they are the sovereign who collectively appoints governments as its agents. In authoritarian and dictatorial regimes, elites hijack the institutions of the state to serve their narrow interests.[6] The ownership of public goods has been widely usurped by local elites who serve their partial interests. In many countries, access to government positions is the fast lane from poverty to personal wealth. This means that the decision to cooperate serves the interests of governing elites, which will not systematically coincide with the collective preferences of citizens. When partial interests oppose the public good, cooperation fails. The distinction between democratic, authoritarian and dictatorial regimes is therefore important for the effective governance of global public goods. The box below shows that the distribution of political regimes around the world is biased towards authoritarian and corrupt governments. Hence, the wider scope of global public goods has not resulted in humankind exerting direct control over their management. This is a major obstacle for the provision of global public goods.

The distribution of political regimes around the world
Political regimes around the world are skewed towards authoritarian and dictatorial regimes. Figure 10.1 shows the distribution of four well-known indicators for democracy, freedom, the rule of law and perceived corruption. In all cases, a high index value indicates high standards of democracy and low corruption. The histogram for each indicator shows that the kernel density is to the left of a normal distribution. This means that low values for democracy, freedom and the rule of law and high values for corruption are more frequent around the world.

---

6   Acemoglu, D., and J. Robinson (2012) *Why Nations Fail: Origins of Prosperity* (New York: Crown Business).

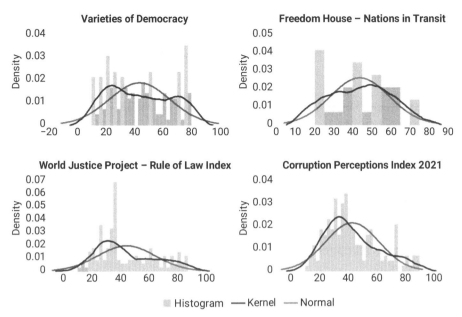

Figure 10.1. The distribution of political regimes.

Varieties of Democracy (V-Dem), the source of the first of these indicators, is a unique approach to conceptualising and measuring democracy. It provides a multidimensional and disaggregated data set that reflects the complexity of the concept of democracy as a system of rule that goes beyond the simple presence of elections. The V-Dem project distinguishes between five high-level principles of democracy – electoral, liberal, participatory, deliberative and egalitarian – and collects data to measure these principles (www.v-dem.net/about/v-dem-project).

Freedom House, the source of the second indicator, is founded on the conviction that freedom flourishes in democratic nations where governments are accountable to their people; the rule of law prevails; and freedoms of expression, association and belief, as well as respect for the rights of women, minority communities and historically marginalised groups, are guaranteed (https://freedomhouse.org/).

The World Justice Project's Rule of Law Index, the third indicator, is the world's leading source for the rule of law. It evaluates 140 countries and jurisdictions around the world. Measuring the rule of law since 2008, the index has been at the forefront of creating positive social change through information (https://worldjusticeproject.org/rule-of-law-index/).

Transparency International focuses on issues with the greatest impact on people's lives and holds the powerful to account for the common good. It publishes the Corruption Perceptions Index – the fourth indicator – and ranks 180 countries and territories around the world by their perceived levels of public sector corruption, scoring on a scale from 0 (highly corrupt) to 100 (very clean) (www.transparency.org/en/cpi/2022).

The difficult governance of public goods

The characteristics and scope of public goods determine the incentives to cooperate. The implications for the governance of global public goods are discussed below. We will look first at the nature of public goods and then at the implications for their scope. We distinguish three groups of public goods.

For the first group, global club goods, the incentives to cooperate are strong, because cooperation generates positive-sum gains out of which potential losers can be compensated. However, the performance and success of such cooperation requires transparency so that each member of the group can observe and rely on cooperation by the others. This trust can be supported by global multilateral institutions. Countries that benefit more than others must take a leadership role in providing compromise positions, and individual countries or coalitions of counties must not have a veto power that would allow them to blackmail others to get compensation.

For the second group, global common resource goods, cooperation is unlikely to emerge, since they generate zero-sum or diminishing gains. Hence, one party's gain is another party's loss. Distributional conflicts are harsh. The efficient management of such public goods requires a global authority that can set binding rules and enforce compliance with agreements on the generation and allocation of public goods.

Similarly, the third group, pure global public goods, also requires global institutions that can set rules and regulate the common interest of humankind. The legitimacy of such an authority must be established by a global compact on the governance of global public goods.

Thus, managing these last two groups of public goods would require a central authority that does not currently exist. Since the Peace of Westphalia in 1648, the world order has been based on the principle of national sovereignty and of not interfering in the affairs of other states. The EU is the most advanced experiment in overcoming this tradition by assuming joint responsibility for common public goods. But in a world overburdened with autocrats and dictators, this model for managing global public goods is unlikely.

Nevertheless, a reform of the governance of the UN could set up mechanisms for imposing solutions when cooperation between states fails. Under the present-day arrangements, the UN Security Council fosters negotiations, imposes sanctions and authorises the use of force, including the deployment of peacekeeping missions. Critics say the Security Council fails to represent many regions of the world and that the increasing frequency of the veto is inhibiting its functionality.[7] Since the Russian invasion of Ukraine, and with the rising systemic conflict between China and the United States, the Security Council has become dysfunctional. The way out of this impasse is to install legislative power in the UN General Assembly. With appropriate majority voting rules (which take into account the distribution of political regimes, discussed above), it would surely be possible to enact and enforce international legislation in the interest of humanity. This reform of the governance of global public goods would primarily apply to global common resource goods and pure public goods.

Aggregating club goods

For club goods, we can take a different approach. One possibility is aggregating groups of states with like-minded governments and then gradually extending the size of the groups and deepening the positive externalities they can generate. Below are seven conditions for aggregation, based on the work of Wolfgang Buchholz and Todd Sandler.[8]

Technologies for aggregating contributions for global public goods
The technology of aggregation determines how countries' contributions determine the global good's overall level for consumption or use. Several options are available.

- *Summation* means each contributor adds equally at the margin to the level of the public good. This encourages free riding and underprovision. Outcomes may be improved by grants and loans, and by multilateral institutions.

7   Ibrahim, S., N. Bussemaker and Z. Rosenthal (2023) "The UN Security Council". Council on Foreign Relations website (www.cfr.org/backgrounder/un-security-council).

8   Buchholz, W., and T. Sandler (2021) "Global public goods: a survey". *Journal of Economic Literature*, 59(2): 488–545.

- *Weighted sum* aggregation means each country's provision is given an empirical weight prior to the determination of the provision levels. These weights reflect objective conditions such as the size of GDP and special or locational factors (e.g. landlocked countries may not contribute to ocean protection to the same degree as coastal countries).

- For *weakest-link* global public goods, the smallest individual contribution fixes the aggregate level of the public good. For example, surveillance for financial crises or disease outbreaks is only as good as the smallest effort made to prevent a crisis. Here, capacity building is essential, and global institutions or dominant country partnerships can assist weakest-link countries.

- *Weaker-link* aggregation for providing public goods is a more moderate form, whereby the smallest contribution has the greatest influence on the global public good's aggregate level, followed by the second-smallest contribution, and so on. This does not prevent crises but can slow down or contain the spread of systemic crises. Insurance schemes can be tools for improving such goods.

- *Threshold* aggregation requires that the overall provision of a global public good meet or surpass some alert level before benefits are generated. Emergency crisis aid falls into this category. Multilateral institutions can induce countries to be threshold contributors and thereby increase individual contributors' willingness to pay.

- *Best shot* global public goods hinge solely on the largest contribution by a country that exerts global leadership and provides public goods as a service to all. Global income inequality promotes this provision by rich countries.

- *Better shot* public goods are a softer variant that allows coalitions of countries to ensure the provision of the public good. This approach for providing public goods is appropriate if no single country is willing to assume leadership. In the EU this function was frequently performed by French–German cooperation.

Effectively, the strategy of aggregation calls for the creation of clubs with different standards, and clubs of clubs that gradually improve the implementation of the SDGs. The important part of this approach is that clubs are exclusive, which means that they can establish conditionality based on fulfilling sustainability criteria. Members of a given club ensure the sustainability of the common goals by jointly providing resources for their achievement. They also impose barriers and sanctions for states that do not cooperate. This creates incentives to join a club that contributes to the efficient supply of global public goods and progress towards the SDGs.

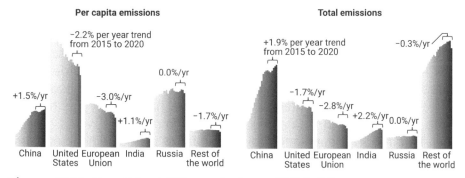

Figure 10.2. Fossil fuel CO_2 emissions, 2000–20.

Source: https://en.wikipedia.org/wiki/Paris_Agreement (accessed July 2023).

The Paris Climate Agreement serves as an example that can be extended to other SDGs. The agreement is a legally binding international treaty on climate change. Countries submit national climate action plans, which take the form of nationally determined contributions towards achieving the agreed goal of limiting global warming to 1.5 °C. Each country must determine, plan and regularly report on its contributions. Over time, goals must become more ambitious. Not all states make the same contribution, but more developed countries provide financial assistance to countries that are less endowed and more vulnerable, while also encouraging voluntary contributions by other parties. However, because countries determine themselves what contributions they should make to achieve the aims of the treaty, enforcement is hardly possible. Figure 10.2 shows that Western democracies have made significant efforts (even the United States, who exited the Paris Agreement under President Donald Trump but have returned under President Joe Biden), while large emerging countries such as China and India and those in the rest of the world have increased their CO_2 emissions. In its present form, the Paris Agreement is toothless: global CO_2 emissions from energy combustion and industrial processes grew by 0.9% in 2022 to an all-time high of 36.8 billion tonnes.[9]

How would the aggregation principle solve this problem? For argument's sake, let's speak of two clubs: emission reducers and emission raisers. The reducers form an SDG club that grants positive incentives to members who wish to reduce CO_2. For example, they provide financial support and subsidies for the costly investment in new technology. At the same time, they would make life more difficult for states who stay outside the club. For instance, they would exclude noncooperating, high-emission states from accessing their internal markets. This can be done efficiently because controlling access to their home markets is within their power. The conditions of financial support need to be carefully considered.

Sustainability clubs can overcome the criticism that has been directed at President Biden's Inflation Reduction Act. This law is the largest piece of federal legislation ever to address climate change in the United States. However, its unilateral protectionist provisions have deeply frustrated US trade partners. In a sustainability club, all club members would agree to keep their markets open and provide funds for the ecological transition, while differentiated regulations (see the technologies of aggregation discussed above) would still address each member state's specific conditions. Sustainability clubs are therefore an improved tool for multilateralism in global affairs. In today's context of renewed competition between liberal and authoritarian states, convincing countries to join a particular club that provides global public goods could reduce global tensions (in accordance with SDGs 16 and 17).

Reforming global economic governance

In his address to the UN General Assembly in 2023, António Guterres declared:

> Something is fundamentally wrong with our economic and financial system. The global financial architecture is at the heart of the problem. It should be the means through which globalization benefits all. Yet it is failing. The global financial architecture does not need a simple evolution; it needs a radical transformation. It is time for a new Bretton Woods moment.[10]

---

9 United Nations (2023) "Progress towards the Sustainable Development Goals".

10 Guterres, A. (2023) "Secretary-general's briefing".

No doubt, the global financial system is fragile and needs reform. However, there are fundamental differences between the present situation and Bretton Woods in 1944. To start with, in the 27 years between 1913 and 1950, the world economy grew by only 1.8% per year. In the 27 years since the wall came down in Berlin, the global economy grew by 3.3%, and between the creation of European monetary union in 1999 and 2015 the rate was 3.6%. At Bretton Woods, monetary instability was identified as the major economic cause for two world wars. The principal goal of the Bretton Woods agreement was to create an efficient foreign exchange system that would prevent competitive devaluations of currencies and promote international economic growth. Today, exchange rate stability between the major currencies is sustained, unemployment is low, and despite a significant inflation shock, financial markets strongly expect that inflation will return to 2%. Hence, today's problems do not arise from inflation, unemployment or a lack of growth. They emerge from the structural change in the world economy that over the last 30 years has generated growing inequalities within states and growing equality between states.

Growing inequalities within states undermine the fundamental consensus that no one will be left behind as the economy grows. If people cannot trust this age-old principle anymore, they will rebel and aggressively defend their partial interests. Solidarity with others, including with victims of disasters and persecution, will vanish.

Growing equality between states is the result of rapid growth in emerging economies, most prominently China. The equality is manifest in catch-up growth in GDP per capita, but it does not extend to social and political values. This economic development undermines the role of the United States as the hegemon providing the security anchor for the system. Instead, competing networks emerge. For example, the share of G7 countries in global GDP has fallen from 50% in the 1980s to 30% today, while the BRIC states have climbed to 31.5%. They now seek to replace the US dollar as the world's anchor currency (presumably with the renminbi), which will inevitably create greater uncertainty and exchange rate instability in the world.

Nevertheless, a decline in the dollar share of international reserves has taken place since the turn of the century.[11] This decline reflects active portfolio diversification by central bank reserve managers; it is not

---

11   Arslanalp, S., B. Eichengreen and C. Simpson-Bell (2022) "The stealth erosion of dollar dominance: active diversifiers and the rise of nontraditional reserve currencies". IMF Working Paper WP/22/58.

a byproduct of changes in exchange rates and interest rates, of reserve accumulation by a small handful of central banks with large and distinctive balance sheets, or of changes in the coverage of surveys of reserve composition. The decline in the dollar's share has not been accompanied by an increase in the shares of the pound, yen and euro – other long-standing reserve currencies and units of account that, along with the dollar, have historically comprised the IMF's special drawing rights. Rather, the shift away from dollars has been in two directions: a quarter going into the Chinese renminbi, and three quarters into the currencies of smaller countries that have played a more limited role as reserve currencies. The evolution of the international reserve system over the last 20 years can thus be characterised as a gradual movement away from the dollar, a recent if still modest rise in the role of the renminbi, and changes in market liquidity, relative returns and reserve management that have enhanced the attractions of nontraditional reserve currencies.

The reason why world trade and finance need a global anchor currency, and only one, lies in the greater exchange rate stability, which supports investment, and the lower transaction costs that come with large volumes of trade. Yet the political values of the countries that challenge the United States are very different, and this must be a cause for concern. The average indexes for anticorruption, rule of law and democracy among the BRICS are roughly half those of the G7 (see Table 10.2). These challengers are seeking to gain supporters. Attracted by the promise of access to new financial resources from a new regional development bank, Algeria, Egypt, Saudi Arabia, Iran, Indonesia, Thailand, Senegal, Argentina and Venezuela would like to join the BRICS. Their average indexes for anticorruption, rule of law and democracy are even worse than those of the BRICS.

Table 10.2. Average indexes.

	Anticorruption	Rule of law	Democracy
G7	71.3	74.0	73.4
BRICS	38.0	34.8	41.3
BRICS candidates	34.7	32.0	31.0

If you give a gun to a gangster, he will shoot you; if you rehabilitate him, you can live in peace. The Bretton Woods institutions – the IMF and the World Bank – provide loans and liquidity on a global scale, but these loans are subject to strict conditionality. This ensures the long-run stability of the global financial system. Of course, severe crises have happened (in Asia in 1998 and the United States in 2007), but in the long run the system has always returned to a steady-state equilibrium. The greatest danger in the global financial architecture is that the emerging challengers to the hegemon will set up institutions that do not impose the financial solidity required for the proper functioning of financial markets. Increased debt may lead to a short-run boom that benefits the elites, but not necessarily the sustained provision of global public goods. It will be followed by financial crises of unknown violence. For this reason, it is important that the reform of the global financial architecture combines the need for investment with the perspective of financial stability, strict conditionality and the need to support the provision of global public goods.

Financing SDGs and global public goods

The need for financing the investment required to achieve all SDGs is massive. An IMF Staff Discussion Note from 2019 found that delivering on the SDG agenda will require additional spending in 2030 of $2.6 trillion (2.7% of world GDP): $0.5 trillion for low-income developing countries and $2.1 trillion for emerging-market economies.[12] However, high-income countries also need to make costly shifts in their economic structures – especially with respect to climate change, energy and food security.

How can these enormous amounts of investment be financed? The easy answer is "more debt". A UN document placed it clearly in context:

> Sovereign borrowing allows countries to invest in the future. Productive investments, including in resilient infrastructure, can improve debt sustainability in the long run: a growing economy helps to raise domestic tax revenue and the capacity to service debt over time. Debt financing is also critical to the financing of crisis responses. Such positive outcomes are, however, only achievable if borrowing and lending decisions are made responsibly, resources are used effectively, risks are well managed, and lending is affordable.[13]

---

12   Gaspar, V., D. Amaglobeli, M. Garcia-Escribano et al. (2019) "Fiscal policy and development: human, social, and physical investment for the SDGs". IMF Staff Discussion Note 2019/003.

13   United Nations (2023) "Reforms to the international financial architecture". Our Common Agenda Policy Brief 6, May (www.un.org/sites/un2.un.org/files/our-common-agenda-policy-brief-international-finance-architecture-en.pdf).

In other words, these new investments stand in the context of SDG 17. This goal calls for a global partnership for sustainable development and highlights the importance of macroeconomic stability and of mobilising financial resources for developing countries. All reform proposals must heed this condition. SDG 17 also stresses the importance of trade and equitable rules for governing it. This sets the difficult path between the Scylla of unsustainable debt and the Charybdis of more rapid growth that destroys natural resources. Only debt that is coherent with these double requirements of sustainability can contribute to the attainment of SDGs. We must distinguish between debt for long-term development, liquidity provision for sound investment and short-term emergency funds.

Long-term development debt

Given the state of political regimes around the world, pumping money into states that are controlled by more or less corrupt elites is unlikely to achieve the SDGs. Simply leveraging public debt with private debt does not change this logic. An alternative could be the decentralisation of lending to target-specific SDG projects with greater technical surveillance.

We suggest setting up investment funds for target-specific SDG projects. For example, one fund would focus on investment for CO_2 reduction; another on energy transition to renewable resources; a third on cleaning up the global oceans, etc. These funds would be professionally managed with a technical focus on achieving sustainability goals. Being constituted with technical missions based on the SDGs, they are politically independent from government bodies – such as modern central banks. Investors in these funds would reflect a variety of stakeholders: international institutions such as the IMF, World Bank, EU and Association of Southeast Asian Nations; a club of willing states; and private investors who are involved in the management and realisation of the SDGs. The fund's management would be authorised to borrow in financial markets at commercial rates and under commercial conditions in addition to the share capital paid up by investors. This keeps up the pressure on improving efficiency. As these funds are target-specific, the fit between material output and finance input is tight – certainly tighter than if one were to transfer money to national governments that then decide what to do with this aid. This cuts short the social elevator of corruption.

The IMF can play an important role in setting up target-specific SDG project funds as a shareholder that invests special drawing rights (SDRs) into the funds' share capital. This requires declaring these new funds "prescribed holders of SDRs". At the moment only a very limited number of institutions outside the IMF can hold SDRs as assets.

Target-specific SDG project funds are a new form of decentralised multilateralism. Traditionally, multilateralism is a form of cooperation between at least three states. Target-specific SDG project funds allow cooperation with a focus on results – cooperation not only between states but between stakeholders who are directly affected by the externalities of global public goods. The funds would therefore change the traditional top-down governance hierarchy. They would work not only across nations but also across higher and lower governance levels, such as regional entities or local municipalities. They could also federate low-level administrations into groups for target-specific cooperation. For example, a coalition of several municipalities could set up a joint programme for waste processing that generates economies of scale, receiving finance directly for the target-specific project fund for waste management without being dependent on national governments.

Short-term liquidity provisions for long-term investment

Sovereign debt has been rising worldwide over the last decade, and in many countries it has once again reached critical levels. The nine least-developed countries and other low-income countries are currently in debt distress, and another 27 are at high risk.[14] Not surprisingly, yields for such debt are rising, which generates a vicious spiral. Yet simply granting debt relief is not desirable, as it would generate moral hazard. Some structural faults in a country's debt dynamic can be solved by debt resolution programmes that involve our suggested target-specific SDG project funds. The surveillance programmes of the IMF, the World Bank, the Bank for International Settlements and others – and, if needed, adjustment programmes – are also crucial for preventing misallocations of funds. However, debt restructuring may require additional short-run funding.

In the national context, liquidity is provided by central banks acting as lender of last resort. In the global context, international liquidity is created by SDRs, issued by the IMF. SDRs are reserve assets for central banks. They are not money. SDRs can be exchanged for currencies among the IMF member countries and therefore soften the hard budget

14   Ibid.

constraint on foreign exchange and increase the flexibility of national monetary policies. Their value is determined by a basket of the five most traded currencies. SDRs play a role if a country with high current account deficits is running out of foreign currency reserves. This is particularly useful when a country is hit by a sudden disaster (say an earthquake, or devastating storms or floods) and there is urgent need for importing resources.

However, if the current account deficit is structural and persistent, the central bank's foreign exchange reserves will be running out, and SDRs would not remedy this. The need for medium- to long-term finance then requires adjustment policies. However, with respect to SDGs, traditional adjustment policies linked to austerity are not enough. They must also consider the structures of foreign trade, and public goods must become a criterion for the sustainability of current accounts. For example, due to heavy government subsidies and large economies of scale, China today has an 80% monopoly in the global solar manufacturing industry. According to the International Energy Agency, this control has emerged as a threat to the huge consumption of solar photovoltaic systems needed to help achieve net-zero emissions across the planet. Countries wishing to switch to solar power must import panels from China, for which they need renminbi. For rich industrialised countries, this is probably affordable, but for less developed and emerging-market economies, such an energy transition requires foreign exchange that they do not have. A new allocation of SDRs by the IMF would not help, as deficit countries would have to switch their SDRs for renminbi (for which they also must pay interest) and China would accumulate the interest income. Diversification is one of the key strategies for reducing supply chain risks. A more balanced structure for solar panel production would enable countries to move to solar energy without balance-of-payments problems.

New SDRs are allocated in proportion to countries' quota shares. The last allocation took place in August 2021 in response to the Covid crisis and was the largest in history, at $650 billion (€550 billion, or 0.6% of world GDP). An initiative was also launched to rechannel SDRs to vulnerable low-income countries, and the IMF is setting up a Resilience and Sustainability Trust that IMF members may stock up with funds, using their SDR allocations on a voluntary basis. The IMF will monitor these funds and ensure that these SDRs are distributed to members on the condition that they implement the necessary economic policies. The EU supports the rechannelling process, in awareness of the looming risks for the stability of the international monetary system if highly indebted and less wealthy countries are not supported in fighting the pandemic and attaining economic recovery.[15] This logic must prevail for SDGs more generally.

Taxation

Fiscal policy has a crucial role for development. Specific SDGs were set in development areas for which public intervention is critical, including ending poverty and hunger (SDGs 1 and 2), improving health and education (SDGs 3 and 4), achieving gender equality (SDG 5), reducing inequality (SDG 10) and enhancing infrastructure (SDGs 6, 7, 9 and 11). This assigns a fiscal role for redistribution, through taxes and income-related transfers, and for equalising opportunity, through in-kind spending.[16]

Typically, tax-to-GDP ratios are less than half of those in advanced economies. This opens a space for raising taxes in less developed countries and emerging markets. Adopting a medium-term approach to raising revenue is critical to achieving and sustaining the much-needed increases in tax-to-GDP ratios. According to the IMF paper, increasing the tax-to-GDP ratio by 5 percentage points of GDP in the next decade is an ambitious but reasonable aspiration in many countries.[17] This would require building broad-based consensus for medium-term revenue goals to finance needed public expenditures; designing a comprehensive tax reform that covers policy, administration and the legal framework; committing to sustained political support over multiple years; and securing adequate resources to support coordinated implementation of the medium-term revenue strategy. Such public consensus is more likely in democratic societies, as authoritarian and dictatorial elites often use tax income for their own enrichment. This danger must be taken into consideration when richer countries commit to aid and transfers. Countries need to spend not only more, but better. Structural reforms at home are often a prerequisite for collecting higher revenues.

---

15 Hallak, I. (2022) "IMF special drawing rights allocations for global economic recovery". Briefing, June, European Parliamentary Research Service.

16 Gaspar, V., D. Amaglobeli, M. Garcia-Escribano et al. (2019) "Fiscal policy and development".

17 Ibid.

Conclusion

Our planet is suffering. Each year, Earth Overshoot Day marks the date when we have used all the biological resources that the earth can renew during the entire year. Figure 10.3 shows that we are running a permanent deficit in global renewable resources. As with a permanent current account deficit that one day turns into a sudden currency crisis, the likelihood of the sudden collapse of the global conditions of material reproduction is rising. It would be nice if governments would act, but the political economy of partial interests blocking the proliferation of public goods and the accomplishment of the SDGs tells us that we should not expect too much from the good will of national governments. Taking power from governments and placing it in the hands of specialised task-oriented agencies that create common club goods might prove a more successful approach.

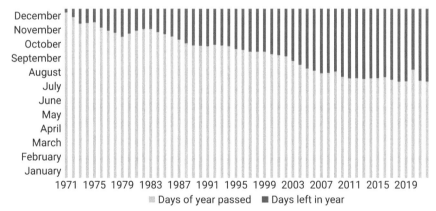

Figure 10.3. Earth Overshoot Day.

Source: Global Footprint Network (2022) "National footprint and biocapacity accounts" (https://data. footprintnetwork.org).

Jo Leinen and Christian Salm

11 | Global governance 2.0: a more democratic and efficient United Nations and a more coherent global governance system for the SDGs

The founding mothers and fathers of the United Nations in 1945 aimed to "save succeeding generations from the scourge of war". Since then, more than 200 wars and conflicts have happened, with millions of people killed. The goal of peace in the world has by far not been achieved. The UN Charter of 1945 envisaged the "promotion of the economic and social advancement of all people" as a common international responsibility. The reality of our world today is an extreme and widening gap between wealth and poverty. Human rights and social cohesion are fracturing in many parts of the world. On top of this, unsustainable debt burdens are a threat to the global economy and the financial system.

After World War II, neither climate change nor biodiversity loss were on the international diplomacy agenda or matters of public concern. One of the most significant gaps in the UN Charter is the absence of any reference to the environment. Planetary systems are close to the tipping points of irreversible changes and breakdowns. For the protection of global common goods, we need the UN's capacity to pass binding legislation with the necessary mechanisms for enforcement and dispute settlement.

Technology has developed at an unprecedented speed, especially since the digital revolution in the 20th century. The internet has enabled global communication and connects individuals, companies and countries around the world. Misinformation and disinformation can damage social cohesion and undermine trust in institutions. The advances in artificial intelligence could present new risks. The UN Charter does not address the digital age. A global rule book on digital devices and services is urgently needed.

The threat of a nuclear war and possible annihilation is still hanging as the sword of Damocles over the planet and humankind. Disarmament has been forgotten, and malignant technological innovations can help kill more effectively.

Most global catastrophic risks are linked to the inability of the current UN system to meet the demands of a rapidly changing and increasingly complex world. A more inclusive and efficient UN is needed. Below, we propose ideas for a renewed UN architecture and a reformed institutional design of global governance for the SDGs, SDG financing, climate and environmental policy, social policy and digital policy.

Empowering the General Assembly

The General Assembly, representing the 193 member states, must be empowered for global rule-making. It is the most inclusive body of the UN. The specific governance system of the General Assembly was intensively debated when the UN was created in 1945. The larger victorious postwar countries wanted to maintain the Security Council as the main locus of power where they could enjoy the veto. To balance the distribution of power between the principal organs of the UN, the General Assembly should have the competence to pass resolutions and recommendations on disputes and conflicts without waiting for a request from the Security Council (and therefore Article 12 should be deleted from the Charter). Like the Lichtenstein Initiative, the General Assembly should request greater responsibility and accountability from the Security Council. Greater effort should be made and new mechanisms introduced to implement General Assembly resolutions.

The General Assembly should play a greater role in selecting the secretary-general. A list of suitable candidates should be presented and an endorsement should be made by the majority of UN members without vetting by the Security Council.

ECOSOC

The world has fundamentally changed since the foundation of the UN in 1945. With 8 billion people on the planet, economic, social and ecological problems are much more connected beyond countries and continents. Peace and security have been the priorities since World War II. We recognise today that peace and security are endangered not only by military conflicts but also by factors such as poverty or the erosion of living conditions through environmental degradation.

The Sustainable Development Goals (SDGs) cover 17 policy fields that define a pathway for a good society and a common future. The weakness of this concept lies in the lack of coordination in implementing the objectives. While the national level is most important, we need a concept of global governance for the SDG strategy. The UN system lacks an operational body that can deliberate and act on nonmilitary global threats. The Security Council does not have the authority or the expertise to address the underlying causes of nonmilitary crises. In the search for a body that would cover a wide range of interconnected challenges – thus dealing with economic security as well as health, food, livelihood, climate and environmental security – there are several proposals for a new coordinating body.

Upgrading ECOSOC (the Economic and Social Council) to an Executive Council or creating a Sustainable Development Council emanating from the General Assembly are ideas being discussed by governments, parliaments and civil society organisations. The word "Council" is used to indicate the operational character of the body and the capacity to make decisions and react with concrete measures to challenges as they arise. Its composition should be representative and reflect the different grades of development among the UN members.

A Global Resilience Council

An effective response to the major global challenges requires innovative structures and actions across sectoral boundaries. Whereas cross-departmental coordination mechanisms exist in governments and large corporations, no global governance institution performs a corresponding function today. The governance system around the UN since the post-World War period has been organised on the basis of the specialisation of institutions and agencies by sectors. A Global Resilience Council could fill that gap. Looking for resilience is key to achieving the 17 SDGs. Bringing together all the relevant stakeholders for analysing and resolving the respective challenges is the core idea of this concept. The Global Resilience Council would act as a body through which the political response to major multidimensional crises could move up from the level of individual specialised agencies to the global community, leading to concerted action across sectoral agendas. Establishing such a multilateral institutional arrangement to ensure human resilience should be part of the negotiations at the Summit of the Future and the process for a UN 2.0 fit for the challenges of our time.

A new Security Council

The Security Council's first purpose was to prevent the emergence of a third world war. It has, in that limited measure, been successful, but it has been unable to avoid or manage regional conflicts that have seen Council decisions blocked with the veto. The body has become largely ineffective. If this situation continues, the UN could be increasingly sidelined, with real power and influence moving to other centres. There is an overall consensus that the Security Council must become more representative and reflect the political and economic reality of today's world. The absence of three continents – Africa, Latin America and Oceania – and the most populous country, India, demonstrates the lack of legitimacy of this body. Giving the veto to an additional set of players would better reflect geopolitics and demographics. Still, it is unlikely to improve the ineffectiveness that has haunted the Council since the beginning of its existence.

A new approach that replaces the veto with weighted voting could overcome the deadlock. As in the Bretton Woods Institutions in 1944, all members of the new, representative Security Council would have a weighted vote and a voice but not a veto. Such a system would guarantee strong representation for large countries. Important decisions would require higher voting thresholds. As the practice in the World Bank and the IMF shows, such systems encourage consensual decision-making rather than the obstructionism that characterises the existing Security Council.

In case the big five are not ready to give up their veto power, a second-best option could be to have a larger number of "new members" to better represent today's world, and to introduce a longer term of 8 or even 16 years and thereby better contribute to the maintenance of peace and security.

The secretary-general

The role of the secretary-general and the UN Secretariat has gradually evolved during the last 79 years. The office has increased in visibility and responsibility, with its activities ranging from coordinating responses to war, famine and disease to advancing new issues such as habitat problems or gender equality. This requires increased accountability in the election process with respect to the capability of the individual chosen as secretary-general.

Unfortunately, history has seen numerous instances in which the autonomy and efficacy of secretaries-general and their offices have suffered under the heavy influence of some member states, particularly the five permanent members of the Security Council, who have dictated not only the activities of the Secretariat but also the appointment of individuals to serve among its ranks. Therefore, the secretary-general appointment process needs reform. The General Assembly should call for applications, as already done since 2016 by Resolution 69/321.

However, applicants remain subject to a process of shortlisting by the Security Council, where the five permanent members retain a veto. As an interim measure, the Security Council should be required to present a list of multiple candidates for a final vote in the General Assembly. Ideally, the General Assembly should undertake the selection via an anonymous vote, without vetting by the Security Council. A second innovation that could enhance the secretary-general's efficacy would be the introduction of a single seven-year nonrenewable term. In this way, the secretary-general would be relieved from being pressured by those who hold in their hands the power to decide a reappointment. Thus, the secretary-general would be effective from day one.

Lastly, the independence of the Secretariat is undermined by the requirement that the member states vet its reports. This process belies a fundamental mistrust of an international system established to promote the wellbeing of all people without prejudice of any kind. Giving the Secretariat greater independence by curtailing the ability of states to affect the content and tone of its publications would enhance the valuable knowledge and insight often contained in its reports.

An Emergency Platform for complex global shocks

Global shocks in the 21st century have taken on new characteristics. They are becoming more complex, and their global impacts and the need for rapid international cooperation are, therefore, more critical. The multilateral system of today is not sufficiently prepared to manage such risks. A complex global shock is an event that has severely disruptive consequences for a large proportion of the global population. Recent examples include the Covid-19 pandemic (2020) and the cost-of-living crisis (2022). They had secondary impacts across multiple sectors and damaged various SDGs. The types of global shocks the world might experience are uncertain. They range from large-scale climatic or environmental events and new pandemics to disruptive activities in cyberspace.

Managing complex global shocks must be part of the Summit of the Future and the action plan thereafter. It starts with a better capability of the UN to anticipate risks through strategic foresight and periodic Futures Lab outputs, issuing Global Risk Reports for awareness and preparedness to strengthen resilience. In the case of a complex global shock, a platform with multidisciplinary and multistakeholder participation can help to better respond. The UN is the only organisation that can fulfil this role. The secretary-general should have the mandate to convene and automatically operationalise an Emergency Platform in the event of a complex global shock of sufficient severity and scale.

Collective global leadership: upgrading the role of regional organisations in the UN system

Seventy-nine years after the foundation of the UN, multiple regional entities have developed in every continent and played a fundamental role in regional governance. New economic, social and political factors explain this major historical change. The current multipolarity is of an unprecedented kind. The global power shift is giving birth to a multipolar global order of a new type. The European Union, the African Union, the Southern Common Market (MERCOSUR), the Association of Southeast Asian Nations and other regional groups, combined with various multilateral formations such as the G7, the G20 and the BRICS, have taken over various functions of common governance. This multipolar world is nevertheless asymmetric and fragmented and therefore not free from frictions, threats and risks. Strengthening and upgrading the common global institutions is the only way to allow containment of a rivalry between the emerging and declining powers, and to prevent an engulfing military confrontation. Institutionalised cooperation within and through the UN system is the answer.

Enhancing the role of regional organisations in the UN decision-making process beyond the current consultation on and implementation of the Security Council's decisions is a necessary issue in the framework of the upcoming UN reform. The legacy of Chapter VIII of the Charter – with its top-down method whereby the Security Council takes decisions and the regions are subordinated – has to be changed. Constructive partnerships between the UN and regional entities must be institutionalised. Biannual meetings of heads of regional organisations, the secretary-general, the president of the Security Council, the president of the General Assembly and, depending on the issue, the heads of select UN agencies could create a permanent framework for discussion and trust building. This proposal would not need a treaty reform but it would need a resolution of the Security Council to upgrade the cooperation between the UN and regions.

Furthermore, the Security Council, on the basis of Articles 31 and 32, could extend a standing invitation to the presiding state of the regional organisation to participate in its deliberations, obviously without voting rights. In the General Assembly, regional organisations are currently admitted as observers and allowed to take the floor, as is the case in UN agencies. Formal membership would require an amendment to the UN Charter. But a review and possibly an upgrading of their actual role should be organised. A UN-coordinated multipolar world will increase legitimacy, coherence and efficiency to achieve a balanced and sustainable world.

Citizens' participation in a reformed UN

The UN Charter begins with the promising words "We the people". However, one would seek in vain for any clause in the document that specifies a means by which the people can play a role in the organisation's deliberations and decision-making.

A UN Parliamentary Assembly

The time has come to give the elected representatives of the citizens a formal role in the UN system. A World Parliamentary Assembly (WPA) – or UN Parliamentary Assembly – should be set up. Below the threshold of Charter reform, the WPA could be created by a majority vote in the General Assembly under Article 22 to establish a subsidiary body. The WPA would help bridge the democratic legitimacy gap and increase the transparency and efficacy of the organisation. Starting as a consultative body, it would draw its members from national parliaments or have them directly elected in member states that want to go ahead. The WPA would engender a fresh perspective on global problems and help build political momentum for their resolution.

A World Citizens Initiative

In this globalised and interconnected world, unresolved international problems can affect people's welfare and wellbeing in many ways.

Citizens should, therefore, have a voice in the UN. A World Citizens Initiative (WCI) would be a dynamic new instrument to put citizens' concerns and aspirations on the agenda of the UN bodies. An organising committee would register citizens' appeals, open the procedure for collecting support and monitor a transparent and fair outcome. A successful WCI would appear on the agenda of the respective UN bodies, depending on the proposal. The General Assembly or Security Council would be obliged to draft a resolution as a response and vote on this resolution. Global politics could thereby become more citizen-centred and improve the credibility of the UN.

The International Court of Justice

Many UN resolutions and conventions suffer from a lack of implementation or from direct neglect and violation. Effective governance needs a strong judicial institution to oversee the members of a political unit and hold them accountable to their obligations. There is a clear deficit on the global level. The International Court of Justice (ICJ) should play a central role in the architecture of a reformed global governance system. To date, the court's role has been restricted to territorial and maritime disputes. The ICJ needs to be empowered to address the great risks facing the global community. More far-reaching improvements could include access for nonstate actors, thus expanding the court's ability to engage in investor–state disputes, human rights cases or interstate disputes. This could result in a more positive shift in states' attitudes to transnational problems and conflicts.

Against the background of the various global catastrophic risks that the planet and mankind are exposed to, a more inclusive and efficient global governance system is badly needed. The Summit of the Future in 2024 must become a restart of common principles and structures that are better suited to the needs of one world and one future for all. Article 109 of the UN Charter opens the door to grounding new objectives, instruments and mechanisms in a UN 2.0.

A better institutional design of global governance for the SDGs

There is an incoherent and insufficient institutional system of global governance for the SDGs. Therefore, there is an urgent need for institutional changes and reforms in global governance in key areas such as

SDG implementation, SDG financing, climate and environmental policy, social policy and digital policy. The following sections build on previous chapters in this book and focus on fundamental institutional reforms in global governance.

A fine-tuned global multilevel governance system for the SDGs

The first reform priority in order to make substantial progress towards achieving the SDGs is a fine-tuned multilevel governance system involving coordination and collaboration between the various levels of governance: local, national and regional levels and the global level. The EU can set an example in this regard with its "whole-of-government" for implementing the SDGs. While the European Commission draws up proposals for new European legislation to implement the SDGs and review the implementation by its member states, the EU member states have the primary responsibility for ensuring sustainable development at the national level by taking steps to integrate the SDGs into national policies and allocating resources to support their achievement. In addition, the EU member states report regularly on their SDG progress through the Voluntary National Reviews. At the same time, many local authorities are increasingly engaging through voluntary local reviews.

A more fine-tuned system, adapted to global multilevel governance, could look as follows. The UN should oversee in a systematic way the monitoring and reporting of SDG progress, provide guidelines and facilitate cooperation among countries. Regional organisations would coordinate SDG implementation across their member states, providing funds, setting targets and monitoring progress. National governments would be responsible for implementing the SDGs within their territories – adapting their national policies, strategies and budgets to their specific social, economic and environmental contexts. Local governments and authorities would need to tailor policies to local needs and engage local stakeholders so as to foster ownership of and commitment to the SDGs by institutionalising the involvement of citizens.

Crucially, the UN sustainable development governance system itself also needs to be advanced and designed in a more coherent way to make it more efficient and to address policies in a more integrated manner. As outlined above, one highly ambitious reform would be to create a UN Sustainable Development Council or Global Resilience Council. A more moderate reform option, which we suggest should be taken in any event, would be to upgrade ECOSOC by reorienting all of its work towards advising the General Assembly on sustainable development. This upgrade should be done by making use of the following instruments:

- a science-based peer review and offer of independent certification of national reports;
- recommendations on prioritisation and timebound instruments, integrating the financing-for-development process with SDG implementation (e.g. by specifying and monitoring commitments and providing written recommendations or reminders);
- calls for proposals and funding for up to six partnerships per year on transformative schemes.

The UN Economic Commissions and the resident coordinator networks should provide a stronger organisational infrastructure for all these processes.

A stronger global financial architecture

The current global financial architecture is far from being optimal for implementing the SDGs. Reforming the international financial architecture so that it tackles future challenges includes three general governance reforms: first, better coordination on financial issues between international institutions; second, greater empowerment and stronger resources for the IMF and the World Bank; and third, strengthening the role of the Global South in international financial institutions.

A fundamental reform is to enable greater coordination between the UN and the international financial institutions (the IMF and the World Bank). Moreover, reforms for better coordination should also include a stronger interface with the United Nations Framework Convention on Climate Change and better coordination with national SDG policy reviews. In addition, interaction with other international forums, notably the G20, should be strengthened. Better coordination and collective action through regular dialogues, joint initiatives and shared platforms for policy evaluation and coordination can align efforts towards SDGs and the financing for their implementation.

Besides better coordination, enabling greater empowerment and stronger resources for the IMF and the World Bank are crucial reforms. This needs to include multilateral development banks, as they represent important financial hubs for guaranteeing global economic stability, reducing poverty and providing financial assistance to developing countries. Thus, greater empowerment and more resources are vital for several reasons, among which are the following. First, strengthening the IMF's resources can effectively address financial instability, preventing systemic risks that could otherwise impede sustainable development. Second, empowering the IMF, the World Bank and the multilateral development banks would further increase support for infrastructure development, healthcare, education and poverty reduction, helping the recipient countries achieve sustainable growth. Third, a well-equipped IMF can respond promptly to crises, minimising their impact on vulnerable economies. Fourth, a stronger IMF and World Bank can enhance their capacity to tackle the increasing debt burden, finding deals for indebted lower-income countries and preventing debt crises that impede sustainable development.

Strengthening the role of countries from the Global South in international financial institutions is crucial to establishing fairness and ensuring equitable representation. It is also important for creating more robust, inclusive and effective global governance structures that can better implement the SDGs. Countries from the Global South are often disproportionately affected by global economic decisions but have had limited influence in international financial institutions. Therefore, strengthening their role in the IMF and the World Bank will ensure a fairer distribution of decision-making power and respect differing national needs in the implementation of the SDGs. For example, creating an African chair on the IMF board is very important in this regard.

A UN environment agency to tackle the triple planetary crisis

The urgency of tackling the triple planetary crisis of climate change, biodiversity loss and pollution also demands a more coherent institutional system of global governance. In other words, a better institutional design of global governance for an effective and enforceable climate and environmental policy is critical to cope with the complexities and challenges of these issues. However, governance structures in this area are fragmented, contributing to policy implementation gaps and varying national priorities, despite agreements such as the Paris Agreement. Therefore, three global governance mechanisms should be established to make the system more coherent: a unified UN environment agency, an interconnected scientific framework and an ombudsman for nature.

It goes without saying that setting up a unified UN environment agency with supranational and binding authority is crucial for streamlining efforts and ensuring coherence in addressing the triple planetary crisis. Such a unified UN agency would consolidate existing UN bodies and programmes related to climate and the environment by fostering collaboration and maximising resources. Moreover, a dedicated agency would provide the necessary institutional framework to oversee and implement comprehensive policies addressing climate change, biodiversity loss, pollution and other critical climate and environmental issues. Crucially, the global economic and financial institutions such as the IMF and the WTO should be turned into implementation agencies accountable to the new UN environmental agency.

For timely and informed policy- and decision-making by a unified UN environment agency, the creation of an interconnected scientific framework is necessary. This framework should integrate data and research across disciplines. It should prioritise knowledge sharing, encourage collaborative research initiatives and establish standardised methodologies for assessing environmental impacts and policy effectiveness. Establishing a global interconnected scientific framework for research institutions would help enhance understanding of complex climate and environmental systems. It would also help to ensure that there is not an exclusive focus on climate change and that issues of biodiversity loss and pollution are also dealt with. Moreover, it can accelerate the development of climate-altering technologies.

An ombudsman for nature would represent an innovative mechanism to protect interspecies and intergenerational equity. It would thus compensate for the lack of existing regulatory bodies and provide the singular focus and authority needed to address climate and environmental issues. While an ombudsman for nature would serve as an independent advocate and oversight body dedicated to safeguarding climate and the environment, it could also help give future generations rights in decision-making processes, in order to rebalance representation and ensure equitable decision-making.

The Global Accelerator on Jobs and Social Protection for a Just Transition

The scarcity of opportunities to access meaningful, stable and decent work, the insecurity of incomes, inadequate conditions of work, and limited social protection for large parts of the population all over the world play an important role in the overall state of the social crisis and in uncertainty, socioeconomic insecurity and mistrust in policies and institutions. In short, despite past initiatives and success, poverty and its eradication – the number one SDG goal – is still a key global issue to be tackled in all its forms everywhere. We propose three advancements for a better and strengthened form of governance to boost jobs and increase social protection worldwide: building up the Global Accelerator on Jobs and Social Protection for a Just Transition, cross-border regulation of employment relationships, and a reform of social and labour governance in global supply chains.

Launched by the UN secretary-general and coordinated by the International Labour Organization, the Global Accelerator's framework consists of better multilateral collaboration, including political and nonpolitical partners on all levels, and strengthened policy integration aligning various policy fields. Through this framework, it aims to address key components of poverty eradication. The first is the creation of jobs through the establishment of integrated national financing frameworks and the mobilisation of public and private domestic and international resources to invest in universal social protection and inclusive, environment- and gender-responsive employment interventions. The second is the in-country development of integrated and coordinated employment and social protection policies and strategies that facilitate just transitions. Crucially, to be more than a pilot scheme, the Global Accelerator for Jobs and Social Protection must fully develop its comprehensive approach.

Improving cross-border regulation of employment relationships as part of addressing poverty is crucial for various reasons: it increases access to decent work, fair wages and labour rights, and it reduces vulnerability and economic instability. By creating a more equitable and just environment in cross-border employment relationships, regulations can uplift individuals and communities, providing them with the means to build a more sustainable and prosperous future. This, in turn, contributes significantly to the global fight against poverty. Among various steps to improve cross-border regulation of employment relationship – such as standardisation, harmonisation, transparency and information sharing – more coherent corporate social responsibility (CSR) standards are needed. By integrating CSR standards such as ethical and responsible business practices, commitment to societal wellbeing and environmental sustainability into their operations, businesses can play a pivotal role in poverty alleviation by contributing resources and leveraging their influence to drive systemic change and promote sustainable development.

Finally, reforms of social and labour governance in global supply chains need to be considered urgently as a central part of global governance reforms. Workers in supply chains often lack access to social protection, adequate protections that ensure they can perform their work in safe conditions, and a voice to bargain for better conditions. Therefore, reforms of social and labour governance in line with environmental and social considerations are crucial for ensuring fair treatment of workers, promoting sustainability and enhancing accountability. The key is to increase coherence, transparency and effectiveness, to close the accountability gaps and to promote workers' empowerment and representation.

Maria João Rodrigues

Conclusion: a New Global Deal for a new development model

The current global challenges can only be overcome with a new development model. But it can only emerge if a more powerful process of international cooperation is launched on the basis of a New Global Deal. These are tasks for the Summit of the Future and beyond.

We conclude for now with a final general assessment and a final set of proposals, building on the collective preparation of this book and the ongoing global debate.

A critical assessment of the current global order

There is an increasing gap between mounting global challenges and the current global governance system. There are increasing inequalities within countries, between countries and between generations in the possibilities to deal with these global challenges. There is also a new geopolitical game. The world is more multipolar, and the US–China rivalry is visible on many fronts; the G7 is too limited to lead the world, but possible alternatives, such as the BRICS, are not credible either. Most countries and the world population do not want to be squeezed into this strategic rivalry and are looking for something else.

We have a weak, outdated and imbalanced global governance system, and it is clear that the only way to repair it is via a more effective, more inclusive and fairer multilateral system that can give it a new and legitimate direction and create hope for future generations. A Pact for the Future is necessary to reform the current multilateral system on different fronts, and one of them is development.

Despite very different political views across the world, the Sustainable Development Goal (SDG) agenda remains one of the few officially agreed agendas that are broadly accepted by all United Nations member states, and it can count on quite large support among the public and different stakeholders. Nevertheless, all the reports show that the implementation of the SDG agenda is lagging behind and not on track to reach its 2030 objectives. And there are countries in which the conditions needed to implement such an agenda, even if they want to do so, are much less established than in others.

A critical assessment to explain these difficulties is urgent, and a frank talk is necessary. The interactions at stake are increasingly complex, and it is important to recognise the contrast between the positive and the negative practices that affect the relationship between developed countries and developing countries.

- In times of an urgent green transition, the negative practice is exporting carbon emissions to developing countries, and the positive one is cooperating with them for this green transition.
- The negative practice is focusing on the extraction of resources, and the positive one is supporting the upgrade of their global supply chains.
- The negative practice is exploiting cheap labour opportunities, and the positive one is building up new skills and improving workers' living standards.
- The negative practice is imposing unbalanced trade agreements, and the positive one is using them for win-win effects.
- The negative practice is blocking developing countries' industrial policy for the sake of free market principles, and the positive one is accepting it, provided it is not just protectionism.
- The negative practice is imposing monopolistic digital solutions to manage data and design algorithms, and the positive one is accepting more tailor-made solutions.
- The negative practice is transferring developing countries' tax resources via profit shifting, tax avoidance or evasion, and the positive one is coordinating global tax rules to prevent this from happening.
- The negative practice is triggering forced emigration only to block it afterwards, and the positive one is organising the comanagement of migration flows.
- The negative practice is giving in to failures in the rule of law and democracy, and the positive one is demanding the improvement of governance standards.

Some actors in the developed countries might assume that these negative practices are still acceptable and that more cooperation is not needed, but this is a wrong assumption because, sooner or later, this negligence will be paid back with increased climate change and exposure to immigration flows, pandemics, and financial, social, security and ultimately internal political disturbances. Can they not see this is already happening?

Why we need a New Global Deal

Development is one of three pillars of the multilateral system and is at the heart of its malaise. On the one hand, developing countries have reached different levels, but many feel – and rightly so – that they are hindered in their possibilities for catching up with developed countries. On the other hand, developed countries are confronted with the need to fundamentally change their mode of development. The problem is no longer just "catching up"; it is moving together to a new development model, and this requires a much higher level of cooperation. This should be the main purpose of a New Global Deal– a deal to achieve an upward convergence towards a new development model, to be cocreated.

The main responsibility of tackling internal social inequalities with a New Social Contract remains at the national level, but if we ask whether all countries have similar chances to implement the SDGs, the answer is no. That is why we need a stronger global support framework whereby developed countries will actively support developing countries in terms of technology, trade and finance, provided the former deliver on their commitments. This should be the central purpose of a New Global Deal. A New Global Deal requires a New Social Contract and vice versa.

An upward convergence process that will shift countries and generations towards better standards and higher targets around sustainable development must be organised at all levels of governance – local, national, macroregional and international.

We need this New Global Deal for three main reasons.

- To deepen cooperation between developed and developing countries according to a win-win approach. If developing countries act to move to a new development model, they should be supported by developed countries. If developed countries agree to support developing countries, they should benefit from new economic opportunities, and also from the improvement of the global context, with more sustainability and fairness.

- To organise the joint and coordinated action needed to provide public goods that can only be provided at the global level: countering climate change, pandemics, large natural and human disasters, global economic recessions, and nuclear and digital threats.

- To include future generations' concerns – and the survival of humankind – in all public and private governance systems at all levels, on the basis of foresight and public debate about possible choices. From a long-term perspective, the needs and interests of the developing countries tend to coincide with the needs and interests of future generations.

A more detailed discussion is necessary about the precise terms of this New Global Deal in different policy fields, and this book proposes key priorities for many of them at the national and global levels. In this conclusion we will highlight the key policy shifts at stake.

Key policy shifts for a new development model

What is at stake is a much higher level of international cooperation to bring about a new development model that should involve the following key policy shifts.

It is important to raise general awareness about new emerging boundaries: the planetary, the human and the technological. They should be called boundaries because they set absolute limits and are signalled by irreversible tipping points that pose existential threats to humankind. This is currently the case for climate change, pandemics, large-scale hunger and migration, and nuclear and cyber weapons, including artificial intelligence. These difficulties are even worse when different boundaries enter into contradiction, such as the contradiction between fighting hunger on the one hand and fighting deforestation and climate change on the other – a dilemma that exists in many regions across the world.

In this context, the main reference for global fairness cannot only be ecological but must also be social. This means that, in international negotiations on climate change, what is to be compared is not only the national amount of carbon emissions but also the per capita carbon consumption and the carbon emissions of the global supply chains that underpin this consumption. The same should apply more generally to the per capita use of natural resources. This means that a sustainable living standard for humankind should be regularly defined in order to achieve an upward convergence towards a fairer world, taking into account these boundaries.

Nevertheless, the current postmodernist calls for a postgrowth economy are not justified. Growth is necessary and possible, but it must be growth of a different kind. Growth is still possible, provided it is less intensive in carbon and natural resources. Growth is also necessary to meet the human needs of an expanding population, and to create jobs and finance social protection. This will also create the kind of purchasing power that is one of the main engines of upward social mobility and of a fair transition to sustainable development.

Considering the new aspirations for wellbeing and respect for the planet, we need to fundamentally change the way we measure prosperity beyond GDP. This will have crucial implications across the board, notably for the way we set standards, attribute value, and remunerate and tax activities, with broad implications for income redistribution. For instance, care activities are increasingly necessary to meet the human needs of an expanding population; hence, their value should be recognised and remunerated accordingly. By contrast, pollution activities or biodiversity depletion reduce value and should be taxed. Sooner or later, our national accountancy systems must be adapted accordingly, and our entire economies made to work in a very different way more aligned with a New Social Contract and a New Global Deal. An international convention to update the terms in which wealth creation is measured is also becoming urgent.

The most powerful reform to drive this new trajectory for sustainable development, reduce social inequalities and build a New Social Contract would be to connect all jobs, whatever their status – permanent, precarious or independent – and from whatever kind of company, sector or region, to a universal social protection system. This social protection system should be able to cover the main risks of ageing, health and unemployment and to count on mandatory contributions from all those who have jobs. This is also the smartest way to formalise informal jobs, in developing countries as well as developed ones, reducing their current share of 60% of the global number of jobs. Connecting developing countries to the Global Accelerator on Jobs and Social Protection for Just Transitions and financing it in a consistent way can make a decisive difference, notably in fighting absolute and relative poverty – a key SDG for achieving all the others (see Chapter 1).

The most powerful area of investment for implementing all SDGs and reducing social inequalities within and between countries remains education, because it promotes upward social mobility, accelerates the dissemination of knowledge and technologies and leads to more inclusive and democratic governance. Access to better educational possibilities can be leveraged by the digital transformation: learning platforms, software and artificial intelligence that are tailor-made for different kinds of participants can provide a new infrastructure for lifelong learning, notably if they are combined with an expansion of digital skills.

Women are not a specific social category, they are half of humankind. That is why their equal access to education and better-paid jobs would be the societal transformation with the most beneficial outcomes on several fronts, not only in terms of respecting human rights and increasing social fairness, but also in terms of increasing total productivity and the human quality of products and services, as well as strengthening social protection and improving governance in order to achieve sustainable development worldwide. A general revision of legislation to promote equality between women and men in all domains is a fundamental task that should no longer be delayed.

Most economic activity is currently driven by global supply chains that need to be envisaged as key economic entities, being led very often by multinational corporations and involving a diverse network of companies and providers. These economic entities should not only be encouraged to contribute to the SDGs but also be made accountable in terms of environmental, social and economic responsibility. As this is typically a matter of global governance, the multilateral system should upgrade its current environmental, social, technological, trade and financial frameworks to deal with these new economic entities.

The increasing role of digital platforms in reorganising all economic sectors requires a regulatory effort to define basic global standards for the security and quality of the devices interfacing with customers, the ownership and management of data, and the basic principles guiding the development of the algorithms that underpin new services and products. This is also relevant for general platforms, which are, in fact, the infrastructures of digitalised economies and societies. Setting global standards and ensuring accountability for these digital platforms will also help to prevent the risk of decoupling, even if alternative platforms should be allowed to meet different social or cultural preferences. The concept of digital public infrastructure is particularly promising for delivering better public services.

Economic decoupling between different economic poles would become a lose-lose game for all parties involved, but a balanced derisking might be necessary to reduce some strategic dependencies. Provided that systemic protectionism is prevented, this might become a new reason for an active industrial policy, in addition to the compelling reason that it would build capacity by combining the relevant productive factors. This new shape for industrial policy, bringing it closer to innovation policy, should be part of a post-Washington consensus for all countries, not only for those who can afford it.

This is one of the reasons why fiscal space matters. Most of the big environmental, technological, digital, educational and social transformations underpinning the implementation of the SDGs require much larger-scale and longer-term investment. There is enough evidence from the recent past that imposing austerity for the sake of a fiscal rebalancing might become counterproductive, since it reduces growth potential and public revenue. Another approach for fiscal rebalancing is necessary to ensure a basic fiscal space for the investments and reforms that are crucial to increasing this growth potential. This should also be the approach for international instruments of financial support, be they for debt reduction, countering shocks or long-term investment, and they should operate based on a positive conditionality: financial support can be given, provided the planned investments and reforms are delivered by the supported country.

The toolbox for international finance must be updated: official development assistance should overcome its postcolonial approach; development banks should be reformed so as to better leverage private investment; new forms of investment partnerships with higher accountability should be introduced; special drawing rights should be redirected to the countries more in need; and global funds such as the Green Climate Fund should be funded not only by intergovernmental contributions but also by new forms of global taxation.

All these instruments should also be used to promote a much higher level of technological transfer and cocreation between developed and developing countries. Nowadays, knowledge production and diffusion are critical factors for quicker upward convergence towards sustainable development.

Global tax coordination is emerging as a key pillar of a new financial architecture. This involves, first, countering tax avoidance and tax evasion, which are depleting national fiscal balances and increasing public indebtedness; second, strengthening the international financial support instruments for upward convergence in achieving the SDG agenda; and third, financing the provision of global public goods and protecting global commons. The recently adopted resolution for a UN Tax Convention is certainly a step in the right direction.

The need for stronger international instruments of financial support is even clearer when there are global public goods that can only be delivered with a higher level of global coordination, such as responses to climate change, pandemics and major natural disasters, or protecting the global commons.

The various policy shifts identified above are also based on the recognition of the spillover effects that the development paths of some countries (notably in the Global North) have on others (notably in the Global South). Several spillover effects have been identified and confirmed by recent analysis, such as the greater carbon footprint of consumption in the Global North, the poorer labour conditions in the developing countries involved in global supply chains, the brain drain and the capital drain from the Global South to the Global North, and the specific advantages stemming from stronger reserve currencies.

These policy shifts should be introduced to reduce these spillover effects or to provide a compensation for them in order to ensure a global governance framework that can better support the implementation of the SDGs for all countries and all generations. This recognition is the basis of the principle of common but differentiated responsibilities when tackling structural inequalities. Recognising different capabilities and the need for solidarity when confronting natural or civil disasters is also an important complementary principle. Both these principles should also be taken into account when building up a global framework to protect the global commons, such as oceans, forests, cyberspace and outer space

A new multilateralism requires not only defining updated global regulations for the big ongoing transformations – the ecological, the digital and the social – but also recognising that states share common but differentiated responsibilities to advance global public goods and protect the global commons. This should be at the heart of a New Global Deal. It requires multilateral public institutions that are accountable to their full membership, open to a diversity of viewpoints and new voices, and able to rely on balanced and legitimate dispute-resolution systems.

The Summit of the Future and a multilateral process for a new development model

A new multilateralism must also be able to provide real opportunities for all those who want to implement the SDG agenda. That is why the Summit of the Future's main outcome should not only be a compelling declaration on a Pact for the Future. It should also be a more powerful process that commits all the relevant stakeholders to changing the way the multilateral system works, to better implementing the SDGs at all levels and to cocreating a new development model. Rebalancing the world will take time and will require a long-term and systematic process driven by a vision of the kind of global governance we need in order to mobilise women and men and meet future generations' needs. This more powerful process should be based on three main building blocks:

- national strategic plans to implement the SDGs that should be monitored and evaluated on a regular basis;
- international support conditions for these plans based on some key instruments that should also monitored and evaluated on a regular basis;
- global governance reforms to provide a stronger political engine to drive this process.

National strategic plans

It is high time to change the approach of the SDG agenda and move from a checklist of 17 objectives to national strategic plans for a new development model, involving several transitions, notably in the energy, food, biodiversity, digital, education and social protection fields. The interplay between the environmental, economic and social objectives of sustainable development must better managed, supported by stronger technological, trade and financial means, and based on better governance solutions.

It is after analysing the key trade-offs and synergies between all these factors that a national strategy to implement the SDGs can be better defined. It is particularly important to analyse the recent trends and identify the main impediments and trade-offs that explain the low level of SDG performance. It is also important to identify the critical factors for increasing synergies, and to identify which improvements depend particularly on a higher level of international cooperation and a New Global Deal.

International support conditions

A better implementation of the SDGs depends on national responsibilities, but also on better international support conditions. Some key instruments for this international support have already been referred to, and they are outlined below.

- A new international instrument pooling and disseminating new knowledge to implement the SDGs via technical assistance and training. Central to this effort should be digital solutions for managing resources, food, climate disasters, energy, transport, urban life and access to health and education.

- Access to knowledge, science and technology with more open systems and with an intellectual-property-rights regime that enables stimulus for innovation but also better diffusion of new technological solutions. New partnerships for technological transfer, cocreation and investment should also be introduced to enable new solutions adapted to each national context.

- A multilateral framework for the digital transformation, defining common standards for the next generation of the web, for the use of big data, for the principles guiding the development of artificial intelligence and for the business models of digital platforms, notably those overseeing access to knowledge, managing markets, supply chains and logistical support, and facilitating social interaction and democratic debate.

- Global trade standards for the development of global supply chains, enabling capacity building in all countries involved, promoting better economic, environmental, social and governance standards, limiting profit shifting and tax avoidance, and promoting technological cocreation.

- A multilateral system to monitor per capita carbon footprints, organise a compensation procedure and push for decarbonisation plans in all relevant sectors

- The Global Accelerator on Jobs and Social Protection for Just Transitions.

- A global long-term investment plan mobilising various private and public components. This, on the one hand, would channel private investment, including investments from pension funds and foreign direct investment, into supporting the implementation of the SDGs. On the other hand, it would strengthen the role of development aid and of regional development banks, as well as exploring new roles for the IMF, particularly by revising the framework for issuing special drawing rights to make it more targeted towards the countries in real need. Debt management and restructuring in countries that are highly indebted or confronted with natural disasters should also be aligned with a better implementation of the SDGs. A global tax framework should underpin all this.

Global governance reforms

The third building block of this process for a new development model should be about global governance reforms. It should define

- how to strengthen the UN's development, social, environmental and digital systems (the last two are more recent and each requires a single strong UN body able to define global rules, provide technical assistance and promote best practices);
- how the global system should function with a multilevel and multi-stakeholder approach, with the higher participation of women and with the multilateral system playing a central role;
- the implications for the composition of governance bodies and the activities of international financial institutions and the WTO;
- a systematic way to use foresight and focus on future generations as a permanent basis for political debate and decision-making.

To ensure the more effective and inclusive implementation of the SDGs, this process should also

- be based on biannual summits reporting on concrete outcomes and defining the next steps;
- involve all the relevant actors from representative and participatory democracy at the national, macroregional and global levels (the relevant UN bodies could also be usefully complemented by other relevant bodies, such as macroregional organisations – the European Union, the African Union, etc. – and the G20);

- be driven by a political engine, an upgraded Economic and Social Council, and a real Executive Council with a representative and rotating composition and with the competence to coordinate all relevant UN agencies and programmes via a stronger UN Secretariat.

Is all this too much? We believe these are just basic conditions to build up world governance for the 21st century that deserve to be discussed.

APPENDICES

Appendix A. UN General Assembly Resolution A/77/L.109

The General Assembly, reaffirming the Charter of the United Nations, and recalling its resolution 76/307 of 8 September 2022 on the modalities of the Summit of the Future, in which it decided that the Summit of the Future would adopt a concise, action-oriented outcome document entitled "A Pact for the Future", agreed in advance by consensus through intergovernmental negotiations:

(a) Decides that the scope of the Summit of the Future will encompass the following elements, and that these elements will be reflected in the outcome document, entitled "A Pact for the Future", comprising a chapeau and five chapters, as follows:

   (i) Chapter I. Sustainable development and financing for development;
   (ii) Chapter II. International peace and security;
   (iii) Chapter III. Science, technology and innovation and digital cooperation;
   (iv) Chapter IV. Youth and future generations;
   (v) Chapter V. Transforming global governance;

(b) Also decides that the 2030 Agenda for Sustainable Development[1] and its pledge to leave no one behind, the commitment to end poverty and hunger everywhere, to combat inequalities within and among countries, to build peaceful, just and inclusive societies, and to ensure the lasting protection of the planet and its natural resources and creating conditions for sustainable, inclusive and sustained economic growth, shared prosperity and decent work for all, taking into account different levels of national development and

---

1   Resolution 70/1.

capacities; as well as the realization of the human rights of all, the achievement of gender equality and the empowerment of all women and girls will be taken into account in the relevant chapters of the Pact for the Future;

(c) Renews its request to the President of the General Assembly contained in paragraph 16 of resolution 76/307 to appoint co-facilitators, one from a developed country and one from a developing country, no later than 31 October 2023, decides that the remainder of the intergovernmental preparatory process of the Summit shall consist of consultations to determine the topics and organization of the interactive dialogues, and negotiations to conclude the outcome document with adequate time for the negotiating sessions, and requests the co-facilitators, in consultation with the President of the Assembly, to designate, as necessary, pairs of coordinators, each comprising one from a developed country and one from a developing country, taking into account gender balance, for specific chapters or elements;

(d) Requests the President of the General Assembly to appoint, no later than 31 October 2023, two pairs of co-facilitators, each comprising one from a developed country and one from a developing country, taking into account gender balance, to facilitate, as part of the preparatory process of the Summit of the Future, open, transparent and inclusive intergovernmental consultations on a global digital compact and a declaration on future generations, which would be annexed to the Pact for the Future if intergovernmentally agreed;

(e) Decides that no meetings of the preparatory process of the Summit will be held in parallel to one another, to ensure a well-coordinated and streamlined process, and that the preparatory process of the Summit shall avoid overlaps and duplications with existing intergovernmental processes.

Appendix B. Political declaration of the High-Level Political Forum on sustainable development convened under the auspices of the General Assembly

18 and 19 September 2023

(1) We, the Heads of State and Government and high representatives, have met at

(2) United Nations Headquarters in New York on 18 and 19 September 2023, at the Sustainable Development Goals Summit, to review progress and accelerate the implementation of the 2030 Agenda for Sustainable Development.

(3) We reaffirm our commitment to effectively implement the 2030 Agenda and its SDGs and uphold all principles enshrined in it. The 2030 Agenda remains our overarching roadmap for achieving sustainable development and overcoming the multiple crises we face. We will act with urgency to realize its vision as a plan of action for people, planet, prosperity, peace and partnership, leaving no one behind. We will endeavour to reach the furthest behind first.

(4) We emphasize that eradicating poverty in all its forms and dimensions, including extreme poverty, is the greatest global challenge and an indispensable requirement for sustainable development.

(5) We reaffirm that the 2030 Agenda is universal in nature and that its Goals and targets are comprehensive, far-reaching, people-centered, indivisible and interlinked, balancing the three dimensions of sustainable development: economic, social and environmental, in

an integrated manner. They seek to realize the human rights of all and to achieve gender equality and the empowerment of all women and girls.

(6) We reaffirm that the 2030 Agenda is guided by the purposes and principles of the Charter of the United Nations, including full respect for international law. It is grounded in the Universal Declaration of Human Rights, international human rights treaties, the Millennium Declaration and the 2005 World Summit Outcome. It is informed by other instruments such as the Declaration on the Right to Development.

(7) We also reaffirm the Addis Ababa Action Agenda as an integral part of the 2030 Agenda. We are committed to its full implementation which is critical for the realization of the SDGs and their targets and to this end welcome the organization of the 2023 High-level Dialogue on Financing for Development back-to-back with the SDG Summit.

(8) We also reaffirm that climate change is one of the greatest challenges of our time. We express profound alarm that emissions of greenhouse gases continue to rise globally, and remain deeply concerned that all countries, particularly developing countries, are vulnerable to the adverse impacts of climate change. We emphasize in this regard that mitigation of and adaptation to climate change represent an immediate and urgent priority.

(9) The achievement of the SDGs is in peril. At the midpoint of the 2030 Agenda, we are alarmed that the progress on most of the SDGs is either moving much too slowly or has regressed below the 2015 baseline. Our world is currently facing numerous crises. Years of sustainable development gains are being reversed. Millions of people have fallen into poverty, hunger and malnutrition are becoming more prevalent, humanitarian needs are rising, and the impacts of climate change more pronounced. This has led to increased inequality exacerbated by weakened international solidarity and a shortfall of trust to jointly overcome these crises.

(10) We commit to bold, ambitious, accelerated, just and transformative actions, anchored in international solidarity and effective

cooperation at all levels. We will promote a systemic shift towards a more inclusive, just, peaceful, resilient and sustainable world for people and planet, for present and future generations.

(11) We will devote ourselves collectively to the pursuit of sustainable development including through international cooperation and partnership on the basis of mutual trust and the full benefit of all, in a spirit of global solidarity, for the common future of present and coming generations.

(12) We reaffirm all the principles of the Rio Declaration on Environment and Development, including, inter alia, the principle of common but differentiated responsibilities, as set out in principle 7 thereof.

(13) We are concerned about the persistent disproportionate and multidimensional impacts from the COVID-19 pandemic. We must strengthen multilateral and international cooperation for developing countries, particularly the poorest and most vulnerable countries, to help them recover from the ongoing effects of the COVID19 pandemic and strengthen resilience including through pandemic prevention, preparedness and response.

(14) We recognize the special challenges facing all developing countries in pursuing sustainable development, in particular African countries, least developed countries, landlocked developing countries, small island developing States, as well as the specific challenges facing middle-income countries and countries in conflict and postconflict situations.

(15) We remain resolved, between now and 2030, to end poverty and hunger everywhere; to combat inequalities within and among countries; to build peaceful, just and inclusive societies; to respect, protect and fulfil human rights and achieve gender equality and the empowerment of all women and girls and to ensure the lasting protection of the planet and its natural resources. We also remain resolved to create conditions for sustainable, inclusive and sustained economic growth, shared prosperity and decent work for all, and equal pay for work of equal value, taking into account different levels of national development and capacities. We take note with appreciation of the Global Accelerator on Jobs and Social Protection for

Just Transitions and encourage all countries to consider supporting its implementation. We commit to ensuring that persons with disabilities actively participate in and equally benefit from sustainable development efforts.

(16) We reaffirm that gender equality and the empowerment of all women and girls will make a crucial contribution to progress across all the Goals and targets. The achievement of full human potential and sustainable development is not possible if one half of humanity continues to be denied full human rights and opportunities. We will ensure full and equal enjoyment of all human rights and fundamental freedoms by all women and girls, without discrimination. We also resolve to eliminate all forms of violence against women and girls.

(17) We reaffirm the role of culture as an enabler of sustainable development that provides people and communities with a strong sense of identity and social cohesion and contributes to more effective and sustainable development policies and measures at all levels.

(18) We commit to stepping up our efforts to fight against racism, all forms of discrimination, xenophobia and related intolerance, stigmatization, hate speech, through cooperation, partnership and inclusion and respect for diversity.

(19) We reaffirm our resolve to realize our vision of a world with access to inclusive and equitable quality education, universal health coverage including access to quality essential health-care services, social protection, food security and improved nutrition, safe drinking water, sanitation and hygiene, affordable, reliable, sustainable and modern energy, sustainable industrialization and quality, resilient, reliable and sustainable infrastructure for all.

(20) We commit to achieving a world in which humanity lives in harmony with nature, to conserving and sustainably using our planet's marine and terrestrial resources, including through sustainable lifestyles, and sustainable consumption and production, to reversing the trends of environmental degradation, to promoting resilience, to reducing disaster risk, and to halting ecosystem degradation and biodiversity loss. We will conserve and sustainably use oceans and

seas, freshwater resources, as well as forests, mountains and dry-lands and protect biodiversity, ecosystems and wildlife.

(21) Sustainable development cannot be realized without peace and security; and peace and security will be at risk without sustainable development. We reaffirm the need to build peaceful, just and inclusive societies that provide equal access to justice and that are based on respect for human rights (including the right to development), on effective rule of law and good governance at all levels and on transparent, effective and accountable institutions. Factors which give rise to violence, insecurity and injustice, such as inequality, corruption, poor governance and illicit financial and arms flows, are addressed in the Agenda..

(22) The 2030 Agenda remains our commitment to the children and youth of today so that they may achieve their full human potential, as critical agents of change and torchbearers of the 2030 Agenda for current and future generations.

(23) We acknowledge the essential role of parliaments in ensuring accountability for the effective implementation of our goals and commitments under the 2030 Agenda.

(24) We commit to enhancing global, regional, national and local partnerships for sustainable development, engaging all relevant stakeholders, including civil society, private sector, academia and youth, recognizing the important contribution they can make toward achieving the 2030 Agenda, and the localization of the SDGs. We also reaffirm the importance of the regional dimension of sustainable development in addressing regional challenges and scaling up action among countries.

(25) Our world has changed drastically since the first SDG Summit in 2019 and since we adopted the 2030 Agenda in 2015. The world was already off track in achieving the majority of the SDGs before the COVID-19 pandemic. Without immediate course correction and acceleration of progress toward achieving the SDGs, our world is destined to face continued poverty, prolonged periods of crisis and growing uncertainty.

(26) We are concerned about the persistent and long-term impacts from the COVID19 pandemic, continued poverty and widening inequalities, and the multiple interlinked crises that are pushing our world to the brink, particularly in developing countries and for the poorest and most vulnerable. The crisis of climate change and its impacts, including persistent drought and extreme weather events, land loss and degradation, sea level rise, coastal erosion, ocean acidification and the retreat of mountain glaciers, as well as biodiversity loss, desertification, sand and dust storms, and pollution, including plastic, air, and chemical pollution, threaten planet and people. Forced displacement, the cost-of-living, water, food security and nutrition, financial and energy crises and challenges are derailing progress on the Sustainable Development Goals.

(27) In many parts of the world armed conflicts and instability have persisted or intensified, causing untold human suffering and undermining the realization of the Sustainable Development Goals. Our efforts to prevent and resolve conflicts and foster peaceful, just and inclusive societies have often been fragmented and insufficient and have been hindered in the current global context.

(28) We acknowledge that the cascading global crises have highlighted and exacerbated existing gender inequality, such as unequal access to healthcare, education, social protection, decent jobs and economic opportunities.

(29) We take note of the secretary-general's special edition progress report on the Sustainable Development Goals, and the Global Sustainable Development Report, recognizing the value of evidenced-based approaches to evaluate progress to date towards the SDGs.

(30) We recognize the positive role and contribution of migrants for inclusive growth and sustainable development in countries of origin, transit and destination, including by enriching societies through human, socioeconomic and cultural capacities. We recommit to cooperate internationally to ensure safe, orderly and regular migration involving full respect for human rights and the humane treatment of migrants, regardless of their migration status, and to support countries of

origin, transit and destination in the spirit of international cooperation, taking into account national circumstances.

(31) We must meet the moment by taking immediate measures to scale
up efforts to achieve the 2030 Agenda and the Addis Ababa Action
Agenda, including through development cooperation, SDG investments, reforming the international financial architecture, supporting sustained, inclusive and sustainable growth, enhancing macroeconomic policy cooperation, exploring measures of progress
on sustainable development that complement or go beyond gross
domestic product, and implementing actions to accelerate sustainable development, in particular in support of developing countries.

(32) We are deeply concerned by the marked increase of the estimated
SDG financing gap and recognize the urgency of providing predictable, sustainable and sufficient development finance to developing
countries from all sources.

(33) We note that there has been positive progress in a limited number
of areas. We recognize the efforts of countries and stakeholders at
all levels since 2015 to realize the vision of the 2030 Agenda and the
Sustainable Development Goals. We acknowledge that important
lessons were drawn from the COVID-19 pandemic in health, culture,
education, science, technology, and innovation and digital transformation for sustainable development.

(34) We are encouraged by the progress achieved in the implementation
of the Vienna Programme of Action for Landlocked Developing Countries 2014–2024, and the SAMOA Pathway for SIDS 2014–2024,
and call upon the international community to take the opportunity
of the Third UN Conference on LLDCs and the 4th International Conference on Small Island Developing States to identify and address
the key priority issues of LLDCs and SIDS respectively, as well as
to forge genuine and durable partnerships, including financial support, that will accelerate the implementation of their respective
sustainable development blueprints. Additionally, we welcome the
Doha political declaration, and the commitments made towards the
timely and full implementation of the Doha Programme of Action for
the Least Developed Countries for the Decade 2022–2031.

(35) We welcome the ongoing efforts of the UN development system to implement the reforms championed by the secretary-general and endorsed by the General Assembly, to better support programme countries in their efforts to implement the 2030 Agenda, stressing the importance of predictable and sustainable funding of the UN development system and its programmatic activities.

(36) We recognize that the Voluntary National Reviews have generated valuable lessons learned and have helped countries monitor progress and integrate the Sustainable Development Goals into national plans and policies.

(37) We commit to taking continuous, fundamental, transformative and urgent actions at all levels and by all stakeholders to overcome the crises and obstacles facing our world. We recognize the urgent need to take the actions necessary to reverse declines and accelerate progress to achieve the 2030 Agenda and implement the SDGs.

(38) We commit to achieving sustainable development and shared prosperity for all by focusing our policies and actions on the poorest and most vulnerable. We will endeavour to identify those who are being left behind and reach those who are the furthest behind first. People who are vulnerable must be empowered. Those whose needs are reflected in the 2030 Agenda include all children, youth, persons with disabilities, people living with HIV/AIDS, older persons, Indigenous Peoples, refugees, internally displaced persons, and migrants. We intend to see the Goals and targets met for all nations and peoples and for all segments of society. We will take action to combat inequalities within and among countries and pursue policies that stem the tide of rising inequality, including through social protection systems and universal health coverage. We look forward to the proposed world social summit in 2025, subject to discussion and agreement by the General Assembly on its modalities, and emphasize that the possible summit outcome should have a social development approach and give momentum towards the implementation of the 2030 Agenda.

(39) We are determined to make all efforts to implement the 2030 Agenda and achieve the Sustainable Development Goals by the target year of 2030 and to revitalize the global partnership for sustainable development. To this end:

(a) We commit to taking comprehensive and targeted measures to eradicate poverty in all its forms and dimensions, including extreme poverty, everywhere, recognizing it is the greatest global challenge and an indispensable requirement for sustainable development. We commit to enhancing and supporting policies and strategies for reducing poverty and inequality, including through international cooperation.

(b) We will accelerate actions to end hunger, food insecurity and all forms of malnutrition, and the realization of the right to adequate food, including through access to sufficient, safe and nutritious foods all year round, the promotion of sustainable and resilient agriculture and food systems, as well as safe, nutritious and healthy diets. We commit to keep trade channels and markets open for the movement of food, fertilizers and other agricultural inputs and outputs, while recognizing the importance of shorter supply chains at the local levels. In this context, we also commit to supporting developing countries to address extreme food price volatility.

(c) We commit to targeted and accelerated action to remove all legal, social, and economic barriers to achieving gender equality, the empowerment of all women and girls including those with disabilities, their full, equal and effective participation in all decision-making processes, and the realization and enjoyment of their human rights. In this regard we commit to eliminating, preventing and responding to all forms of discrimination and violence against women and girls in public and private spaces both in person and in digital contexts, and call for women's full access to justice and effective legal remedies.

(d) We will continue increasing investment in inclusive and equitable quality education and life-long learning opportunities for all, including early childhood education, youth and adult literacy programmes and initiatives, digital education, cultural education, education for sustainable development, digital technologies for education, skills enhancement, affordable higher education and vocational training, education in emergencies and teachers' continuous professional development. We recognize that early childhood education and care can generate substantial benefits for children. We will address barriers to girls' education, gender and disability gaps and promote gender equality and the empowerment of women and girls in and through education and safe, healthy and stimulating learning environments that enable all learners to achieve their full potential and physical, mental and emotional well-being. We also take note of the 2022 United Nations Transforming Education Summit.

(e) We will continue to take action to bridge the digital divides and spread the benefits of digitalization. We will expand participation of all countries, in particular developing countries, in the digital economy, including by enhancing their digital infrastructure connectivity, building their capacities and access to technological innovations through stronger partnerships and improving digital literacy. We will leverage digital technology to expand the foundations on which to strengthen social protection systems. We commit to building capacities for inclusive participation in the digital economy and strong partnerships to bring technological innovations to all countries. We reaffirm that the same rights that people have offline must also be protected online. We look forward to the elaboration of a Global Digital Compact to bridge the digital divides and to accelerate the achievement of the Sustainable Development Goals.

(f) We will address water scarcity and stress and drive transformation from a global water crisis to a world where water is a sustainable resource, ensuring the availability and sustainable management of water and sanitation for all. We note the importance of the mid-term comprehensive review of the implementation of the International Decade for Action, "Water for Sustainable Development", 2018–2028 and the water-related goals and targets of the 2030 Agenda, and we commend the convening of the UN 2023 Water Conference.

(g) We will ensure healthy lives and promote well-being for all at all ages, including by strengthening health systems and achieving universal health coverage and all other health-related targets and leaving no-one behind. We will address gaps in preventing, preparing for, and responding to current and future pandemics and health emergencies, including in the development and distribution of timely and equitable access to medical countermeasures such as vaccines, therapeutics and diagnostics.

(h) We commit to making cities and human settlements inclusive, safe, resilient and sustainable, including through the implementation of the New Urban Agenda, to contribute to the achievement and localization of the 2030 Agenda for Sustainable Development, and enhancing financial and technical assistance to plan and implement sustainable urbanization and human settlements programmes and projects, and we will promote access for all to adequate, safe and affordable housing.

(i) We recommit to making fundamental changes in our consumption and production patterns, including by transitioning to sustainable economic and business models, the implementation of the 10-Year Framework of Programmes on Sustainable Consumption and Production Patterns, and by providing support to developing countries to strengthen their scientific, technological and innovation capacity. We recognize that local and national zero-waste initiatives can contribute to achieving sustainable consumption and production.

(j) We will ensure universal access to affordable, reliable, sustainable and modern energy for all, including through enhanced international cooperation to assist developing countries and through sustained investments, advancing research and development, and promote investment in energy infrastructure and clean energy technology. We will increase substantially the share of renewable energy in the global energy mix by 2030.

(k) We recommit to the full implementation of the Sendai Framework for Disaster Risk Reduction 2015–2030, and recall its Mid-term review, as disasters have become more frequent and intense. We acknowledge that its implementation will require capacity building and technical and financial assistance in order to be effectively implemented by developing countries. We will promote a disaster riskinformed approach to sustainable development at the local, national, regional and global levels and accelerate progress on integrating disaster risk reduction into policies, programmes and investments at all levels. We recognize the need for a broader and a more people-centred preventive approach to disaster risk reduction, and that disaster risk reduction policies and practices need to be multi-hazard and multisectoral, inclusive and accessible in order to be efficient and effective. We will promote effective local, national and regional multi-hazard early warning mechanisms.

(l) We stress the urgency of enhancing ambition for climate action in the implementation of the UNFCCC and the Paris Agreement[2] in relation to climate mitigation, adaptation and the provision of the means of implementation, especially finance to developing countries. We urge the implementation of the decisions adopted at COP 27 held in Sharm El-Sheikh. We will take concrete steps toward the operationalization of the new funding arrangements for responding to loss and damage by COP 28. We commit to continuing our work to accelerate our action to address climate change. In this regard, we also look forward to the first global stock take of the Paris Agreement to take place at COP 28.

(m) We emphasize the need for a balanced and enhanced implementation of all provisions of the Convention on Biological Diversity, including its three objectives. We will take urgent action to halt and reverse biodiversity loss by 2030 to put nature on a path to recovery for the benefit of people and planet by conserving and sustainably using biodiversity and by ensuring the fair and equitable sharing of benefits from the utilization of genetic resources, while providing the sufficient means of implementation to support developing countries. We welcome the CBD COP15 and its outcomes, including the Kunming Montreal Global Biodiversity Framework and call for the timely implementation of these outcomes and in this regard we welcome the establishment of the Global Biodiversity Framework Fund. We call for its timely operationalization and capitalization from all sources, including international

2 Adopted under the UNFCCC in FCCC/CP/2015/10/Add.1, decision 1/CP.21.

financial resources from developed countries, philanthropic organizations and private sector, and to progress towards implementation as soon as possible.

(n) We commit to continue urgent efforts to implement the strategic objectives of the United Nations Convention to Combat Desertification, affirming that combating desertification, land degradation, drought and floods, as well as sand and dust storms, and achieving land degradation neutrality are essential and have emerged as a pathway to accelerate progress towards achieving the SDGs.

(o) We will decisively and urgently mobilize action for sustainable ocean management, recognizing the central role of a healthy, productive and resilient ocean. We commit to an integrated and coordinated approach to conserve, protect and restore the ocean, its ecosystems and its biodiversity. We emphasize that our actions to implement Goal 14 should be in accordance with, reinforce and not duplicate or undermine existing legal instruments, arrangements, processes, mechanisms or entities. We affirm the need to enhance the conservation and sustainable use of oceans and their resources by implementing international law as reflected in the UN Convention on the Law of the Sea, which provides the legal framework for the conservation and sustainable use of oceans and their resources, as recalled in paragraph 158 of The Future We Want. We look forward to the third UN Ocean Conference, to be held in 2025, to scale-up ocean action and accelerate implementation.

(p) We will support the global efforts to address plastic pollution, and the work of the Intergovernmental Negotiating Committee (INC) to develop an international legally binding instrument on plastic pollution, including in the marine environment by 2024.

(q) We commit to bridging the science, technology and innovation divides and the responsible use of science, technology, and innovation as drivers of sustainable development and to build the capacities necessary for sustainable transformations. We reiterate the need to accelerate the transfer of environmentally sound technologies to developing countries on favourable terms, including on concessional and preferential terms, as mutually agreed. We will take action to enhance the ability of developing countries to benefit from science, technology, and innovation and address the major structural impediments to accessing new and emerging technologies including through scaling up the use of open science, affordable and open-source technology, research and development, including through strengthened partnerships. We aim to increase funding for SDG-related research and innovation and build capacity in all regions to contribute to and benefit from this research. We will seek to better realize the benefits and address the challenges of artificial intelligence. We undertake to increase the use of science and scientific evidence in policymaking.

(r) We pledge to take action to strengthen international, national and local data systems efforts to collect high quality, timely, relevant, disaggregated and reliable data on SDG progress and to intensify efforts to strengthen data and statistical capacities in developing countries. We will continue to strengthen our efforts to collect, analyse and disseminate relevant, reliable and disaggregated data for better monitoring and policymaking to accelerate the achievement of the 2030 Agenda. We commit to increasing the availability of SDG data and closing SDG data gaps at all levels, increasing financing for data and statistics, and enhancing capacity building support to developing countries.

(s) We will continue to integrate the SDGs into our national policy frameworks and develop national plans for transformative and accelerated action. We will make implementing the 2030 Agenda and achieving the SDGs a central focus in national planning and oversight mechanisms. We will further localize the SDGs and advance integrated planning and implementation at the local level. We encourage all relevant actors to better address interlinkages, synergies and trade-offs between the Sustainable Development Goals, enhancing policy coherence for sustainable development.

(t) We commit to accelerate the full implementation of the Addis Ababa Action Agenda and to take further actions to scale up financing for sustainable development, and provide means of implementation for developing countries, including the following:

(i) We will ensure significant mobilization of resources from a variety of sources, including through enhanced development cooperation, strengthening the capacity to mobilize domestic resources and private sector investment in order to provide adequate and predictable means for developing countries, in particular the least developed countries, and to implement programmes and policies to end poverty in all its forms and dimensions and to create decent jobs.

(ii) We urge developed countries to scale up and fulfill their respective ODA commitments, including the commitment by many developed countries to achieve the target of 0.7 per cent of gross national income for official development assistance (ODA/GNI) to developing countries and 0.15 to 0.20 per cent of ODA/GNI to the least developed countries.

(iii) We call for improved international debt mechanisms to support debt review, debt payment suspensions, and debt restructuring, as appropriate, with an expansion of support and eligibility to vulnerable countries in need. We commit to continuing to assist developing countries in avoiding a build-up of unsustainable debt and in implementing resilience measures so as to reduce the risk of relapsing into another debt crisis. We recognize the importance of new and emerging challenges and vulnerabilities in regard to developing country external and domestic debt sustainability. We call for strengthened multilateral actions and coordination by all creditors to address the deteriorating debt situation.

(iv) We welcome the secretary-general's efforts to address the SDG financing gap through an SDG stimulus. We will advance the secretary-general's proposal, in a timely manner through discussions at the United Nations as well as other relevant forums and institutions, to tackle the high cost of debt and rising risks of debt distress, to enhance support to developing countries and to massively scale up affordable long-term financing for development and expand contingency financing to countries in need.

(v) We call for scaling up debt swaps for SDGs, including debt swaps for climate and nature, and debt swaps for food security, as appropriate, while recognizing that debt swaps cannot replace broader debt treatments in unsustainable debt situations, to allow developing countries to use debt service payments for investments in sustainable development.

(vi) We recommit to preventing and combating illicit financial flows and strengthening international cooperation and good practices on assets return and recovery. We reaffirm our commitment to strive to eliminate safe havens that create incentives for the transfer abroad of stolen assets and illicit financial flows. We will implement our obligations to prevent and combat corruption, bribery and money laundering in all their forms enshrined in the existing international architecture, in particular in those prescribed in the United Nations Convention Against Corruption and the United Nations Convention Against Transnational Organized Crime.

(vii) We call for an urgent voluntary re-channeling of Special Drawing Rights to countries most in need, including through multilateral development banks, while respecting relevant legal frameworks and preserving the reserve asset character of Special Drawing Rights. We will explore ways for future allocations of Special Drawing Rights to benefit those countries most in need.

(viii) We support reform of the international financial architecture. We also support international financial institution and multilateral development bank reform as a key for large-scale Sustainable Development Goal-related investments in order to better address global challenges. The international financial architecture, including its business models and financing capacities, must be made more fit for purpose, equitable and responsive to the financing needs of developing countries, to broaden and strengthen the voice and participation of developing countries in international economic decisionmaking, norm-setting, and global economic governance. We commit to engage in inclusive inter-governmental discussions on the reform of international financial institutions in forthcoming processes, including at the United Nations, taking into account current and ongoing initiatives.

(ix) We urge multilateral development banks to bring forward actions to mobilize and provide additional financing within their mandates to support developing countries to achieve the SDGs. We support multilateral development bank reform efforts and call for tangible progress in this regard, including through securing increases to grants and concessional finance, better leveraging their capital bases and considering ways for the respective boards of the MDBs to increase their capitalization and encourage dialogue between multilateral development banks and other financial institutions.

(x) We recommit to the promotion of a universal, rules-based, non-discriminatory, open, fair, inclusive, equitable and transparent multilateral trading system, with the World Trade Organization (WTO) at its core, as well as meaningful trade liberalization. We underscore that the multilateral trading system should contribute to the achievement of the Sustainable Development Goals, providing policy space for national development objectives, poverty eradication and sustainable development, consistent with relevant international rules and countries' commitments, and promote export-led growth in the developing countries through, inter alia, preferential trade access for developing countries, targeted special and differential treatment that responds to the development needs of individual countries, in particular least developed countries, and the elimination of trade barriers that are inconsistent with World Trade Organization agreements. We welcome the commitment of WTO members to work towards the necessary reform of the organization, with the aim of improving all its functions and effectively addressing the challenges facing global trade. We look forward to concrete and positive results at the 13th WTO Ministerial Conference.

(xi) We confirm our political commitment to explore measures of progress on sustainable development that complement or go beyond gross domestic product to have a more inclusive approach to international cooperation and reaffirm our call to engage in United Nations-led intergovernmental discussions in consultation with relevant stakeholders.

(xii) We encourage the international community to consider multidimensional vulnerability, including the potential use of a multidimensional vulnerability index, as criteria to access concessional finance.

(xiii) We look forward to the deliberations on convening a fourth international conference on financing for development in 2025.

(xiv) We look forward to the beginning of inter-governmental discussions in New York at United Nations Headquarters on ways to strengthen the inclusiveness and effectiveness of international tax cooperation.

(40) We recognize that the integrated nature of the Sustainable Development Goals requires a global response. We renew our commitment to multilateralism, to find new ways of working together and to ensure that multilateral institutions keep pace with the rapid changes taking place. We further commit to finding peaceful and just solutions to disputes and to respecting international law and the purposes and principles of the Charter of the United Nations, including the right to selfdetermination of peoples and the need to respect the territorial integrity and political independence of States.

(41) We commit to fully support the UN development system, including the RC system and the Joint SDG Fund, to deliver better in support of programme countries and their efforts to implement the 2030 Agenda and its SDGs. We support the United Nations in playing a central and coordinating role in international development cooperation.

(42) We commit to using the review of the high-level political forum at the 78th session of the General Assembly to further strengthen the follow-up and review of the implementation of the 2030 Agenda, harnessing data to track progress in implementing the Sustainable Development Goals and targets, strengthening analysis of the inter-linkages across the Goals and targets, including policy implications of their synergies and trade-offs.

(43) We look forward to the Summit of the Future in 2024 as an important opportunity to, inter alia, accelerate the implementation of the 2030 Agenda and its SDGs.

(44) We commit with united efforts, political will and firm actions to advance concrete, integrated and targeted policies and actions to fulfill the vision of the 2030 Agenda and achieve the Sustainable Development Goals. We pledge to act now, for present and future generations, turning our world towards a sustainable and resilient path by 2030, and leaving no one behind.

About the authors

AZITA BERAR AWAD ――――――――――――――――――――――――――

Azita Berar Awad is a political economist and global policy advisor on inclusive social and economic policies with extensive experience in international development cooperation and the United Nations system. She has held several senior leadership positions at the International Labour Organization, including director of the Employment Policy Department from 2006 to 2017. She is currently the chair of the board of UNRISD (the United Nations Research Institute for Social Development) and the director of policy at the Global Labor Organization. She is a member and the current chair of the OHCHR board of trustees on technical cooperation in the field of human rights. She teaches in various universities and executive education programmes. In 2020 she founded the first Global Interdisciplinary Policy Research Network on Youth Transitions, bringing together academia and policy actors.

JOHANNAH BERSTEIN ――――――――――――――――――――――――

Johannah Bernstein is the senior policy lead for Earth4All. She is an international environmental lawyer with over 30 years of professional experience advising UN organisations, national governments, international NGOs and the private sector. Her work has always been focused on multilateral environmental diplomacy processes, about which she has written extensively. She has also taught international environmental law at universities in Europe and North America. She holds a BA degree in human ecology from the College of the Atlantic and law degrees from Osgoode Hall Law School and Oxford University.

CÉLINE CHARVERIAT

Céline Charveriat is an expert researcher in environmental policy and sustainable development. She is the director of Pro(to)topia Consulting and an adjunct professor at the Paris School of International Affairs (PSIA). Previously, she was the executive director of the Institute for European Environmental Policy – a Brussels-based sustainability think tank – and the advocacy and campaigns director of Oxfam International. She began her career in Washington DC as a researcher at the Peterson Institute and the Inter-American Development Bank.

DAVID COLLESTE

David Collste is a researcher and modeller at the Stockholm Resilience Centre focusing on the future of human development in the Anthropocene. He studies feedback between human development, the economy and planetary boundaries. David co-leads the graduate module on systems thinking of the Stockholm Resilience Centre's master's programme and leads an undergraduate course in ecological economics. David was the 2022 recipient of the Donella Meadows prize.

STEFAN COLLIGNON

Stefan Collignon is research professor at Chulalongkorn University, Bangkok (competitive track), and visiting professor at the European Institute, London School of Economics, where he taught from 2001 to 2005. During 2005–7 he was visiting professor at Harvard University. From 2007 to 2022 he taught as Professore ordinario at the Sant'Anna School of Advanced Studies, Pisa. His research has focused on European monetary economics and the political economy of regional integration. Having contributed to the creation of the euro, he worked from 1999 to 2000 as deputy director-general of the German Treasury. He has recently published several books on the transforming economy of Myanmar and is presently working on a new book with the title *The Political Economy of Liberty and Money*.

SANDRINE DIXSON-DECLÈVE

Sandrine Dixson-Declève is copresident of the Club of Rome and divides her time between leading the Club of Rome, advising, lecturing and facilitating difficult conversations. She currently chairs the European Commission's Expert Group on the Economic and Societal Impact of Research and Innovation and sits on the European Commission's Mission on Climate Change and Adaptation. She also sits on several non-executive and advisory boards including those of the EDP, BMW, the UCB, Climate-KIC, the Leonardo Centre and Imperial College London, and she is a senior associate and faculty member of the Cambridge Institute for Sustainability Leadership, an ambassador for the Energy Transition Commission and the Wellbeing Economy Alliance, and a fellow of the World Academy of Art and Science. Sandrine is a TED global speaker and recently published *Quel monde pour demain?* (Editions Luc Pire) and *Earth for All: A Survival Guide for Humanity* (New Society). She was recognised most recently by Reuters as one of 25 global female trailblazers and by GreenBiz as one of the 30 most influential women across the globe driving change in the low-carbon economy and promoting green business.

ENRICO GIOVANNINI

Enrico Giovannini is full professor of economic statistics at the University of Rome. He was Minister of Sustainable Infrastructures and Mobility in the Draghi government (2021–2) and Minister of Labour and Social Policies in the Letta government (2013–14). He is cofounder and scientific director of the Italian Alliance for Sustainable Development (ASviS). He was director of statistics and chief statistician of the OECD and president of the Italian Statistical Institute. In October 2014 the President of the Italian Republic made him "Cavaliere di Gran Croce della Repubblic Italiana" and in January 2023 he received a honorary PhD in sustainable development and climate change. He is the author of more than 130 articles published in national and international journals and seven books on statistical and economic topics.

ARANCHA GONZÁLEZ LAYA

Arancha González Laya is a lawyer and currently the dean of the Paris School of International Affairs at Sciences Po. She served as Minister of Foreign Affairs, the European Union and Cooperation in the Spanish government of Prime Minister Pedro Sánchez. Earlier in her career, González served as assistant secretary-general at the United Nations and as executive director of the International Trade Centre.

PAOLO GUERRIERI

Paolo Guerrieri is visiting professor at the Paris School of International Affairs, Sciences Po (Paris). He was a Senator of the Italian Republic in the 17th legislature (2013–18). As a member of the Commission for European Affairs, he worked on relations with the European Parliament and the European Commission. He is a former full professor of political economy at the Sapienza University of Rome, where for many years he taught courses on the "Economics of European integration". He is president of the Scientific Council of the Rivista Economia Italiana, director of the Economic Policy Observatory of the Agenzia di Ricerche e Legislazione (AREL), president of the Scientific Committee of the Centro Europa Ricerche (CER) and scientific advisor of the Istituto Affari Internazionali (IAI). He has worked as a consultant for many international institutions and organisations, including the European Commission, the World Bank, the OECD and the United Nations Economic Commission for Latin America and the Caribbean (ECLAC). He has been a visiting professor at the University of San Diego Business School; the University of California, Berkeley; the Université Libre de Bruxelles; the College of Bruges and Natolin (Brussels and Warsaw); and the Esade Business School (Barcelona). He is the author of numerous books and articles on international economics, European economic integration and technological change.

FRANCESCO LAPENTA

Francesco Lapenta is the founding director of the John Cabot University Institute of Future and Innovation Studies. He is also a Mozilla-Ford Research Fellow and the technical editor of the IEEE P7006 standard on Personal Data Artificial Intelligence Agents. His research focuses on

emerging technologies, innovation, technologies' governance, standardization processes, ethics and impact assessment, and future scenario
analysis.

JO LEINEN

Jo Leinen is a German politician who served as a Member of the European Parliament from 1999 to 2019. He was the chair of several European
Parliament key committees, such as the Committee on Constitutional
Affairs. He served as Minister of the Environment for the German Saar-
land. He has published many works on European and international politics, including a book outlining a vision for global democracy.

PIER CARLO PADOAN

Pier Carlo Padoan was Italian Minister of Economy and Finance and
Member of the Chamber of Deputies of the Italian Republic, and he has
been chairman of UniCredit since April 2021. He was chief economist
and deputy secretary-general at the OECD, and executive director at the
IMF. He is a full professor of economics (retired) at the La Sapienza University of Rome. He also covers the following positions: vice president
of the Istituto Affari Internazionali (IAI); board member of the Institute
of International Finance (IIF); member of the board of directors and the
executive committee of the Associazione Banche Italiana (ABI); and
chairman of the High-Level Group on Financing Sustainability.

MARIA JOÃO RODRIGUES

Maria João Rodrigues, former Portuguese minister under PM António
Guterres, is a European politician with a long track record in different
European institutions: EU Presidencies, the Council, the European Council, the European Commission and, more recently, the European Parliament. She is currently the president of FEPS, a European political foundation located in Brussels, which is financed by the EU budget to support
EU policy-making and has UN observer status and a network of partners
across Europe and the world. She played a relevant role in several important European and international initiatives: the EU's development agenda;

the interface with EU strategic partners Africa, China, Brazil and India for sustainable development; the EU's Lisbon Treaty; and, more recently, the European Pillar of Social Rights. She was also involved in the economic plans to respond to the financial crisis, the pandemic and the climate crisis. She coordinated a large project on a New, Inclusive and Fair Multilateralism, and is now coordinating another on a New Global Deal. In academic terms, she was professor of European economic policies at the European Studies Institute (Université Libre de Bruxelles) and at the Lisbon University Institute. She was also the chair of the European Commission Advisory Board for socioeconomic sciences. She is author of more than 100 publications, including 11 books.

CHRISTIAN SALM

Christian Salm is a researcher at the Foundation for European Progressive Studies. He worked as a science officer at COST (European Cooperation in Science and Technology) and as a policy analyst at the European Parliamentary Research Service of the European Parliament. He obtained a PhD from the Centre for European and International Studies at the University of Portsmouth (UK) and was postdoctoral researcher at the Institute for Social Movements at the Ruhr-University Bochum (Germany). Christian has published on several issues pertaining to European integration, EU policymaking and policy areas such as development cooperation, defence policy, research policy and international trade agreements.

NATHALIE SPITTLER

Nathalie Spittler is a postdoctoral researcher at the Center for Global Change and Sustainability at the University of Natural Resources and Life Sciences, Vienna, where she currently co-leads the Foresight Group. She also works as a sustainability analyst for the Millennium Institute and is an active member of the Austrian chapter of the Club of Rome. Her focus lies on the application and teaching of systems thinking tools to address global challenges and find ways to ensure wellbeing within planetary boundaries. Nathalie holds a PhD in environment and life sciences from the University of Iceland and a PhD in economics from CERDI at the Université Clermont Auvergne (France) as well as a master's in socioecological economics and policy from the Vienna University of Economics and Business.

GERHARD STAHL

Gerhard Stahl started his professional career at the German Ministry of Finance. He was secretary-general of the European Committee of the Regions for over 10 years. Furthermore, he worked in leading positions in the European Parliament and the European Commission. He was a professor at the College of Europe in the Economics Department. Currently, he is visiting professor at the Peking University HSBC Business School in Shenzhen, China.

ROBERT SWEENEY

Robert Sweeney is Head of Policy at the think tank TASC (Think-tank for Action on Social Change). He researches and publishes on a variety of topics relating to international and European governance, labour markets and housing. He has a PhD in economics from the University of Leeds.

About the partners

EARTH4ALL

Earth4All is a vibrant collective of leading economic thinkers, scientists and advocates, convened by the Club of Rome, BI Norwegian Business School, the Potsdam Institute for Climate Impact Research and the Stockholm Resilience Centre. Earth4All builds on the legacies of *The Limits to Growth* and the planetary boundaries frameworks. *Earth for All: A Survival Guide for Humanity* was published in September 2022 and presents the results of a remarkable two-year research collaboration.

FONDATION JEAN-JAURÈS

Fondation Jean-Jaurès is the leading French political foundation, which works not only as a think tank but also as a grassroots actor and a historical memory centre at the service of all those who defend progress and democracy in the world.

FRIEDRICH-EBERT-STIFTUNG – NEW YORK

The Friedrich-Ebert-Stiftung New York office works at the intersection of the United Nations in New York, the international financial institutions in Washington DC, FES field offices and partners in developing countries. It aims to strengthen the voices of the Global South, labour and other progressive actors. We work closely with academia, civil society, multilateral institutions and their member states.

FUNDACIÓN PABLO IGLESIAS

Fundación Pablo Iglesias contributes to intellectual debate at national and international levels by organising international seminars, exhibitions, publications, conferences, debates and round tables in which politicians, academics, representatives of culture and opinion leaders discuss contemporary social, political, ideological, cultural and historical issues, and the history of socialism in Spain.

KARL-RENNER-INSTITUT

The Karl-Renner-Institut is the political academy of the Austrian Social Democratic Party. It is a forum for political discourse, a centre for education and training and a think tank on the future of social democracy.

OLOF PALME INTERNATIONAL CENTER

The Olof Palme International Center is the Swedish labour movement's umbrella organisation for international solidarity. The organisation work globally for democracy, human rights, social justice, peace and sustainability through a just transition – in the spirit of Olof Palme – and supports progressive social movements and parties that change societies and people's everyday lives.

TASC

TASC (Think-tank for Action on Social Change) is an independent think-tank whose mission is to address inequality and sustain democracy by translating analysis into action. TASC's Constitution presents its main objectives as promoting education for the public benefit and encouraging a more participative and inclusive society.